FROM A PARK
TO A STADIUM
TO A "LITTLE PIECE OF HEAVEN"

CULTURAL CHANGES
AS SEEN THROUGH
THE ST. LOUIS CARDINALS'
BASEBALL DIAMONDS

CONNIE F. SEXAUER

Hope you enjoy this.
Uncle Carl & Aunt Lois
GO CARDS!

From a Park to a Stadium to a "Little Piece of Heaven"
Cultural Changes as Seen Through the St. Louis Cardinals'
Baseball Diamonds

Author: Connie F. Sexauer
Foreword: Chuck Korr
Contributing Editors: Lyda Rose Haerle, Marla McKenna
Associate Editor: Griffin Mill
Cover Design and Interior Layout: Michael Nicloy

ISBN-13: 978-1945907401

Published by Nico 11 Publishing & Design,
Mukwonago, Wisconsin
www.nico11publishing.com

Be well read.
Quantity and wholesale order requests can be emailed to:
mike@nico11publishing.com
or be made by phone: 217.779.9677

ACKNOWLEDGEMENTS

This book has been more than twenty years in the making. My love of the game and fascination for the St. Louis Cardinals began in 1957 when my friend, Marilyn Smith invited me to a game. I took that interest home with me, and the George and Connie Fields family started on a life-long path of following the hometown team. Since women were not a part of the game, I could not imagine a professional role that would connect me to the club. Then one day in 2003 I presented a paper at a conference of the Society for American City and Regional Planning History. Even before I delivered the paper, I was approached by a representative from Northern Illinois Press. She was interested in publishing my book. I explained it wasn't a book, it was simply a 30-page academic paper. She contacted me three times before it finally dawned on me that perhaps there actually was a book. That enlightenment led me on a fascinating journey of pure pleasure. The research included numerous trips to St. Louis, as well as Cooperstown, New York. Over the years I have delivered several sections of the book at history conferences. What a joy to find a professional path that connected with a team I have long admired.

Thanks to Dr. Chuck Korr for opening my mind to the idea that professional sport is and has always been a business. I remember in a sports history class at the University of Missouri – St. Louis he brought up that idea and most of the students, including myself, balked. But under his expert guidance, and much support for his argument, he convinced us.

A small segment of this book began in a graduate class at the University of Cincinnati with Dr. Wayne Durrill. He presented the historical importance of place. He guided the class to see the world of physical space in a fuller context.

I am extremely grateful for friends who have read parts of the manuscript through the years to include: Joan Sabers, Ann Watts, Rene Whitaker, Lynn Kordus, Brad Cross, Pam Sanfilippo, Clint Terry, Kirsten Gardner, Michelle Lewis, Chuck Korr, Mike Sexauer, Angela Kolkmeier, Tom Sabers, Pat Fox, James Veninga, Zane Miller, Suzy Wampler, Darrell Meadows, Chad McGee, and Joe Minson.

Thanks to Ann Watts for her warm hospitality during several spring training trips to Jupiter, Florida. Also, thanks to my friend, Deborah Henry for a place to stay several times on my trips to St. Louis, as well as my sister, Mary Anne and her husband Al Hagedorn.

I appreciate the interest throughout the years that the St. Louis Cardinals archivist, Paula Homan has shown in my work and the conversations we have had about the history of the club. I am greatly indebted to Charles E. Brown of the Mercantile Library in St. Louis and

Teresa Militello of the National Transportation Museum in St. Louis for their help in locating some outstanding photos for the book. Thanks to Josh Phillips for his encouragement and expert advice on the world of publishing.

Thanks to Judy and Fran Dwyer, Roger Drake, Sharon Maniaci-Melton, Michelle and Rick Lewis, Judie Campana, Isabelle Lenhardt, Jane Devine Pilkington, Mary Anne Hagedorn, and George Fields II for sharing their thoughts of the game. These are included in the book and I hope I have done justice to their accounts. I am grateful to my colleagues at the University of Wisconsin-Marathon County for their support. I appreciate the professional funding the history department and the campus provided for research trips and presentations.

I am indebted to Nico 11 Publishing for bringing this book to life. I appreciate Mike Nicloy for his enthusiasm for this project, as well as Lyda Rose Haerle's, and Marla McKenna's editing expertise. It was a joy to work with them.

Thanks to everyone who has patiently waited for the release of this book and encouraged me along the way. I hope you all consider the wait worth it and enjoy the read.

Dedicated to My Fields Family
and
Angela, Michelle, and Michael

FROM A PARK
TO A STADIUM
TO A "LITTLE PIECE OF HEAVEN"

TABLE OF CONTENTS

FOREWORD

More than fifty years ago, the English playwright and sports journalist, Arthur Hopcraft, described the importance of football (soccer): "Not a sideshow of this century. What happens on the field matters, not in the way that food matters, but as poetry does to some people and alcohol does to others; it engages the personality." If the reader substitutes the word "baseball" for "football", Hopcraft's comments provide the context for Connie Sexauer's history of professional baseball in St. Louis. The major focus is on the St. Louis Cardinals—how the club was created, maintained, and changed since the last quarter of the nineteenth century. We meet both the men who set the pattern for how the team was run and understand why the team meant so much to millions of fans over the years. Unlike so many baseball histories that are built around the story of games played and players who thrilled (and many times disappointed) their fans, this book has an added dimension. It recognizes that any history of the Cardinals would be incomplete without paying attention to the various ball parks/stadiums that provided homes for the teams in St. Louis. They were special places for the crowds that came to see the team as an extension of themselves. Sexauer made it a point to spend some time writing about the "other St. Louis teams", including the Browns. The Browns left St. Louis in 1953 and spent much of their time at the bottom of the American League standings. But they were the team that owned Sportsman's Park for much of its existence and were the landlords for the team that spent its time in the higher regions of the pennant races.

Baseball fans approaching this book might think they are going to be informed by another fan who will explain why the Cardinals are credited with creating a "Cardinals way of playing the game" and why it has been one of the most successful teams in baseball. Much of the success of the club was turning spectators into fans, people who would identify with the team even when it was unsuccessful on the field. The Cardinals have a fan base that far exceeds the St. Louis community. To many people the team is the first thing they identify with St. Louis.

Historians will look at the book hoping to understand the role that the teams have played in the life of the broader community and what the location and setting of a baseball park can tell one about the changing nature of a metropolitan area in the middle west. In fact, both groups will find what they want and have the bonus of being exposed to much more than they expected.

Until the 1960's the ball parks that were home to the St. Louis team were in residential neighborhoods. The parks reflected the culture of the city in all its rich diversity and its racially segregated reality. Some of the questions raised about what should take place during a game are still subjects of discussion to this day. What should be the role of alcohol and how should gambling be tolerated. The first successful owner, Chris Von der Ahe boasted that "beer was a focal part of his stadium" He did little to discourage gambling taking place so long as it presented no direct impact on what happened on the field. He was not alone in that approach. (I remember going to games at Shibe Park in Philadelphia along with other twelve-year-olds. A police officer who was a relative told us where to sit in the bleachers. He assured us that we would be safe since the area was patrolled by a few policemen to ensure that no one would cause trouble in the ongoing craps games and blackjack.) Von der Ahe also turned part of the stadium into an amusement park atmosphere with lawn bowls, hand ball, picnic tables, and celebratory fireworks. He anticipated the changes that present-day teams would boast were novel and forward thinking.

Along with a chronicle of the players and an appreciation of on the field actions, Sexauer understands how club owners, from Von der Ahe to Gussie Busch set the tone for the team and established a relationship with its fans. When Anheuser-Busch brewery bought the team, Gussie Busch became both the president of the team and its biggest fan. Busch understood how much his new purchase could be an asset to his business of making and marketing beer. He was living a fan's dream. They could only talk about changes that should be made, Gussie could do it. Busch was very much a "hands on" owner, a quality that many thought might better be described as meddling.

Busch had a complicated relationship with his players and the changing nature of American society in the 1960's. He purchased a motel in Florida to ensure that players at spring training would not have to follow the state's segregated housing laws. At the same time, he was the fiercest opponent to any efforts by the players in their post-1966 union to challenge how he did things. His tirades against the union had the effect of convincing the players how much they needed a union. His anger at players who rejected his contract offers in the 1970's led to a set of disastrous trades that probably cost the team more than one pennant. As much as fans loved their star players, most fans supported Busch because they knew that he would not harm the chances of the team without good reason.

When the new multi-purpose stadium was built downtown within sight of the Gateway Arch, the team showed a new awareness of the role it might play in the rejuvenation of downtown St. Louis. When Busch's successor as the head of the brewery decided to sell the team, there were fears that the new owners would run it strictly as a business. If anything, the current owners have built an even stronger relationship with both the region and its fans.

Sexauer also recognizes the unique ties the Cardinals had to generations of fans who might never have seen them play in St. Louis. For more than sixty years, the Cardinals were the most western and most southern team in Major League Baseball. I took a friend of mine to a Cardinals' opening night in the mid-70's. He had been a passionate fan for forty plus years but had never seen them play. He did have a mental picture of what would happen since he had listened to the broadcasts at his home up-river from New Orleans. Fan loyalties were reinforced by the most potent radio network in the history of baseball, one that reached across the western half of the country and much of the south.

In her final chapter, Sexauer brings together the various threads of the book in ways that will be appreciated by both baseball fans and readers who want to understand how the sport has reflected changes in American society. She weaves together the tragedies of drunk driving, the business nature of baseball, and fans' reaction to the loss to free agency of an iconic player (Albert Pujols). She describes the politics of new stadiums as part of a narrative that shows how a baseball team must change. The trick is how to deal with changes in the broader society while at the same time maintaining many of the traditions that has made baseball and an identification with a team matter to millions of people over more than a century and a half. The book might be summed up best in the phrase used so often by Jack Buck, the team's great radio play-by-play announcer, "That's a Winner."

Chuck Korr is a professor emeritus of history at the University of Missouri-St. Louis and the author of the award-winning book, *The End of Baseball as We Knew It*, a history of the major league baseball players union.

INTRODUCTION

L eisure space and popular traditions help shape American culture. The physical space of amusement parks, circus tents, dance halls, vaudeville playhouses, and motion picture theaters serve to encourage mingling of classes, genders, and ethnicities. It is the same with the cathedrals of baseball. The American icon, baseball, appeals to diverse populations who congregate at a common site to share their love and passion for the game. This unity of purpose thus helps to produce a cultural identity. This unifying spirit is worthy of examination.

For over a century, baseball has served as a trope to inculcate immigrant groups into 100-percent Americans; it appeals to men and women, and especially the rising middle- and working-class.[1] Baseball has a prominent place in the American social scene; investigating the history of a city's baseball stadiums over time reveals historical significance.

Beyond the architectural structure and the neighborhood setting, one can better understand society by inspecting the culture of place and its connections to society. The buildings helped to change the culture, but so did those who owned the buildings, played the game, and followed the activities on the playing field. Stories focused on place show how spaces are "planned, designed, built, inhabited, appropriated, celebrated, despoiled, and discarded;" as such they are focal points to better understand the cultural identity within a community.[2] By the late nineteenth century the St. Louis community embraced baseball as a major entertainment venue in ways that helped intertwine the fragments of a public social space and produce a kinship.[3]

This study inspects an interchange of actors within cultural spaces in St. Louis, Missouri, where the history of the Cardinals baseball teams played out: Solari Park/Sportsman's Park (1866-1893) at Grand and Dodier; New Sportsman's Park (1893-1899) League Park (1899-1911) Robison Field (1911-1917) Cardinal Field (1917-1920) at Natural Bridge and Vandeventer; Sportsman's Park (1920-1952) Busch Stadium (1953-1966) at Grand and Dodier; Civic Center Busch Memorial Stadium at Seventh and Spruce (1966-2005); and Busch Stadium (III) located at 700 Clark Avenue (2006-present). While the Cardinal organization officially uses 1892 as the beginning of Cardinal history, this study begins in 1866 as Sportsman's Park dates to this time period.

The argument presented here is that the built environment of place matters in historical context and serves to form a community of factors that help shape the culture of the day. The development of the ballpark design, the space, and place of the ballpark parallel the general cultural development of American urban design and reflects the political, technological, social, economic, and cultural changes in the history of

America. Specifically, baseball went from a poor man's exercise of fun to a multi-billion-dollar industry in the course of a century as it intertwined with the culture of an age to influence society and citizens. The changes are noted by studying the historical connections of all actors associated with the game and the space where the action took place to acknowledge the synergy across the ages between place and the cultural players.

This book centers on the site of play, the neighborhood landscape, and more specifically, the interconnection of human factors to get a clearer understanding of the power and symbolism of the relationship between organizations and their communities.[4] The intention is to note the changes that have occurred over the years based on the complex interchange of society at large and specific arenas of place to show how the American culture changed from the late nineteenth century to the early twenty-first century. The focus is on the city of St. Louis, Missouri, and specifically what has become known as Cardinal Nation.

CHAPTER ONE

BLEST ST. LOUIS FANS AND PLAYERS

For those who love the game of baseball and follow it faithfully it is a holy and consecrated institution. The sport of baseball is something pure and special in its relationship to traditional American culture. There are numerous media outlets devoted to keeping fans up to date on all the happenings with books, poems, movies, and songs that have contributed to cultural outlets to educate and enlighten an interest in the sport. Baseball's dramatic sport closely ties the nation together, especially on opening day and in the Fall Classic. It provides rich memories of unity. As sports author Rich Wolfe noted many share the insular experience of "feverishly opening newly purchased baseball cards, our first uniform, learning to keep score, the dew and mosquitoes, the sounds of the radio or our first big league game."[5]

Baseball purists form a microcosm of society from young children, old-timers, rich, poor, and all those in between. Baseball followers belong to their own world. The St. Louis Cardinal fans are a nation unto themselves, the Cardinal Nation. St. Louis, a town noted for hot, humid summers and cold beer, has long been known as "the best baseball town in the world" with the greatest fans.[6] That proclamation has been bestowed by the *Sporting News*, ESPN, *Sports Illustrated*, and other national media. In 1998 *Baseball America* magazine named it the "Best Baseball City."[7] At his retirement as Commissioner of Baseball, in 2015, Bud Selig proclaimed St. Louis as "the best baseball town in America."[8]

Each generation has established its rituals and embraced its own memories. That hallowed tradition, the spirit and connectedness continue. Members of the Nation easily recognize the uniqueness of each age: the Gas House Gang, the Swifties, Whitey Ball, the La Russa era, and the Matheny Style. They may disagree on what era was the best, but fans idolize the heroes of the Red Bird uniform; respect holds the Nation together.

St. Louis-native Joe Buck, son of renowned broadcaster Jack Buck noted, "Baseball, it's more than just a game; it's a way of life. Nowhere is this belief more evident than in St. Louis." He stressed, "In America's heartland the spirit of this game echoes beyond the playing field... Baseball has become a part of this city's soul." As a national sports commentator he follows the geographical settings of the game. Buck views St. Louis as "one of the greatest baseball cities the world has ever known."[9]

Bob Costas, a huge Cardinal fan, stated that during the 1998 home run chase, between Mark McGwire and Sammy Sosa, a *Newsday* writer summed up the essence of Cardinal fans: "the combination of passion and civility…is what makes it the best baseball town in America." Costas added St. Louis fans "are extremely knowledgeable. The Cardinals have a rich history which the fans very much appreciate." What you very rarely see in St. Louis is an "ugliness and mean spiritedness" that other stadiums might exhibit.[10]

Hall-of-Famer, Stan Musial spent his entire twenty-two year career with the franchise, and remarked "From the first time I put on a St. Louis Cardinals uniform, I knew I was part of something special…St. Louis is a special town and the fans of the Cardinals are something special…They understand the game, but most important, they love the game. And they love the Cardinals. You can't teach that. It has to come from the heart."[11]

Well-known former Baltimore Orioles manager Earl Weaver grew up in St. Louis in the era of the thirties and forties where he dreamed of playing for the Cards. He followed both hometown teams, in fact, his dad did the dry cleaning for the clubs, so Earl was privy to the clubhouse. He went to Beaumont High School (a site where the Cardinals used to play) which was only about a ten-minute walk from Sportsman's Park. In 1944 the fourteen-year-old skipped class, walked over to the game, bought a bleacher ticket, and watched his first World Series game. He signed with the Cardinal organization in 1948 and bounced around their minor leagues until 1957. Though he was inducted to the Hall of Fame on his managerial abilities, Weaver has stated, "one thing I'm really proud of is that I was put on the St. Louis Cardinals roster in 1952." He only played eighteen games but that meant the world to this St. Louis native.[12]

Some players might not have been happy going to the Cardinals, but most changed their mind once they arrived. Leo Durocher, when traded to St. Louis from Cincinnati in 1933, told General Manager Branch Rickey "I won't play for your chain gang." Rickey assured the shortstop he knew of his reputation for being cantankerous, but he made the trade because he knew Durocher would help the team "win a lot of pennants." It was not long before Durocher began to see Rickey's wisdom and admitted being upset by "all the viscous slanders that certain people have been spreading about this brilliant baseball man, this keen judge of talent, this biblical scholar." Yes, even Durocher came to enjoy his four seasons in St. Louis.[13]

Red Schoendienst so wanted to be a Cardinal that "he slept on a park bench outside the St. Louis train station the night before his tryout"[14] and became emotionally upset years later when he was traded. Tim McCarver, from Memphis, was elated to sign with this team. He knew the club history, especially the catchers, and he was honored to be a $75,000 "bonus baby."

Players recognize the game has a "coldhearted" side as a trade is always possible, but for most players it still is an emotional shock and a disappointment to leave St. Louis. When Gussie Busch acquired the team in 1953, he assured Enos Slaughter that he was "a credit to the game" and would always remain with the team. Yet, Slaughter was traded to the Yankees in 1954. Slaughter acknowledged, "I cried, and I don't mind admitting it, because I had a tender heart, and I don't think anybody who ever put on a Cardinals uniform tried to give the Cardinals any more than Enos Slaughter did."[15] Bob Uecker played for many teams but said of St. Louis "I played in the best baseball city in America...Those were two of the greatest years of my life."[16] Richie Allen noted, "St. Louis is baseball All-American style. Not like Philly, not like New York, not like anywhere else. In St. Louis, the fans care about the game...they talked strategy, the hit-and-run, the squeeze play, the defensive alignment."[17]

Mark McGwire remarked, "When the baseball season starts in St. Louis, they bleed (Cardinal) red. Everybody told me I would love St. Louis, and no wonder."[18] He continued to play in St. Louis when he could have made more money elsewhere and noted, "I don't think it was too hard to fall in love with St. Louis...It makes me float every time I come to the ballpark and play in front of these fans. I've never been treated that way as a baseball player."[19] He was also credited for convincing Jim Edmonds what a great time he would have playing in St. Louis.

Rich Wolfe, author of numerous books about sports fans, grew up in St. Louis during the 1950s listening to Jack Buck and Harry Caray. He sees those days as "a great era in America." Kids flocked to diamonds every chance they got and "a trip to a major league baseball park...was magical." Before the 1960s expansion, with schedules of one hundred fifty-four games, major league baseball consisted of only sixteen teams divided into two leagues. It was easy to know all the team rosters. Trades made history and mattered on a personal level. Hopes and dreams for success hinged on the victories and defeats, the stats, and the league standings. Those outcomes seemed to affect the mood of fans more than the players themselves. Many fans so identify with their team that the won-lost record reflects a personal character quality as staunch fans often refer to the accomplishments of the team as "we."[20]

The physical space of being in the park is extremely important to fans, but over the years, radio has connected Cardinal fans around the nation too. Fans outside of St. Louis have gone to great lengths just to hear a Cardinal broadcast. In the mid-twentieth century some recall positioning their cars to get better reception of the play-by-play feed going to the highest points in their town for the best reception. By the twenty-first century, with Major League Baseball online and satellite radio, fans can get the game anywhere in the world.

The purity of the game is remembered as a time of innocence without agents, Astroturf, designated hitters, collective bargaining, free agency, mega salaries, arbitration, inter-league play, play-offs, wild cards, or championship night contests. Many view the game as perfection, though it cannot be denied that negative elements also exist. Baseball banned black players, held racist policies, and had to deal with the reserve clause, drugs, alcohol, and steroids. Over more than a century times have changed, especially with integration, technology, league expansion, television revenues, the union, the overall big business of the game, and Congressional hearings, but baseball still holds a special place in American culture.[21]

Many may dispute the popular draw to baseball as simple nostalgia but for millions the love of the game is a part of the American heritage. In St. Louis, at the 2009 All-Star game, President Barack Obama noted that baseball "has been at the center of our national life" for generations and "has always embodied the values that make America great: hard work, leadership, passion and team work."[22] The American flag flies over the fields and the custom of beginning games with the singing of the "Star-Spangled Banner" dates to before the First World War.[23] Baseball tradition continues as families pass along the inherited American legacy across generations.

St. Louis baseball moves beyond a simple summer pastime; it is an all-season sport that begins with February spring training, continues throughout the heat of summer, erupts in pennant fever in the fall, and then picks up for the hot stove league in winter. "Wait 'til next year" is a common mantra heard throughout the land as fans bide their time waiting to once again hear "play ball."

St. Louis fans become totally involved in the game. They keep score, cheer their team, converse with the players, and bring their gloves to grab a souvenir. These fans have a reputation as the least likely to boo the opposition, unless it is the rival Chicago Cubs or opposing players who talk smack about the Cardinals. Then those friendly fans will show their displeasure as they defend their team.[24]

Die-hard enthusiasts of baseball see the game as a sacred religion, a spiritual experience. Like religious ceremonies, attending a game is ritualistic with repetitive motions for fans and players. Stadiums are "much like a cathedral, where domed roof or open-air parallels the vaulted roof of a medieval cathedral built to approximate the eternal vault of the heavens" and provide sites for pilgrimages to holy grounds with annual excursions as fans journey to witness where players perform.[25]

The shrine in St. Louis has always been a favorite stop on the baseball circuit. To those frequenting the new Busch Stadium it is "a little piece of heaven" to witness baseball "as it ought to be" played, in open air with natural elements. A summer just would not be complete without catching a game or two on the home field. If a trip to St. Louis cannot be worked out, fans reluctantly settle for trekking to the closest baseball field to catch a game and to cheer on their Cards. St. Louis contests held in blue cities of Kansas City, Chicago, and Milwaukee demonstrate a sea of red, that rivals the blue that home fans sport.

In St. Louis, the devotion to the hometown team does not fit just any baseball franchise; even when the Browns held court in the river city the Cardinals held favor. Cardinal fans see the team as family. They do not come out to the game as mere spectators or to "turn the spotlight on themselves." They worship the team with a passion. Cardinal fans "wear red, they come from all across the baseball watching world, and they keep the Cardinals faith." Within the last 20 years or so "more than three million fans show up annually to see the Cardinals play at home." [26]

Even when not in the stands, loyal fans get involved in the game. They yell at their radios and televisions as the team comes out on top or when they think the manager should make a change. After a St. Louis victory, the sound of honking horns can be heard throughout the metropolitan area as a celebratory trumpet that announces victory. The bliss of triumph has people jumping up and down and screaming in living rooms, bedrooms, kitchens, and local bars. This activity may seem foolish to those not involved in the ecstasy, but these are fanatics and if anyone does not understand their antics then they just have not found their way to Cardinal Nation.

Up to 1958, when the New York Dodgers and Giants moved westward, "the Cardinals were baseball's southern and westernmost franchise, and they drew swarms of players and fans from the vast stretches of baseball's heartland." [27] That devotion continues into the twenty-first century. Early on fans tracked the team via the "Voice of St. Louis," KMOX radio broadcasts that had 50,000 clear watts. Throughout the middle of the twentieth century the station had virtual coast-to-coast coverage after sundown.

Noted author John Grisham brought his love of the Cardinals to print in *A Painted House*, where the main character "is a young boy who dreams of playing for the Cardinals when he grows up." In fact, that was Grisham's dream, too. In Mississippi he saw playing ball as a way out. "I picked cotton, chopped cotton and worked in the fields and dreamed of playing for the Cardinals because I wasn't going to be a farmer." [28]

Until 1954, when the Browns moved to Baltimore, growing up in St. Louis was either Browns or Cardinals. Brownie fans never lost their devotion or forgot their happy moments; nor have Red Bird followers.

St. Louis kids grow up on baseball and they possess special memories of how they got hooked on the sport. Some never attended games but listened on the radio and followed the box scores in the *Star Times, Globe-Democrat* or *Post-Dispatch*. Others were members of the infamous Knot Hole Gang, or attended games with family members, friends, or even alone. John Ulett, Cardinal announcer for several decades, lived within biking distance of the stadium and recalled that he and his friends rarely paid admission. They would wait until "they opened the gates for fans to exit the game in the seventh inning… [to] watch the final 12 outs."[29]

Cardinal fans, like Sharon Maniaci-Melton of Virginia, may leave the city of St. Louis, but they never lose the attachment for the hometown team. She grew up in the St. Louis area and holds fond memories of her Aunt Connie George who gave her an appreciation for the game and taught her never to leave early. Sharon passed that love onto her nephew. Her fondest memories date to the 1970s and Busch II. She remembered when she worked for the police department that officers and first responders received courtesy tickets from the Cardinals. Transplanted fans remain faithful. A trip to St. Louis to catch a game has a spiritual aspect that "is coming home."[30]

Some folks never lived in St. Louis, yet somehow, they become avid Cardinal fans. That would be understandable if they resided in a city that did not have major league baseball, but it is astonishing to think that someone who had baseball in their own backyard still chose the Cardinals. Many out-of-town fans share their stories of conversion and faithfulness. Joe Maddon, manager of the Chicago Cubs, grew up in Pennsylvania, but it was not the Pirates, Phillies, or any other east coast team that won his favor. It was the St. Louis Cardinals.[31]

Another east-coast fan's story of induction to Cardinal Nation gives insight to the life of living in enemy territory. Roger Drake, a successful businessman now living in New York, grew up on the east coast among a family of Yankee fans. It was the 1967 World Series of the Cardinals against the Boston Red Sox that captured the attention of this seven-year-old. He recalled he sat on the living room floor in front of the black and white television as his mom ironed. They saw Game One when Lou Brock got four hits and the Cards won 2-1. The Cards went on to take the championship in seven games. That was it; young Roger was hooked. The Cardinals became his team from then on.[32]

Drake continued to follow the team throughout his life, and in fact saw one of the longest games in major league baseball history when he attended a Cards-Mets game in 1974, a birthday gift. Roger said his dad wanted to leave in the ninth, but he would have none of that; after all, it was his birthday, and these were his Cardinals. In the bottom of the ninth, with two out, Ken Reitz stepped up to the plate with two strikes against him and lined a homer to take the game into extra innings. Baseball commissioner Bowie Kuhn attended and left in the tenth inning; but Roger stayed to see the Cardinals win 4-3 in 25 innings. The game lasted seven hours. Now that is a real Cardinal fan, whether a St. Louis native or not.[33]

The goal for all fans is to be in the park to worship in comfortable surroundings, yet sadly for some, the physical sites of play have changed over the years and fans take it hard when asked to move on. Fans mourn the diamond where they witnessed their first game, but they always seem to pack up their sentiments, along with the ghost of their special heroes, and continue to follow the team to the new site. They want to add to their memories, so they take the spirit of the former playing field to the new shrine. For fans the park is the physical representation of the team, and tradition. Many of the old stadiums face bulldozing once the new temple is in place; perhaps that is good so fans can transition easier to letting go of the past and supporting the new venue.

Baseball unites complete strangers and connects generations of families and friends. For devoted fans, place is powerful in eliciting personal memories. Long after the place has changed its physical appearance of an architectural monument, the musing of by-gone days and that spirit of memory rests to create a special ambience. American culture and edifices have changed over the last one hundred forty years but a unifying spirit in the community of Cardinal Nation has been, and continues to be, baseball and the franchise of the Cardinals.

Cardinals show their appreciation to the fans by winning. No National League team has won more World Series championships than the St. Louis Cardinals; even when they lose, they typically play competitive ball and give fans reason to believe. Fans and players alike know they are lucky to have found the Cards to share an appreciation for the game and pledge their loyalty. It is a proven fact throughout baseball that St. Louis is a great town to play in and players speak openly about the privilege to play for the St. Louis Cardinals.

Everyone, whether player or fan, knows St. Louis baseball is epitomized by the caliber of Stan the Man, "baseball's perfect warrior... baseball's perfect knight."[34] The legend of Stan continues, long after his playing days. In 1963, when Musial retired, sculptor Carl Mose crafted a ten-foot statue of The Man. That memorial sat outside the first downtown Busch Stadium and moved to the new location in 2006 where it greets loyal fans and foe alike. It fits with the idea of place being special. The statue serves as a welcome sign that works to tie generations of Cardinal Nation together. The stance of the man has become a great landmark for fans to meet up before or after a game.[35] It is a perfect representation of the franchise that honors its hero and the site where the community converges as a nation of believers. But the story of place begins long before Busch Stadium III. The origins date to the late nineteenth century at renowned Grand and Dodier.

CHAPTER TWO

THE EARLY YEARS AT GRAND AND DODIER

Baseball has been a popular pastime since the middle of the nineteenth century where businessmen controlled the public space of the diamond and found ways to profit. Early days were a simple past-time enjoyment of a bat and ball, sans gloves or other protective equipment. Day games were played under an open sky, on rough fields that lacked a professional manicure and racking up hundreds of errors in one season was considered the norm. Rules were sparse.[36] The games were simplistic events, before official announcers and scorekeepers, team mascots, radio, television, computers, and cell phones. There was no fast-paced automobile transportation, super-rail, or airlines. Newspapers covered the teams, but to really follow and enjoy the game one had to be present.

The Cardinals first field at Grand Avenue and Dodier Street sat on nine acres of pastoral land in "the wilds" of a rather undeveloped suburban area of north St. Louis, approximately six miles from the center of town.[37] In 1866, August Solari built a simple, wooden, closed field structure to house sporting events. It was called Grand Avenue Grounds and later changed to Solari Park.[38] The stands held about 800. "Less expensive, unprotected seats consisted of unpainted, sun-bleached boards (bleachers.)" Seating was limited. When more fans showed up and seats were filled, they would "congregate along the foul lines… [or] in front of the outfield fences," hence the term "standing-room." This presented problems though, as fans tended to sneak in closer to the action and sometimes interfered with play. A few wealthy spectators "view[ed] the game from the comfort of their carriages parked in the outfield."[39] Women's fashion styles of the day were the Gibson Girl look of long dresses or skirts that went to the floor with a high collared, long-sleeved top. Some women carried parasols to guard against the sun. Men wore trousers, long-sleeved white shirts and suit jackets. Many folks caught sight of the game sitting on the ground around the field or they captured it from housetops, light poles, and treetops.[40]

Solari Park's main revenue came as a shooting club, though it was also used for baseball games and picnics. The area served as an escape from the city, drawing pedestrian traffic, passengers in horse-drawn carriages, and others from the Grand Avenue trolley. The site became a popular spot in Victorian days and soon top amateur baseball teams made this their home.

The origin of the Red Birds can be traced to the original Brown Stockings big league team. They held to nationally accepted baseball rules that changed throughout the years. The roots of the early Cardinals were brown. The teams started out with white woolen uniforms trimmed in brown with brown caps and stockings. The new color, a vibrant shade of cardinal red, only burst forth at the turn of the twentieth century.

The team played at Solari Park from 1875 to 1877.[41] This club, formed by John R. Lucas, played in the National Association. He hired national, as well as local talent. Lucas became upset and disbanded the team in 1877 when he learned that some of the recently signed players had been accused of throwing games and found guilty of taking bribes for playing carelessly and recklessly down the stretch of the season while they were with the second-place Louisville team. Subsequently, league president William Hulbert banned the players for life. Lucas did not want to tarnish his own reputation with a scandal and separated himself from the club. The team became independent for the next few years under the sponsorship of the St. Louis Sportsman's Park and Club Association.

That organization raised funds to help support the team, and brothers Alfred H. and William Spink, both reporters for competing newspapers, oversaw the day-to-day operations.[42] Businessmen aligned to the sport sought to avoid a negative image as they recognized the important ties to the sport in helping to attract people and businesses to the city.

It soon became obvious that baseball could promote more than just the action on the field. In 1881, Christian Frederick "Chris" Von der Ahe, a twenty-nine-year old heavily accented German immigrant, "paid $1,800 for 180 of the 200 shares" of the recreational Brown Stockings.[43] The other 20 shares were held by Alfred H. Spink, who eventually established the bible of baseball, the *Sporting News*. Von der Ahe brought the city to major competition on the baseball circuit.[44] The team won the association pennant four consecutive seasons, 1885-1888, and took the coveted World Series in 1886.[45]

In 1851, Von der Ahe, born in Hille, Germany, found his way to St. Louis at the age of sixteen. He left his homeland at a time of economic downturn and to avoid being drafted by the Prussian Army. By the early 1870s he had settled at Grand and Vandeventer Avenues near the ball park. He owned property in the area where he built rooming houses for working-class German immigrants. In 1874, at the corner of St. Louis and Grand Avenues, he opened the Golden Lion Saloon and a grocery store. Von der Ahe knew nothing about baseball, but Eddie Cuthbert, his bartender talked baseball all the time. He finally convinced his boss there was something to the game and suggested that Von der Ahe bring his beer to the fans.[46] He did a brisk business at the saloon but noticed that the bar virtually emptied during the afternoon hours of a game. Von der Ahe decided beer and baseball might be a good combination. He faced a roadblock in getting the rights to sell the beer at the game, though, as the St. Louis Sportsman's Park and Club Association and the Spink brothers supported the growing Temperance Movement. The association would not approve of the sale of alcohol at the ballpark. Consequently, the young entrepreneur decided he would buy the team and run it the way he wanted, which meant selling beer.[47]

Von der Ahe rented the playing field at Grand and Dodier from Solari, invested $6,500 in the semi-pro St. Louis Browns, and obtained a place for them in the American Association (AA). The puritanical National League prohibited Sunday games and the sale of beer, but the AA allowed both. In fact, a host of brewery owners held positions on the board of directors of many of the AA teams. This association went against Victorian standards of propriety by allowing the sale of beer at the games and promoting Sunday games.[48] The AA also notoriously hired "contract jumpers and blacklisted National League players." In February 1884 "the leagues made peace…by signing a national agreement. They recognized each other's contracts, initiated a post-season championship, or World Series, and together with the minor Northwestern League, set up an arbitration committee to settle disputes."[49]

A Missouri law, dating from 1839, prohibited labor from being performed on Sundays but exempted "places of amusement." Since 1882 Von der Ahe's team played games in St. Louis on Sundays without interference, but in 1887, Von der Ahe was arrested at a Sunday game for breaking the Sabbath Law. The ump called the game. The case went to court and a judge ruled that baseball was a form of amusement and therefore exempt. Play continued for the Browns on Sundays "without interference from law enforcement officials."[50]

Von der Ahe, with rights to the ballpark concessions, sold beer in the beer garden and hired vendors to canvass the crowd with tall steins of the cold beverage. He looked at the sport as part "spectacle as it was game;" some of his moneymaking ventures to draw people to his beer garden and other amusements included horse races and lawn bowling. In the late nineteenth century battles over 'wickedness and sin,' St. Louis was an open fun city. The French, Irish, and German residents observed "The Browns' ball games were played around a keg of beer and a barrel of pretzels." Admission to the game cost twenty-five cents and a beer could be had for a nickel.[51]

Though Von der Ahe learned to love the game, other baseball club owners never respected him. Al Spalding, the tyrannical owner of the National League Chicago White Stockings and a baseball purist, saw him as a "proprietor of a pleasure resort in the suburbs of [St. Louis], and he came to be interested in Base Ball from the fact that games constituted one among other attractions in his place."[52] Baseball purists saw Von der

Ahe as a buffoon; that did not stop the flamboyant owner from taking on this business venture. To him, America supported free enterprise, and no one had the right to stop him. With help from Alfred H. Spink, he expanded the park and renamed it Sportsman's Park.[53]

Von der Ahe was a rotund playboy and a flashy dresser. With a pronounced German Accent, he referred to himself "der boss president," and called the players his "poys." He sported a stovepipe hat, "checked slacks, spats, gaudy waistcoats, and diamond stickpins," usually with an expensive mistress in tow and his pet greyhounds. He traveled by rail with the team and lived a lavish lifestyle, staying in prominent hotels along the way. He did not really know the game of baseball in a sense to guide it, but he certainly saw himself as the expert of the game and constantly interfered with the overall operations and running of the game. He fired managers at will and several times tried to call the action on the field himself.[54]

In those days most of the teams did not have clubhouses so the players dressed off-site, usually at a hotel. While railroad cars transported teams from city to city, the common mode of transportation for teams coming to the ballpark was horse-drawn bus-wagons that resembled prison vans known as a tally-ho. The extravagant Browns' owner shuttled his "poys" in grandeur. The horses, draped in St. Louis Brown blankets, led stylish open carriages. The owner proudly showed off his players before they ever took the field.[55]

In 1882, Von der Ahe's Brown Stockings, along with five other teams (Baltimore, Cincinnati, Louisville, Philadelphia, and Pittsburgh) joined the American Association to begin a stretch of ten seasons before they folded into the National League. Most of the players did not use equipment such as gloves, but by the end of the century barehanded play faded out. New forms of equipment were introduced such as "the catcher's mask and chest protector, shin guards, and small, lightly padded, pocketless gloves."[56]

One of the Brown's earliest player acquisitions proved to be an asset. In 1882, they acquired talented and combative first baseman Charlie Comiskey from Chicago. The following year he took over as player/manager. He steered the team to four straight pennants and a world championship. Comiskey knew how to get fans into the ballpark. He, like many in the history of the game, believed "first place is the only subject of conversation."[57] He expected his men to be tough, play hard, and do whatever it took to win the game as "one decision sometimes may mean the loss of the pennant." His players were known to distract opposing pitchers from the foul lines as they ran back and forth and shouted obscenities. With Comiskey on-the-field fights were common, he never backed down.[58] Abusive play led to exciting baseball, though inhospitable behavior. The press referred to a Comiskey team as bad boys, demons, and hoodlums."[59] The fans loved it. Wagering on games was common practice. Fans supported controversial players who fought and complained over the plays and the calls. Fighting hard, chatting, and taking on the lone ump proved the way to take a stand and show spirit for the game.[60]

In 1882 Von der Ahe hired his bartender, Eddie (Ned) Cuthbert as skipper of the team. Opening day drew a crowd of 2,000 to cheer the team to victory. That year the Browns finished in fifth place with a 37-43 record, but more importantly to the owner, they were second in AA attendance finishing with 135,000 attendees.[61] In days before electrically lit fields these daytime outings attracted a diverse following of mainly white-collar men whose work allowed them the leisure to attend the events in the middle of the day, in contrast to manual workers. The twenty-five to fifty-cent admission price, the necessity of working twelve-hour days with only Sunday off, and the price of transportation may have kept some working-class men away during the week; though weekend and holiday games brought out those "who normally were confined to shops and factories."[62]

Von der Ahe hired vendors to sell beer in the stands and fans hung out in the beer garden guzzling the brew and enjoying the game. After the game, fans stayed at Von der Ahe's saloon as it was a popular site that players frequented.[63] Spink noted "it was a turning point for the history of sport. Thereafter, beer would provide bucketsful of money for virtually every professional team in the land and for hundreds of colleges as well."[64] In spring 1882, when Von der Ahe first fielded a team in Sportsman's Park, the seating capacity was 6,000. Many times, the crowd rose to twice that number. Two decks stretched behind home plate from first to third base.[65] In 1883, the AA expanded the schedule to 98 games as they added teams in New York City and Columbus, Ohio. Baseball proved even more popular in St. Louis as the team doubled its opening game attendance. A hot pennant race drew a crowd of 16,000 for a single game. They finished one game behind the Philadelphia Athletics as the excitement of the season attracted 243,000 Browns' fans.[66]

The Browns faced competition in 1884 when a new eight-team Union Association took umbrage with the policy of the reserve clause that barred players from talking with another team unless they had already been let go outright or their contract had been sold to another team. It basically gave the exclusive right to the player's services for their whole career. If the team decided to trade a player, that contractual right passed to the new club. Those who established the new league saw that practice as "undemocratic, un-American and made serfs of the ballplayers."[67]

This new group formed under the tutelage of St. Louis millionaire Henry Lucas; he saw the restrictions on the players as "undemocratic, un-American and made serfs of the ballplayers" and he felt no compunction with luring current players to his new association.[68] In order to keep up with this new rivalry, the American Association opened its league to four other cities, Brooklyn, Indianapolis, Toledo and Washington (the team playing in D. C. moved to Richmond, Virginia.)

Lucas put together a good team, the Maroons; they took off with a 20-game winning streak and ended with the remarkable record of 94-19. He established a new park closer to the city in Kerry Patch, the Irish section of St. Louis at Cass and Jefferson. It was quite a lavish park that accommodated 10,000 fans. Around the league it became known as "The Palace Park of America" with "upholstered folding opera chairs," a billiards table in the clubhouse, and other amenities. Fans came out, but the Browns still outdrew them in attendance 212,000 to 116,000. The new league only lasted one season. Other teams did not draw enough fans to economically survive. The Maroons and the Cleveland team folded into the National League.

Financial disasters struck Lucas. The new ballpark, uninsured, burned to the ground, and play moved to a lot at Natural Bridge and Vandeventer. He managed to hold onto the team for another year. The Browns were hot and winning American Association pennants while the Maroons rested either at the bottom or close to it. The National League did not allow Sunday games and refused to let alcohol be sold at the games. Those restrictions garnered more fans to the American Association and financially hurt Lucas. He sold the Maroons to Indianapolis businessman John T. Brush who moved them out of town.[69]

Baseball events attracted large crowds as evidenced by the near 250,000 who came out for a St. Louis night-time parade on October 7, 1885, to honor the pennant-winning team that defeated the National League champion Chicago White Stockings.[70] In 1885 Von der Ahe put in "what is believed to be the first women's restroom in an American sporting facility."[71] In 1886 bleachers were added to the outfield areas and increased the seating capacity to 12,000. The "outfield distances were 350 feet down the left-field line, 460 feet to center, and 285 feet to right."[72] When he converted a two-story house in the right field corner into a beer garden it brought an amusement atmosphere to the game. For additional entertainment Von der Ahe provided "lawn bowling, handball courts, and picnic tables,"[73] and initiated a celebratory tradition of "Japanese fireworks" in the lawn area. Firework displays became a custom for baseball events in St. Louis.[74]

Some seasons the team had reason to celebrate with fireworks. Under the leadership of player/manager Charlie Comiskey, Von der Ahe's team won four pennants (1885-88), tied one World Series championship (1885) and won one (1886.) Von der Ahe, an interfering, difficult man to work for, caused some managers to resign, including Comiskey. They just did not want to put up with his antics. He also hired and fired managers at will. Numerous times the "brilliant" boss attempted to manage the team but that proved unsuccessful.[75]

A manager for the Browns certainly did not have it easy. Players used him as a protector and buffer from the controlling owner, and Von der Ahe expected a manager to be his whipping boy, to follow his "suggestions" and enforce tyrannical dictates. The inept owner "believed he knew far more about the game than he actually did...saw himself as the brains behind the baseball team...'the greatest feller in baseball.'"[76]

Von der Ahe's ambition, to win at all costs, supported players' efforts when it suited his mood. He did not interfere when in 1883 a group of angry players, upset by their pennant loss to the Athletics, beat up on fellow teammate, third-baseman Arlie Latham. They approved of Latham going after the opposition, the owner, and the umps with his caustic remarks, but they drew the line when he directed his sarcastic comments at them. Strangely, Latham's talent helped the team stay in contention and he continued to play for the Browns until 1889.[77]

Misbehavior by team members caused problems for management. Quite a few big leaguers tended bar in the off season and many operated saloons when their playing days ended. Increasing numbers of the young fellows came from the working-class stock of Germans and Irish who enjoyed drinking and brawling on and off the field.[78] Owners had their hands full trying to curtail the antics of their charges. Prior to the 1880 season the National League issued a stern warning in an "Address to Players." It cautioned players to stay clear of drink as the league would not "tolerate drunkenness" and players "would be 'absolutely shelved'" for such actions.[79]

In September 1887 race relations became a problem and a turning point for the Browns. From 1883-1898 "at least fifty-four...blacks played on racially integrated professional teams."[80] Yet, on a fateful 1887 autumn day segregation won the day. Previously, the magazine *Sporting Life* voiced several opinions on the race question, noting in 1885 of black player John "Bud" Fowler "the poor fellow's skin is against him...With his splendid abilities he would long ago have been on some good club had his color been white instead of black." Real competition for playing spots surfaced with the introduction of the minor league International League that fielded black players. By the latter part of the nineteenth century many teams objected to playing with blacks on the field and they received the support of the magazine when it questioned "how far will the mania for engaging colored players go?"[81]

The Browns decided to defy Von der Ahe's lining up a game that fielded black players. They refused to take the field in New York to play an exhibition game against the Cuban Giants, a team of black players. The day before the game the St. Louis players sent Von der Ahe a telegram that read "We, the undersigned members of the St. Louis Base-Ball Club do not agree to play against negroes to-morrow. We will cheerfully play against white people any time and think by refusing to play we are only doing what is right, taking everything into consideration and the shape the team is in at present." It does not appear that the players faced repercussions for that stance.[82] It was a time when throughout the United States segregation became the norm and eventually led to the support of the Plessey v. Ferguson, separate but equal Supreme Court decision of 1896; by the 1898 season blacks were banned from "white professional baseball."[83] The racist policy in professional baseball continued until 1947 when Jackie Robinson broke the color line.

Owners virtually reported to no one. Von der Ahe, no saint in his dealings, used an iron fist in conducting his relations with the team. He found ways to go after his players. He fined them for poor performances, as well as dirty uniforms. In one case, Von der Ahe called on Ted Breitenstein to pitch relief in the second game of a doubleheader after he had completed the game opener. Breitenstein claimed exhaustion and refused to enter the game. Von der Ahe fined him $100 and suspended him indefinitely even though he was one of his best pitchers.[84] By the end of the 1887 season Von der Ahe displayed irritation with the team. The Browns joined other teams looking for ways to cut costs and make profits. They sold some of their players for $5,000-10,000.[85]

The German owner exhibited his tightwad moments. When the team tied for the championship against Chicago in 1885, he did not pay them for their work. Von der Ahe decided not to pay his 1887 team for their postseason play that was scheduled to be a fifteen-game contest. By the time the Detroit Wolverines had taken the eighth win both teams disbanded thinking the contest was settled. The owners demanded the players stick around to play four exhibition games and the teams were justifiably upset. Perhaps the play was not that stellar. In any case, Von der Ahe decided that the team played so horribly and they had lost the World Series, so he just kept the $100 he had promised them.[86] When the Browns lost six to the New York Giants and went on to play three more exhibition games in 1888 post-season play, Von der Ahe pulled the same stunt, calling his team "chumps."[87]

Most association players made about "thirteen hundred to sixteen hundred dollars, about four times the typical nonagricultural worker, with stars getting up to twenty-five hundred dollars" but what they earned covered only the short playing season.[88] Players were also responsible for paying for uniforms, keeping them clean, and other expenses that ate into their pay. Vondy made money off his team in many ways. He insisted players live in rooming houses he owned, and they should drink "only in his establishments."[89] In 1898, when Von der Ahe faced desperate financial troubles, intensified by a severe fire at the ballpark, he paid his players sporadically.

Players in the American Association were American-born whites, primarily city boys. They found playing ball a thing to do for a few years and then settled down somewhere doing a regular job. It was clear the tyrannical owner thought he controlled the players. Fines for things that upset Von der Ahe became common place to include dirty uniforms, tardiness, laziness, and losses, virtually anything that displeased him. He viewed players as his employees to be rewarded or punished as he saw fit.[90]

Some of Von der Ahe's antics infuriated fans who talked of boycotting the games, but good baseball on the field always brought them back as the owner knew it would. A consummate businessman, Von der Ahe had a product the fans wanted. Owners held power to sell players and the reaction of fans mattered little as they continued to come to the ball park.[91]

The latter part of the nineteenth century and into the early twentieth witnessed an unruly atmosphere at the ball parks. Though Victorian society frowned on activities associated with "saloons, vaudeville, variety shows, billiard halls, gambling emporiums, and brothels," open gambling on the games was commonplace.[92] By the 1890s groups of bettors hung out around the grandstands. Fans, as well as owners and those on the field, bet on the game and "no longer made serious efforts to disguise their own betting." With the habit of betting, fans became more actively involved in following the game and the officials' decisions of the play. Gambling helped to involve the spectators for more than just the outcome of the game as they wagered on "statistics such as hits and runs and even the call of a pitch."[93]

Fans viewed baseball as more honest than horse racing or boxing and they bet freely. With bets on the line they voiced opposition to what they considered bad calls or bad play on the field. They screamed, yelled, and shouted obscenities and insults to communicate their displeasure. Some threw things on the field or took to physical attacks. Players were known for rough play, too, and use of profanity. Things got so out of control that in 1897 the National League issued a paper to address and curtail behavior on the field entitled, "A Measure for the Suppression of Obscene, Indecent and Vulgar Language upon the Ball Field." Players could be fined or even banished from the game if they spoke to another player or an umpire in a "filthy" way.[94]

A clever marketing strategy emerged when Von der Ahe introduced Ladies' Day games. Women got into the games for free. Perhaps he believed the presence of women would clean up the game and a moral responsibility of the game might emerge. He attracted a new group of fans. Men were the usual patrons, as photos of the time period attest, but women were becoming more interested in this social outing. It made sense to expand the appeal to garner a new crowd. On opening day, 1887, Von der Ahe declared a Ladies' Day game. He presented the ladies with a souvenir white silk handkerchief embossed with a picture of eleven baseball players, one Victorian lady waving a handkerchief, and the wording: "Souvenir of the opening of Season 1887 to the Lady Visitors, St. Louis Browns, with compliments Chris Von der Ahe." When the ladies entered the park, they found the free seats in a hot, sunny section on plank bleacher seats. They had to pay a quarter if they wanted a seat in the shady grandstand.[95]

At the end of the 1891 season, when faced with dire financial straits, some AA owners offered their players a chance to sign on with the National League. Disheartened with the owner of the St. Louis club, many of the Brown's players and their manager, Charles Comiskey, took the opportunity to jump to the National League and flee the irrational harassing Von der Ahe.

On December 17, 1891, the American Association folded and Von der Ahe moved his franchise to the National League. The schedules were arranged by the league, and teams played each other a set number of games per season. The league also instituted rules that handled disputes and supervised paid umpires. Stricter control of the operation took hold; for a new team to form they had to receive the permission of the existing clubs. It was agreed they would allow only one team per city and in order to qualify for admission the city had to have at least 75,000 people. The teams within the league could only compete against others in the league. Fearful that richer teams would buy up the best talent in the league, since 1879 they all had a reserve clause, "which gave teams an option to renew, trade, or release a player, without any reciprocity on the team's part." Baseball became an important tool for putting a city on the map.

Concerned about cleaning up the game and presenting a good image, the National League set out on a moral crusade banning gambling and Sunday ball, as well as drunkenness and raucous behavior. It was believed that politeness, respectability to the game and attracting women would clean up the game. The minimum admission cost of fifty cents was to discourage the rowdy element and encourage the better sorts to support the game. However, Von der Ahe obtained league permission to continue Sunday games and the right to serve beer.[96]

Opening day in baseball has long been a day of rituals to usher in spring with displays of patriotic American red, white, and blue, parades, marching bands, and honoring players. Die-hard fans find ways to skip school or work to show support, enjoy a day out, and cheer their players. A long tradition holds that a public official throws out the first ball to sanction the rite of spring with the pronouncement of "play ball."[97]

On April 12, 1892, St. Louis kicked off a new season in fine style with the franchise now a part of the National League. The occasion was a time to promote the city and galvanize attention and pride. A marching band led the festivities of a street parade featuring Browns players, Chicago opponents, and noted celebrities, including world champion boxer, John L. Sullivan, St. Louis mayor, Edward Noonan, Missouri Governor David Francis, and actress Lillian Russell. The team faced defeat 14-10 before a crowd of 10,000. Then five days later, on Easter Sunday, the National League hosted its first Sunday game as more than 10,000 spectators watched Cincinnati take the Browns 5-1 at Sportsman's Park.[98] When attendance fell, Von der Ahe lost money so he docked players' salaries and made it retroactive to the beginning of the season.[99] The season went downhill from there. The franchise finished eleventh out of twelve teams, yet boasted an overall attendance of over 192,000, third in the National League.[100]

Looking for a larger venue to garner profits, in 1893 Von der Ahe moved the team a couple of blocks north to 3852 Natural Bridge Avenue, an estate owned by Jesse G. Lindell, a real estate broker. The Maroons of the Union Association had played there before they moved to Indianapolis. Von der Ahe signed an eight-year lease at $1500 per year.[101] The park sat at the corner of Natural Bridge and Vandeventer Avenue, directly across from the Fairgrounds racetrack and was named New Sportsman's Park (1893-98).[102]

A $45,000 recreational area was constructed at the site. Dimensions of the new park were larger than the former playing field, 470 feet down the left-field line, 500 feet to straightaway center field, 290 down the right-field line. Seating capacity of the wooden structure was 14,500. The Lindell Railway Company built a streetcar loop across from the main gate of the park. The new home, described as "the finest park in America," advanced from simple grandstand seating to "private boxes, a clubhouse, a pavilion, a rooftop press box, and a Ladies' powder room. A long bar located on the ground floor sold beer and sandwiches for a nickel."[103]

Another spectacular parade, led by two brass bands, ushered in the 1893 season. Carriages lined the streets for blocks to see players, noted city and state officials, and prominent citizens such as beer tycoon Adolph Busch leading four of his finest black Arabian horses. Buildings along the route sported foliage and flags, while patriotic bunting donned the new ballpark. Players entered in horse-drawn carriages as crowds cheered. The ceremony included the burial of a time capsule under home plate, speeches by dignitaries, and the playing of the "Star-Spangled Banner."[104]

Losing seasons kept away some faithful fans, but other commercial entertainment distractions of the theater, picnics, circuses, dance halls, and saloons drew audiences as baseball alone did not draw the crowd Von der Ahe needed for enough revenues. Around 1896 Von der Ahe, known for his flair and extravagance, looked for ways to use this park on a year-round basis. Sometimes, in desperation to draw crowds, Von der Ahe combined the playing season with other events, such as a Wild West Show featuring Buffalo Bill, Sitting Bull, 40 cowboys, and 50 Sioux Indians. The show ran in conjunction with the regular baseball game but did not prove to be a financial success. Von der Ahe added a honky-tonk bar, a "wine room," and an amusement park with rides that included a low roller coaster that circled the field. He referred to the park as the "Coney Island of the West" complete with "carousels, carnival rides, band concerts, girl singing groups, and boxing matches before and after each game."[105] Von der Ahe added a racetrack. These enterprises upset baseball purists; yet the league had no rules that forbid such events. Other owners took note.

Von der Ahe came under attack in the 1890s when Spink's *Sporting News* published, "The Prostitution of a Ball Park" that showed displeasure with Von der Ahe's enterprising adventures. Charlie Spink personally affronted the showman; calling him "Von der Ha Ha... 'maggot' instead of magnate and later he referred to him as 'the tricky Teuton.'" Spink advised "baseball should rid itself of the thing that smells to heaven in the nostrils of every honest lover of the game."[106] In defense of the hostility from his fellow owners, Von der Ahe became intimidating. He called other owners "thieves and crooks, porch-climbers and sandbaggers" out to get him. There was not much they could do to stop his gauche antics but once he left the game and they controlled access to the league, the memories of this river city showman guided future decisions.

Von der Ahe continued to promote other entertainment venues to include a "chute the chutes" water ride, bicycle races, horse racing, winter ice skating and a Civil War reenactment. Most of the endeavors did not reap financial benefits. Lawsuits for non-payment to contractors and patent infringements put him near financial ruin. In addition, some of these events were quite destructive to the playing field, upset the players, and did nothing to improve play. Finally, by opening day 1898 Von der Ahe had converted the playing field to a baseball only venue.

For most of the nineties Von der Ahe's teams did not finish higher than tenth in a twelve-team league and "averaged 45 victories and 91 losses."[107] In fact, the last full season under his tutelage the team rested in the cellar and posted a deplorable 29-102 record. Since moving to the esteemed National League, the Browns were virtually the laughingstock of the circuit never finishing higher than ninth in a twelve-team league. The attendance over those same seven years never broke 200,000. Eventually, the lackluster results helped determine a change of ownership.[108]

As time progressed, safety and profit steered major changes to national ballparks. The wooden stands of the late nineteenth century, haphazardly and cheaply erected, brought frequent hazardous fires; by the turn of the century a rash of ballpark fires and lawsuits took their toll. Five major fires sparked at Sportsman's Park alone in the 1890s. The structure was partially rebuilt on three separate occasions and once had to be completely rebuilt.[109]

On Saturday, April 16, 1898, the second game of the season, a fire broke out in the second inning. Players spotted the blaze first under the grandstand and stepped off the field. Along with the umps they tried to clear the stands, but fans assumed some confrontation between drunken spectators had halted play. They yelled for the game to continue. Crowd panic set in once the fans realized there was a life-threatening emergency. City firemen arrived in horse-drawn wagons and doused the fire.

Close to a hundred of the 6,000 in attendance suffered injuries from burns or trampling. Most of the ballpark faced complete destruction at a cost of $60,000. The grandstand, half of the bleachers, the saloon, and the clubhouse office burned along with most of the owner's personal possessions. Von der Ahe lost team trophies as well as cash. Insurance only covered about half the cost to rebuild the park and the owner faced numerous lawsuits for personal damage. Von der Ahe, financially unstable at the time, never fully recovered. Determined not to miss a game because of the fire, he enlisted the services of more than a hundred carpenters, and ordered manager Tim Hurst and his players to work throughout the night cleaning up the damage and helping to construct stands to ensure a game the next day.[110] No one could say for sure how this duty affected their play the next day, but the team committed eleven errors in the fourth inning and the opposition scored ten runs. The Browns lost to Chicago 14-1. The stands had to be rebuilt. Many games that season had to be played in other cities. The Browns finished in the basement.[111]

One-time millionaire Chris Von der Ahe saw himself as an astute businessman, but over the years he squandered his money and could not hold onto his wealth. His extravagance and egotistical attitude included commissioning a life-sized statue of himself. Then in 1894, his son Eddie sued him over a property dispute; between 1895 and 1898 the scandalous owner married and divorced twice due to "infidelity and physical and mental abuse." His first wife sued for divorce; his girlfriend, Anna Kaiser sued him $10,000 for breach of promise because after his divorce Von der Ahe married another woman, Della Wells. He divorced Wells and ultimately married Kaiser.[112]

Financially, the flamboyant Von der Ahe's lavish spending and his misdeeds finally caught up with him. Things got so crazy financially that former Pittsburgh Pirates owner William Nimick hired a private detective to kidnap Von der Ahe and bring him back to Pennsylvania because of a seven-year-old debt of $2,500. The 1898 season was the final one for Von der Ahe. The expenses incurred to rebuild the park and settle the lawsuits caused Von der Ahe, who had been involved in the business of baseball for seventeen years, to file bankruptcy and go into receivership. The National League, only too happy to have the bumpkin out of the game, paid his debt to Nimick.

Von der Ahe lost his franchise on January 26, 1899, on foreclosure to The Mississippi Valley Trust Company. On March 14, 1899, the bank acquired a court order to sell the club at auction for $33,000 to G. A. Gruner. A disgruntled Von der Ahe acknowledged "I didn't care who got the property, just so that...Robison did not." Gruner promptly realized a $7,000 profit as he resold the club to St. Louis attorney Edward C. Becker acting on behalf of Frank and Stanley Robison, transportation magnets from Cleveland, Ohio who had made their fortunes with the local streetcar industry in Cleveland and Fort Wayne, Indiana.[113]

Furious at being outfoxed and losing his team, Von der Ahe took the National League officials to court to regain control of the Browns. He argued the team was stolen from him and he demanded restitution of $25,000 from other team owners. A trial ensued where his old friend Al Spink testified against him, convincing a judge that the owner had agreed to hand over the team. Von der Ahe lost his claim. Charles Spink took credit for running the owner out of the game and mockingly reported in the *Sporting News*, "Chris Von der Ahe is a baseball corpse."

The former Browns' owner never again found the path to financial success or stability. In fact, he was in such desperate condition financially that in 1908, in an effort proposed by Charles Spink, the Cardinals held a benefit for him. Von der Ahe died June 5, 1913, of cirrhosis of the liver. He was buried at Bellefontaine Cemetery in St. Louis; four of his former players and Al Spink served as pallbearers. Fittingly, his grandiose, larger-than-life statue adorns the gravesite.[114] For baseball purists it is worth a trip to the cemetery.

Baseball in St. Louis at the end of the nineteenth century was a simple time directed to get a profit for the owner at the expense of the players—at all costs. Fans supported the endeavor for pure entertainment value and needed more than baseball to bring them to the ballpark. It was a time of rowdiness and vulgar behavior that involved drinking and gambling. Rules were slowly implemented to bring some semblance of civility to the game, yet it would take new owners to clean up the sport in St. Louis.

PLAY AT LEAGUE PARK/ROBISON FIELD/ CARDINAL FIELD

At the turn of the century, cities were places of high culture and economic growth. St. Louis, overall a city of first-generation Americans and German-born newcomers, boasted a population of 575,000. It was a growing city where one could hear English and German spoken on the streets and read newspapers in both languages. About 6 percent of the population was African American. Folks found jobs building skyscrapers, working as clerks, managers, phone operators, or part of a cleaning crew. Some worked in the automobile industry, at the shipping docks, on trains, or shoeing horses. It was an industrial town noted for making shoes, brewing beer, printing newspapers, and rolling steel. The garment industry flourished on Washington Avenue and jobs thrived in the shopping districts. The professional class consisted of newspaper publishers, physicians, entrepreneurs, lawyers, and teachers. City boosters searched for ways to increase population numbers and to sell the benefits of living in this city by the river.

St. Louis ranked as the fourth largest city in the United States behind New York, Philadelphia, and Chicago. Like those places it was a dangerous place, run by the manipulation of political bosses. The St. Louis boss system fell to Irishman, Ed Butler who controlled city elections for many years.[115] The wealthy businessmen held social standing and played into the corrupt practices that helped get things done through bribes and graft.

Fear presided, especially for the north and south side working-class plagued by urban problems of political corruption, overcrowded waterfront conditions, slums, filthy unpaved alleys and roads. The smell of the city reeked with garbage in the streets and "the odor of formaldehyde used as a disinfectant and insect powder spread to kill and destroy vermin." A real problem rested with the water supply that produced "liquid mud flow into wash-basin or bath-tub."[116]

In addition, 1900 saw numerous bloody strikes. The disturbances proved violent and by summer at least fifteen men had been killed.[117] One confrontation involved a streetcar strike that ensued when the company refused to recognize the workers union.

Lincoln Steffens, a muckraker, documented these problems in articles published in *McClure's Magazine* and later reprinted in a book, *Shame of the Cities*, in 1904. He revealed St. Louis as a city going through problems of greed brought about by growing industrialism and an influx of more people to the city. He showed the way to cleanup cities came through exposing the dishonesty of the boss system and finding folks willing to stand up to corruption. The answer seemed to be social reformers, and circuit attorney Joseph W. Folk, who won office in 1902. His mission was to clean up the city, throw the crooks out, and present "a world on display" for the upcoming Louisiana Purchase Exposition Fair and the Olympics, both to be held in St. Louis in 1904. Folk took on corruption. He prosecuted at least twenty-four of the crooks, including Butler. Peace reigned during the summer of the World's Fair and beyond with the installation of streetlights, pavement of more city streets, and cleanup that included improved water purification. It became a time when folks felt comfortable strolling the streets, riding bicycles, and maneuvering horse drawn wagons.

During this era, the professional baseball team transferred to two successful businessmen with baseball experience, Frank and Stanley Robison. The brothers also owned a National League team in Cleveland, the Spiders.[118] A few years earlier the Robison's had come close to owning the Browns, but they refused to allow Von der Ahe the beer concessions.[119]

New ownership changed the team. These men supported baseball but not the other entertainment distractions surrounding it. The first hint that things would be different came with the announcement, "No beer waiters, peanut venders or score card [sic] boys will annoy patrons during games. Boys may sell score cards [sic} only before games, none after." It was clear that play on the field was prominent to the Robison brothers.[120]

Entertainment competition existed overall in the field of music and drama, as well as horse racing, billiards, boxing, rifle championships, bowling, and automobile tournaments. Therefore, the new owners searched for ways to draw fans to their enterprise. Attendance at the Robison's Cleveland games never reached high numbers even though they fielded strong teams that included the phenomenal pitcher, Cy Young, who posted 30 or more victories in three seasons.[121] Frank Robison spent a lot of money on the competitive Cleveland team and he thought the city never appreciated all he did to give them such an entertaining club. Looking to present a successful and profitable team to the sports-loving city of St. Louis, the Robison's swapped Browns and Spiders players that included future Hall of Fame members Jesse Burkett, Bobby Wallace, and Cy Young. They also installed the Cleveland player/manager, a hard-hitting St. Louis native, Oliver "Patsy" Tebeau.[122]

The rowdy St. Louis fans, often "crass and crude, careless, abusive and explosive in their language to the players on the field…were the breed which would take a fighting ball club like the transplanted Spiders to their hearts."[123] In the swap fans got rough-and-tough baseball from colorful, aggressive pros out to win at all costs. The feisty team of 1899, and especially its manager, took on umpires and thought nothing of beaning batters, spiking opposing players, using obscene language or getting into fist fights. Fans got caught up in the antics too. Occasionally police had to break up unruly mobs upset with on-field incidents, miscalled plays, and games called for darkness or rain.[124]

On Saturday, April 15, 1899, the festivities of opening day got underway. Close to 5,000 people assembled to witness a parade of players usher in the ritual of baseball's return. Frank Robison greeted prominent citizens, including St. Louis mayor Henry Ziegenhein, in the lobby of the Southern Hotel to predict winning the pennant. "Beyond a doubt, St. Louis is the most enthusiastic baseball city in the country and with a team this capable of playing the game for all that is in it, we surely have a winning combination." A marching band led the parade assembly of twenty-five carriages to escort Mr. and Mrs. Frank Robison and Stanley, as well as dignitaries and players. The procession ended up at the Southern Hotel for a luncheon and then resumed for a trip to the ballpark on Natural Bridge Road.[125]

Hoping to change the image of the team from the drab Browns, who had only won 30 percent of their games over the last four seasons, Robison started fresh with bright red trim to the team's uniforms.[126] The color and the transfer of personnel proved a good move. In less than two hours the new team defeated Cleveland 10-1.[127] At the park, close to 500 well-dressed women and 17,500 men, the largest St. Louis crowd to witness a professional baseball game, eagerly embraced the team. These owners brought something fans had only fantasized about, an excitement to win.[128] Fans soon got over the replacement of their old players. Pennant fever hit when the team won its first seven games.

At the end of May, when the club fell out of first place one fan could not believe it had anything to do with the playing on the field. The players had not let the fans down. No, typical of a loyal fan, he found fault with the officiating. "The umpiring was unsatisfactory at all stages. Burns' judgment on strikes and balls was frequently questioned and Smith's base decisions were accepted to so often that the spectators tired of his yellow work…Think of it requiring two hours and fifteen minutes to play six innings in one of the games! What better proof of the inefficiency of the umpires!" On another occasion police found it necessary to escort a game official to safety when St. Louis fans chased a respected National League umpire Hank O'Day into the clubhouse and someone "appeared with a rope."

Fans enthusiastically enjoyed the new ownership and becoming part of the activities of the game. Attendance soared from 151,700 in 1898 to

373,909 the following year.[129] This was not the same team as the one a year ago that only attracted 2,100 to a game and finished in twelfth place. This team brought enthusiasm and promise of winning. They finished the season in fifth place, fifteen games out of first, with an 84-77 record. Cleveland had a disastrous season finishing 20-134 and disbanded at the end of the 1899 season. Louisville, Baltimore and Washington dropped out, too.[130]

The St. Louis club continued to play at Natural Bridge–Vandeventer. They changed the name of the field to League Park (1899-1911). The following year the original lease (dating back to Von der Ahe's ownership) expired and the brothers bought the property from Lindell for $60,000.[131]

A striking change ensued when the team changed the color of their uniforms to red. Since the National League already had a Cincinnati team called the Red Stockings, the St. Louis name became the Perfectos. That did not last long. By the end of 1899, sports reporter for the *St. Louis Republic* William McHale suggested the brothers rename the club the Cardinals and by the start of the 1900 season, they did. Originally, the change in name was not connected to the cardinal bird but when the team changed the uniform trim and stockings to a bright red McHale heard a woman remark of the team's attire, "What a lovely shade of cardinal," and over time the name stuck.[132] McHale used the name in print and over the years it became official.

Baseball continued to be a revenue-based venture that benefited owners if they could cut costs and share expenses. Some things influencing attendance were out of their hands, though. In May 1900, a streetcar strike hit St. Louis that virtually shut down transportation throughout the city. On May 8th only two hundred people came out for the Cardinals-Reds game. Believing the strike would end soon, the May 9th game was postponed, but the strike continued for close to another eight weeks. Convinced the strike could affect attendance, the team acquired two major players, John McGraw and Wilbert Robinson. Fans enthusiastically joined the brass band welcoming committee at the train station and watched these two superb players take the field. They did not let a transportation strike foil their plans.

On May 12th, in a game against the Dodgers, close to 7,000 fans flocked to League Park. The "crush of wagons around the park made a sight long to be remembered." The traffic jams of 1,500 to 2,000 horse drawn wagons, as well as a few of the first automobiles to hit the streets, caused quite a stir and brought chaos "beyond description."[133]

Meanwhile, fire continued to endanger parks. In a game against the Cincinnati Reds on May 4, 1901, a raging blaze at League Park, caused by a careless smoker, took most of the wooden structure except the bleachers.[134] To escape injury excited fans ran onto the field. The fire spread quickly and leapt to a nearby racetrack and set ablaze some streetcars outside the structure. The home-stand continued the next day, but at nearby Sportsman's Park. That park, known for cycling races, had not been used for baseball in quite a while though it served its purpose for the day to accommodate a crowd of 7,000 who watched the game from behind roped off areas.[135]

A road trip ensued as basic reconstruction of the mammoth park finished to open a home-stand on June 3rd. Reconstruction of the playing field had not changed much from its earlier days simply because the field was rather landlocked on an oddly shaped rectangular lot. Evidently, this configuration fit the early twentieth century team where play was dominated with hit and run, base stealing, and sacrifices.

In December 1901, the newly established American League transferred the Milwaukee Brewers team, owned by Robert Lee Hedges, to form a new St. Louis Browns team. Hedges worked to present a safer environment to clean up the rowdy image of baseball; he hired security guards, banned alcohol and promoted Ladies' Day. This new approach proved exciting news for St. Louis baseball fans, but ultimately Hedges' team had devastating results for the Robison's investment. The reserve clauses seemed to vanish, and the new St. Louis team lured away seven prime players from the Perfectos (Cardinals).[136]

It was not difficult to entice the players to leave Robison as many saw him as a cold, calculating owner. At the end of the 1900 season, he withheld full salaries from all but four of his players.[137] To justify this shortage Robison sent a letter to the players stating, "In your contract for the past playing season of 1900 said contract called for [a certain amount of money] per month for playing and producing first class baseball for the American Base Ball and Athletic Exhibition Company of St. Louis, Mo. This you have not done."[138] Within two years the new league managed to "steal" fourteen of the Perfecto players, resulting in Robison's team ending the 1902 season 44.5 games behind the first place Pittsburgh Pirates. For the next eight years they never finished higher than fifth and averaged close to 50 games behind the pennant winner. Meanwhile, the Browns, at least for those first few years, fielded contending teams and they drew more fans than their competitor.[139]

Baseball's popularity led owners to recognize the financial necessity to build sturdier facilities, increase the seating area, and beautify the grounds to attract larger crowds. The troublesome fires that ignited the wooden stands presented problems that scared away fans and halted playing schedules. One solution pointed to the National City Beautiful Movement that supported urban planning and community living.

It promoted ways to bring together the street grid of the modern city with green spaces and magnificent architecture in the industrial cities of America. Akin to the other construction of the day to include railway terminals, emporiums, skyscrapers, amusement parks, office buildings, city administration buildings, and theaters these parks were "edifices that local residents proudly pointed to as evidence of their city's size and achievements." In addition to providing a park to view the sport of baseball, they "served as retreats from the noise, dirt, and squalor of the industrial city." Names of these new buildings, Sportsman's Park, Fenway Park, Ebbets Field, Shibe Park, spoke to the idea of a tranquil, rural setting denoting an escape from the urban chaos.[140]

Between 1909 and 1915 thirteen of the sixteen major league teams built new architecturally attractive, fireproof baseball parks of steel and concrete. Owners were somewhat hampered in constructing these projects without the aid of public funding or eminent domain. They either erected these new parks in sites they already used or they acquired land further from the downtown area, keeping in mind the trolley, streetcar and subway lines.[141] In October 1905, Stanley Robison announced that within the next fifteen months the owners would erect a new concrete and steel, fireproof grandstand and pavilion at the site of League Park to double the seating capacity and bring the fans closer to the playing field.[142]

The newly formed American League St. Louis Browns moved into the original Sportsman's Park. In 1908, the rickety, combustible wooden stands at Grand and Dodier were replaced with a steel and concrete grandstand, and the following year a sturdy upper deck was built.[143] Overhauled many times over the next forty odd years, the Browns continued to use this park until they left St. Louis at the end of the 1953 season.

In a time of economic prosperity baseball became an American feature in which "every city, town, and village in America" had its team to support and point to with pride. To be considered a big-league city, and have a place on the map, one had to have good railway transportation, as well as fine cultural establishments that included public parks, museums, symphonies, and universities; but cities did not measure up unless they had a major league baseball team. Many of the bigger cities had two teams. Every up-and-coming city wanted to be a major league city to attract settlers as well as tourists.[144]

At the height of America as a melting pot, immigrants came to ballparks to learn the game and be considered all-American. The two major league rosters excluded blacks and few of the latest immigrants found a place on the team, but over the first quarter of the twentieth century the teams became more diverse. In addition to urban Irish and German working-class, there were a couple of Native Americans and a few white Cubans; but the biggest difference from earlier teams seemed to be more players from rural Midwestern small towns and some from the Deep South.[145] Most of the youngsters had little or no education; about a quarter of the players had a college education and their presence helped to garner a cleaner image of the game, as did the attention given to players who did not smoke or drink. The hero examples provided more opportunity for second-generation immigrants to make the team in the years that followed. Kids playing street baseball with "sticks and makeshift balls" as well as those lucky enough to play "sandlot ball" found a path of "assimilation into the American mainstream" through baseball.[146]

The sport was gathering support among traditional conservative Protestants and the nation's upper class, but baseball was not necessarily seen as a respectable occupation. Many thought it was nonsense and lazy to play a sport for one's job. It was all right to work in the factory or attend school and play for the fun of it, but one needed to "work" for a living and not loaf around. In some cities it was difficult to get hotel rooms for the players, especially in the finer establishments. Even restaurants were quick to push them off to the back or into corners to avoid offending other patrons.[147]

Not everyone thought poorly of the game; some admired it for what they saw it could do for America. Baseball came to the attention of the American public in 1888 when the *San Francisco Examiner* printed the poem, "Casey at the Bat" by Ernest Thayer. The piece became well known when actor William DeWolf Hopper recited it on a New York stage; according to Hopper he repeated that feat at least ten thousand times. The same year *Spalding's Official Baseball Guide*, which included league rules and statistics, came out. It stressed the cultural importance of the sport noting, "It is very questionable whether there is any public sport in the civilized portion of the world so eminently fitted for the people it was made for as the American national game of base ball...It is full of excitement, is quickly played, and it not only requires the vigor of constitution and a healthy physique, but manly courage, steady nerve [and] plenty of pluck." The sport was recreational activity for American boys with a strong national heritage and seen to help civilize the masses. Many saw it as a "Good Thing for America."

Baseball was America's sport during the early twentieth century. Newspapers, magazines, and baseball fiction encouraged a following to help foster love of the game and produce heroes. The literacy rate rose throughout the early part of nineteen hundred. Beginning in 1908, the monthly publication *Baseball Magazine* garnered a huge following that brought extensive baseball news into the home. Kids enjoyed reading the Burt Standish series on young hero Frank Merriwell and novels of Zane Grey, known for his Western stories, but he also "had a long association with baseball," thereby combining two of the most American forms of entertainment.

The *American Boy* magazine, in May 1916, featured Christy Mathewson on the cover, showing him as a hero that encouraged "traditional qualities as fair play, discipline, and rugged individualism." Baseball became a way to educate boys with skills needed in modern society, a life that included teamwork and self-sacrifice. To see players excel set an example of what was being a good American.

Throughout the country, World Series contests brought crowds in the streets to watch the play-by-play reported on boards in front of newspaper offices. With increased popularity, a theme song emerged. Jack Norworth wrote the music and Albert von Tilzer the lyrics in 1908 for the hit song "Take Me Out to the Ball Game." Baseball was the rage, especially when it received the endorsement of U. S. President William Howard Taft in 1910. He set the "precedent for the ritual of the president opening each season by throwing out the first ball."[148]

Baseball became a more controlled sport as time went on. Play altered when rules changed around the turn of the century.[149] Other changes were an increased use of bullpen pitchers, not necessarily relievers or closers, but if the starting pitcher seemed to be blowing the game they brought in another starter. If the starter pitched well, he usually stayed in the whole game. Pitchers threw whenever it was necessary, no matter if they had just pitched the day before.

Another improvement was attention to the conditions of the field; benefits showed the "average errors per team fell from more than 400 in 1894 to 265 by 1908."[150] Most games only fielded one ump. It was difficult for him to catch all the plays and equally difficult for players and fans to hear all the calls, so umpires began to use hand signals to designate the call.[151] The strategy and tactics of the games demonstrated improved hitting and running, base stealing, and bunting. *Baseball Magazine* noted that the sport "year by year [has] grown more scientific, more a thing of accepted rules, of set routine."[152] All of these changes helped promote the game and garner audiences.

Throughout the first decade of the twentieth century the Cardinals and Browns fielded losing teams. A fair share of fans came out as both teams played on Sundays, a day that brought spectators. For the first decade of the twentieth century the Cardinals averaged an attendance record of over 230,000. The Browns also racked up high attendance records, including their opening season in 1902 with a record of 272,283.[153] As the 1907 season unfolded, the *St. Louis Globe-Democrat* called the fan base of the river city Dementia Americana for the spell bound attraction of baseball in St. Louis.

Tragedy struck the Cardinal family on September 25, 1908, when Cardinal co-owner, Frank De Hass Robison, age 54, died of a stroke at his home in Cleveland. His brother Stanley had already taken over the management of the franchise two years earlier. Not much changed in the operation of the club.[154] In the off-season the Cardinals acquired player/manager Roger Bresnahan from the New York Giants. Bresnahan was one of the best catchers in the game. He did not like losing. His presence excited fans eager to see winning baseball brought to the city.[155]

To be sure of garnering more fan support, Robison and Bresnahan worked to govern the objectionable and abusive language at the park. The skipper saw this behavior of disrespectful rants lacking good sportsmanship. Bresnahan had a salty tongue of his own that spurted out "every expletive known to the human ear" but that was beside the point.

He did not want fans tossing that language about. At the beginning of the 1910 season he issued a formal statement against fans who shouted insults and abuses to the players noting that both home and visiting teams deserved respect for their efforts. The club posted signs supporting a new policy that persons abusing players or umpires would be thrown out of the park and they could face prosecution.[156] In keeping with Robison's desire to improve the game and keep order, the decision was made to remove the bar so that "everything that would interfere with baseball as a sport was eliminated."[157]

Stanley Robison controlled the team mainly the way Frank had. The team brought entertainment to the city, yet it never finished higher than seventh place. He paid his players decently, but he also faced some financial troubles that necessitated his living in the ballpark clubhouse.[158] Then on March 24, 1911, in Cleveland, Stanley also died at age 54 of heart failure. Stanley, an admired gentleman of the game, was a courageous owner who moved the sport to a respectable position of good clean fun and who, along with Frank, elevated the game to "a high-class basis" away from the "old days of rowdy ball."[159]

Stanley Robison, a bachelor, divided his estate between his sister, Frank's widow, and thirty-two-year old Helene Robison Britton, Frank's daughter. Stanley's niece loved the game. She inherited majority of the St. Louis Cardinals team. The attractive brunette, married to an attorney, had two children, an eight-year-old boy and a four-year-old girl. Britton became the first female owner of a professional sports franchise. At the time American culture supported the notion of separate spheres and followed the cult of domesticity where women were placed on a pedestal for their piety, morality, and self-sacrifice. Wives were obliged to covet the domestic sphere, managing the household and raising the children to be upright, moral, and responsible citizens while men held forth in the public sphere of politics and the economy.

Church authorities supported this role for women and spoke from the pulpit about the "proper behavior" for women. Cardinal James Gibbons of Baltimore and others warned women tempted to step out of their prescribed bounds to steer clear of wayward women who moved into the traditionally male sphere of business, politics, and sports, as they neglected their traditional domestic role. For sure, the idea of a woman running a baseball club would not sit well with the male-dominated National League.[160]

Following Stanley's funeral, the *Sporting News* declared "it was made clear soon after the announcement of his death that the Cardinals will not be owned, or controlled by women."[161] The Cardinals announced that the Robison family would not sell the team and that Britton would not be active in the running of the club. Within a few weeks the front office was restructured. E. A. Steininger of St. Louis served as president of the association. He was a local resident and would oversee the daily operations. Mrs. Britton would serve as the elected vice president with G. H. Schofield, former vice president of the team, taking over as secretary and Herman Seekamp remaining as the treasurer.[162]

Britton, an educated socialite from Cleveland, lived in a guarded mansion bordering Lake Erie. While she readily admitted to not knowing "the game as intimately from a playing standpoint as a man might" she proved to be a woman who would not back down easily. After all, she had grown up with baseball, had played the game, learned at an early age to keep score, and "had mastered the details of the game."[163]

In 1911 women did not have a major presence in the male dominated public sphere. They did not even have the right to vote until 1920 with the passage of the Nineteenth Amendment. "Lady Bee," as she became known, supported women's rights, especially suffrage. Though she had no professional experience she had been around the business of baseball most of her life. In the years her father and uncle owned the Cleveland and St. Louis teams they taught her baseball, introduced her to scorekeeping, and to following the standings. She willingly embraced this new adventure and was determined to show her capability. Britton daringly challenged the place ascribed to her by men and society at large. She was "a new woman" of the modern age.

The death of Stanley shocked Britton but inheriting the club did not. In fact, in an interview with a female reporter for the *St. Louis Post-*

Dispatch, Britton noted that she and Stanley "were more like father and daughter…I was always my uncle's favorite…he could spend his affection on me. I often accompanied him on his tours with the team until my duties here at home became so numerous [and] I found it difficult to be away." The sentiment expressed in the interview was not only of a financial matter, but also the legacy of "sentimental assets and liabilities." She felt duty-bound and saw the bequest as a "pleasure and advantage not to shrink from doing everything in my power to further the interests of the Cardinals."

Britton saw this as an opportunity "to take a positive stand and actually aid the prosperity and popularity of baseball by very reason of my sex." She remembered that Stanley presented ways to make the sport attractive to women. He removed alcohol, improved the experience, and made the game more appealing. She noted having women in attendance helped to bring a "civilizing effect."[164] Britton supported "Ladies Day" games long before it became a popular practice and saw it as a way for "the fair sex to come out and see the Cardinals play!"[165]

Originally, Britton stayed in Cleveland and continued her responsibilities of tending to her children and running her mother's home. She expressed pleasure in the way Manager Roger Bresnahan was leading the team and remarked he had, "a nice wife. They have visited us here and we found her such an attractive woman." Britton did not know the players personally and remarked that she would enjoy getting acquainted with them.[166]

Much to the chagrin of other National League owners and some of the Cardinal front office, Britton ran the club in her own way. She took the reins immediately to become a force to be reckoned with; she became the head of the organization and made important decisions.[167] Throughout the years she attended all National League meetings in New York where "dressed in the height of fashion;" she held a front-row seat in the smoke-filled council room as well as appeared in the annual picture of club owners. Her presence was said to have "a salutary effect on some of the boisterous boys who then made up the National League's family of club owners."[168]

The change of ownership was good for the team. They played the best ball in over a decade and throughout the summer seemed in real contention for taking the pennant, something they had yet to achieve in the National League. Even though they finished in fifth place, they produced a winning record 75-74 and brought exciting play to the city. Attendance reached an all-time high of 447,768, a record that would hold until 1922. The club hit a bonanza financially, the best in their history to date. The profit of $165,000 allowed the team to settle all debts and go after new players. Delighted and confident of the winning path laid out by player/manager Roger Bresnahan, Britton signed him to a five-year contract.[169] The agreement assured him $10,000 a year salary with 10 percent of the profits.[170]

The 1912 season got off to a dismal start. The Cardinals lost 16 of their first 21 games; but for Britton things appeared bright. From the start she and Steininger had not agreed on running the club so she took him to court for control of the team. It was decided that Steininger had "overstepped his authority as the administrator of the estate, and a judge agreed" that he should step down. Britton took complete control of the Cardinals on May 20. She appointed her attorney, James Jones, to take over as president of the club.[171]

Play on the field was not as successful, though. By early June the team was already 30 games out of first. Pressures mounted as Britton took to advising Bresnahan on ways to pull the team out of the slump. He did not hold back. He spoke to her the way he would her father or uncle, in crude and offensive language. He stood his ground and informed her that "no woman was going to tell him what to do." She retorted "That's no way to talk to a lady." Caustic diatribe between the two continued.

As attendance dwindled undercurrents of tension swirled around Britton and some of the men. They simply were not used to a woman being in a power position, and they did not like it. The *Sporting News*, reported that she was referred to as "a weak woman," but the essence of the article favored her, stating, "Despite everything, Mrs. Britton has been at her post of duty, on the firing line, encouraging by word, if not by deed, her athletes. Some game spirit when so many troubles beset at home. Mrs. Britton may be only a weak woman, but she is doing more than many a strong man would think of doing."[172]

Bresnahan wanted her gone. He set out to buy the team from under her for $500,000. She would not hear of such nonsense; this was her team and she intended to keep it and run it.[173] She proved better prepared for the public sphere occupied by men than most had given her credit for. Britton, her children and her husband, Schuyler, an executive for a printing firm, moved into a St. Louis mansion, at 4215 Lindell, not far from the ballpark where she attended every home game from her private box.[174] That same year she renamed the ballpark, Robison Field.[175]

Things got testy in August when Bresnahan attempted to trade one of Britton's favorite players, Miller Huggins. She blocked the deal. At the end of the season Britton reached her limits. She invited the manager to her home to evaluate the season and devise a strategy for improvement. Bresnahan wanted no part of her interference and asked, "what the hell any goddammed woman can tell me about baseball."[176] Curtailing her anger until he left, Britton quickly contacted the club attorney and president, James Jones. She instructed him to fire the manager. Jones informed Britton that he could not release Bresnahan; he still had four years left on his contract and the team would owe him $40,000. The incensed owner replied, "I do not care if we have to buy up his contract— if we have to pay him in full for four years; I do not want him running my club any longer."[177]

The club dismissed Bresnahan in October and replaced him with Huggins. The excitement and confidence Britton displayed a year before proved short-lived and costly. The fired manager struck back. He hinted at an affair between Lady Bee and the bachelor Huggins but got nowhere.[178] Bresnahan asserted his rights to compensation. The club settled for $20,000.[179] The ordeal brought ire from many fans, players, reporters, and minor stockholders who backed the former manager. During the off-season Schuyler "Skip" Britton, husband of the owner, became team president. To many, her antics proved that women had no place in the male bastion of business, especially in sports.

Britton enthusiastically embraced the new season. Always eager to attract more women she celebrated opening day by giving flowers to the women and free scorecards to all the fans. She hired a male singer to croon between innings. Her son served as the mascot of the team as she had in her youth for the Cleveland Spiders. It was clear she was not going to be a silent force and demonstrated it was her team.

Rumors circulated that Huggins would not last the season, but the boss stuck by him. Britton, looking to the future with hope and anticipation announced that before the next season she would present the fans with a new ballpark, but she was not be able to procure the funding. Within the year the Federal League would come along to raid both major leagues of prized players, resulting in increased costs for the other leagues.[180]

The Federal League began in 1914. They set up teams in St. Louis, Baltimore, Brooklyn, Buffalo, Chicago, Kansas City, Indianapolis, and Pittsburgh. St. Louis fielded the Terriers, owned by Philip Ball, an ice plant manufacturer and Otto Stifel, a brewer. The president of the new club was Edward Steininger, the former Cardinals executive. Britton, without strong financial cash reserves, became vulnerable. Raids ensued when new teams offered substantially more money. Overall, more than a third of major league players jumped to the new organization as did many minor-leaguers.[181]

The Terriers opened at Handlin's Park with a seating capacity of 12,000. Located at the corner of Grand and Laclede, not far from Robison Field and Sportsman's Park, the new team competed for fans. It was not clear if St. Louis could support three major league teams, but the Terriers brought excitement to the city and opened to a crowd of 18,000.

Fans did turn out to support all three St. Louis teams in 1914. One was Miss Anna Gene Witzig, an artist, who attended an exhibition game between the Cardinals and the Browns. It was her first baseball game. Her illustrations of the game appeared in the *St. Louis Globe-Democrat*. Witzig reported the game "dull and uninteresting" but she attended "to see the hats, the new gowns, and the hundred and one things that occur when thousands of persons are congregated in a baseball park." Evidently Britton's son no longer served as the team mascot for Witzig noted in her drawings and writing that one thing that impressed her was "the antics of a cute little negro boy, who is the official mascot of the Cardinal players...Hops about like a clown."[182] A few days earlier the newspaper reported that the mascot, a "negro lad [was] about the height of a baseball bat" and that "the Browns need a full-sized buck negro for theirs."[183] Blacks were not allowed to play on the professional teams with whites but evidently serving as mascot did not offend the rules. Witzig's remarks on the fashion of the day and the pleasure of seeing the mascot spoke volumes of what society thought women were supposed to value at the games, as well as the accepted language in reference to blacks.

By the end of August, the Cardinals were in the heat of a pennant race. A midweek doubleheader against the Giants produced a crowd of 27,000 and set a record for the largest weekday crowd in St. Louis to date. They split the doubleheader, but the team was not able to keep up the pace and ended the season in third.[184]

December 22, 1915, saw the demise of the Federal League. National and American League owners agreed to pay the defunct league holders $600,000. As part of this agreement, Phil Ball, owner of the Terriers, received assurance that he could purchase one of the remaining St. Louis teams. He wanted to purchase the Cardinals. Britton resolutely refused to sell even after, or perhaps especially after, being "pressured by her fellow NL owners to do so." Once again owners had a difficult time removing an owner that they believed unsuitable to run a St. Louis franchise.

Ball acquired the Browns from Hedges for $425,000. He fired Branch Rickey as team manager and brought in his old skipper from the Terriers, Fielder Jones. Rickey stayed throughout the 1916 season with the Browns and then began a long, successful career with the Cardinals in 1917. Another important point of the attempt of the Federal League to establish a place in American sports was that the Baltimore team "balked at the settlement and sued organized baseball under the Sherman Antitrust Act...The case eventually went to the Supreme Court." In 1922, the majority opinion of the court, written by Justice Oliver Wendell Holmes,

Jr., defended baseball as "not a subject of commerce" and basically "exempted organized baseball from antitrust legislation."[185]

Ever bold in the public sphere Britton took control of the club and assumed the role of president. She filed for divorce in November 1916. She had previously filed suit in 1911 but she and Skip reconciled. This time, in defense of her position, she boldly presented private aspects of their relationship, asserting her husband was lax in his financial responsibilities, physically aggressive, and lacked affection. As well he was "addicted to drink and [his] associates are bad...many of whom were loud, vulgar and uncouth manners and of ill repute."[186] Britton stated, "Anyone who cared for my welfare would not have acted as he did." She contemplated her predicament. As the first female owner of a professional baseball team in which she held seventy-five per cent of the stock and her mother held the remaining twenty-five per cent, she had never been accepted by the other owners, and she felt she had not been given the respect afforded her.

Britton's financial situation was not good. She fielded too many losing teams, and after the fiasco with the Federal League, she welcomed a chance to give up the club. She summoned Huggins and Jones to her home to inform them, "Gentlemen, I want to get out of baseball. I guess I have had enough. I want you to be the first to know it, in case you should be interested in buying the club yourselves." Huggins wanted to purchase the team and looked to Cincinnati for financial backing from Max and Julius Fleishmann, wealthy yeast manufacturers. They arranged to back his deal but before they could present the package to Britton, on March 5, 1917, she agreed to sell the team to her attorney, James Jones.

Helene Britton left St. Louis for Boston where she became the wife of Charles S. Bigsby, an electrical appliance distributor. She died January 8, 1950, in Philadelphia.[187] She was survived by her daughter, Marie R. Britton, and her son, Frank De Haas Britton, and four grandchildren.[188] Upon her death Britton's body was returned to Cleveland, Ohio, and she was buried at the Lake View Cemetery.[189]

Cardinal Field

James Jones, Britton's legal adviser, afraid the Cardinal franchise would leave St. Louis, bought the team and ballpark for $375,000. He viewed the purchase as a civic investment for a betterment of the community. He setup a community-owned team where he arranged to have 1,200 investors purchase stock in the club in $25 increments with a maximum purchase of $10,000. Stockholders, mainly eminent St. Louis businessmen, received the option to offer a season pass to "a deserving underprivileged youngster between the ages of 10 and 16." This began the Knot Hole Gang, set up to curtail youth run amuck.

The program was part of the greater boy's movement that allowed kids to come into to the bleachers on weekdays for free.[190] At the same time it was thought that distribution of tickets to the kids would help assure their allegiance to the Cardinals and turn the youngsters into lifelong supporters. The company worked with numerous St. Louis organizations and offered membership to the Knot Hole Gang through Catholic churches, Protestant Sunday schools, Jewish welfare associations, the YMCA, and black boy's club. In 1920, 64,000 St. Louis kids attended the games for free. If the kids got out of control, they were booted from the game. It is not clear if girls were included in this promotion early on but by 1940 there had formed a Cardinal Girls' Club associated with the YMCA.[191] Two rules applied with the passes: The child needed his parents' consent and could not play hooky to attend a game.[192]

Another shrewd move by the club that year was convincing thirty-five-year-old Branch Rickey to join the front office, a position he held for the next twenty-five years. Rickey acquired two hundred shares of the team. Though a staunch Methodist, who did not drink and would not attend Sunday games, everyone in the game respected and admired his baseball expertise. He could do it all, "a natural-born organizer, promoter, trader, [and] lawyer." Rickey was "crafty, even brilliant…two or three moves ahead" of others. He knew the game, and better yet, he knew players. The man was a baseball genius with an uncanny sixth sense for judging talent. Rickey built "baseball's first extensive farm system," and under his brilliant leadership the Cardinals became a full-fledged contender that "would go on to win nine National League pennants and six World Series Championships from 1926 through 1946."[193]

Jones changed the name of Robison Field to Cardinal Field. Not much money had been put into the wooden structure in the past few years, so the park had become dilapidated. In fact, the city building commissioner declared the left field bleachers upper deck unsafe and ordered it removed, thus eliminating 1500 seats.

In 1917, the United States entered World War I. Patriotism flourished in opening day ceremonies when the Cards opened in Cincinnati where fans displayed over 10,000 flags. The season did not see much change in personnel, but things changed the following year as the war escalated. Teams fielded whomever they could suit up, old-timers and kids alike. The game went on. The new owners brought in male cheerleaders with megaphones to rev up the crowd, as was the custom at college football games; the fad did not take hold.[194] The team garnered 82 victories, the most any St. Louis team had won since 1899, but they finished in third place. Huggins, upset at not being able to own the team, resigned at the end of the season and went on to a successful managerial career with the

New York Yankees.[195] The confidence Helene Britton had in him and his abilities proved astute.

The year 1918 ushered in the first season that the nickname "Cardinals" appeared on the team's uniforms instead of STL.[196] Rickey had attended a gathering where he saw "red cardboard cardinals on the tablecloths" and that prompted him to find a way to display the bird as an official symbol of the team. Edward Schmidt, a local artist, designed the logo of a "red bird perched on a bat in front of a large baseball."[197]

The season saw drastic changes on the playing field with World War I and the draft. The Cardinals alone lost eleven players to the armed forces. Patriotism and support for the troops was clear, though the team fielded was not much to watch. On May 13th the team sponsored "Bat and Ball Day." Part of the gate receipts went to buy baseball equipment for the soldiers fighting in France. On the 20th of July, in a pregame contest, Jefferson Barracks played the Great Lakes Naval Training Station for the Midwest title. Army won 6-5. The gate proceeds went to the St. Louis Tuberculosis Society for "soldiers and sailors who contracted the disease during World War I."[198] Total attendance for the season, which ended one month early, was 110,599 and the club finished in eighth place.[199]

The war officially ended November 11, 1918, and baseball was fully back in business, but things at the ballpark changed with the passing of the Eighteenth Amendment. Prohibition was the law of the land. St. Louis was definitely "not a temperance town." Since the mid-nineteenth century the city was known as "the Rome of the New World" because there were so many Catholics living there. Catholics simply did not support temperance nor did the many beer breweries in the city.[200]

Meanwhile, fire destroyed the last major league ballpark constructed of wooden stands, Cardinal Field, on June 6, 1920. The Cardinals found their way back to Sportsman's Park at Grand and Dodier. In an astute financial deal, the club sold the bulk of the Cardinal Field property for $200,000 to the St. Louis Board of Education to build Beaumont High School and a smaller parcel of land went to the Public Service Corporation for $75,000 to erect a streetcar loop. Then instead of investing in a new ballpark, which they had threatened to do, they used the proceeds internally.

The Cardinals established baseball's first farm system, which ultimately transformed the Cardinals organization and fed young players to the parent club, a practice that continues to turn out winning combinations. The program set up a series of minor league teams to train players for future play and competition. The Cardinals signed scores of players at low salaries, put them in different levels of minor league teams, and watched the talent develop.[201] The mastermind behind this program was baseball executive Branch Rickey.

In the beginning, players widely criticized the program as a "chain gang" as they saw the work as a useless endeavor to keep them from playing in the big leagues. What they wanted was to immediately move into the majors. Baseball purist John McGraw noted it as "the stupidest idea in baseball." Eventually, though, it proved a spark of brilliance that all major leagues followed. Rickey saw it as "no sudden stroke of genius... It was a case of necessity...Other clubs would outbid us; they had the money and the superior scouting system. We had to take the leavings or nothing at all."[202] Consequently, in a time of financial desperation, Rickey, a poor farm kid from Ohio, came up with an idea to grow his own team through the ranks of the farm system and the program paid off in dividends for Cardinal talent that served the parent club ever since.[203]

The Progressive Era was a time to clean up cities and find ways to end political corruption; those same ideas worked on the popular sport of baseball with rule changes and accountability for fan behavior. Respectability for the game was important to the Robison family when they owned the team (1899-1916). In addition, the popular culture of the day found ways to promote the sport and garner a following. Place became an important consideration as well with ways to make the parks safer while trying to accommodate more spectators.

By the close of 1920 the Cardinals officially moved to Sportsman's Park. For the next thirty-three years they would share space with the St. Louis Browns as they battled for hearts of the local fans. Overall, the move proved beneficial to the Redbirds and eventually they came to own the address at Grand and Dodier, but it was a slow journey.

Meanwhile, the organization found ways to ensure future strength of the team through the farm system established under the leadership of Branch Rickey. All the changes since the days of Von der Ahe helped solidify a close relationship between owners, players, and fans. Place would continue to help form a community of supporters who came out to cheer the St. Louis Cardinals.

CHAPTER FOUR

SHARED SPACE AT GRAND AND DODIER

By the 1920s St. Louis no longer held sway as the fourth largest city in the United States, it dropped to sixth; though people continued to flock to the city where warehouses, factories, business offices, shops, entertainment and residential buildings provided modernization with new technological advances. Industry diversified with the auto industry and electrical products; but Prohibition caused an economic slump in St. Louis, especially in the Soulard district where breweries shut down production.

Despite the passing of Prohibition, the decade of the 1920s proved to be exciting for St. Louis with cars, planes, telephones, jazz, motion pictures, and radio. High-rise structures such as the new buildings of Shell Oil Company and Bell Telephone changed the architectural landscape. When voters approved the passage of a 1923 major $88 million bond issue, the city itself caught onto the modern era hoping to make a name for itself with the installation of electric streetlights, and the widening and repaving of streets to accommodate the popularity of the automobile. The Cardinals added to the highlights by winning their first World Series and participating with the New York Yankees in the first national radio broadcast of that 1926 Fall Classic. To top off the decade, the 1927 radio broadcast of Charles Lindberg's successful flight across the Atlantic in the *Spirit of St. Louis* brought international acclaim to the city.[204]

In the 1920s, professional baseball anchored in industrial cities serviced by railways with eleven of the sixteen teams in the American and National Leagues holding rivals in their hometowns. That included two each in Boston, Chicago, Philadelphia, and St. Louis. New York had three teams. The other towns with major league presence were Cincinnati, Cleveland, Detroit, Pittsburgh, and Washington. To be considered a big city one had to house a major league team.

Fans leisurely traveled from city to city with game schedules set up to coordinate with train schedules. In the early days of baseball, the telegraph, print media, and railroad helped "spread the ideas and activities" of the sport nationwide. Long-distance competition thrived on the dependency of rail transportation and trains were glad to have the business. They offered special rates to the teams and featured them in their advertisements. The team's private cars hooked to the trains. Road games produced a special bonding between the players and sportswriters traveling with them. It presented an opportunity for players, owners, and sportswriters to get to know each other on a personal basis. They shared food, drink, played cards, talked baseball, and played practical jokes.

The relaxed traveling provided a chance to see the United States from St. Louis to New York and everything in between.

Train life was not all that glorious, though. To get fresh air on hot nights one had to open the train windows which meant "you'd be eating soot and cinders all night long. If you closed the window you'd roast to death. Get off in the morning either filthy or without a wink of sleep. Usually both." Some arrived in town rested and ready to play ball, but others found it difficult to relax in small sleeping compartments. Once they arrived, they would have to get their own luggage, hail a cab, and check into the hotel. In the days before air conditioning the summer heat could be unbearable, and they played in major industrial cities that were filthy with smoke.

Players shared hotel rooms and that could be problematic if one proved hard to get along with or had some strange quirks. Did one like the window open, who showered first, did one like to stay up late, how about the annoying habit of snoring, was one an early riser, was one a drinker or smoker, what about entertaining in the room? Players had to adjust to each other and try to get along. Sportswriters had an unwritten law of presenting the players as heroes and consequently, even if they were privy to scandalous information about a player's private life, it was off-limits.[205]

In 1920, with the move to Sportsman's Park, the Cardinals were back where they had gotten their start. They signed a ten-year contract, became tenants of the Browns, renting the field and office space at Grand and Dodier from Ball for $20,000. The Browns' front office address read 2907 Grand Avenue, and the Cardinals, around the corner, was 3634 Dodier Avenue.

The administration offices sat over the ticket windows of the main entrance. Each club had its own staircase separated by a common walkway. Browns' owner Ball was not receptive to the idea of sharing his ball park as his financial situation looked healthy at the time but after the Cardinals started rumors of building a new ballpark Ball figured he could control them, and the rent would help him expand and modernize his park.[206]

Early on, the St. Louis Cardinals captured an avid fan base that extended beyond the local area. St. Louis was the most western and the most southern major league city. That meant a solid geographic following of baseball for the winning Cardinals. Fans picked up scores in their local papers and faithfully followed the games on KMOX radio. With a 50,000 watt clear channel, the station had a far-reaching frequency that touched fourteen southwestern and midwestern states to include Arkansas, Colorado, Iowa, Oklahoma, Tennessee, and Texas and other far off regions.[207]

The Cardinals opened at Sportsman's Park to an overflow crowd of 20,000 on July 1, 1920. Though they lost 6-2 to the Pittsburgh Pirates, they finished the season in fifth place with a 75-79 record and posted attendance of 326,836. The following year, with Rogers Hornsby leading the club in all hitting categories, the promise of better years seemed imminent. The team finished in third, seven games from first, posted an 87-66 record, and drew over 50,000 more fans than the previous year.[208]

The 1922 season brought some changes, a new direction to the team and a major stockholder. Though he did not don a Cardinal uniform, Sam Breadon emerged as the catalyst of those changes. Breadon grew up a New Yorker at the turn of the century where he acquired an elementary school education. He was a go-getter who started his nest egg with profits earned from selling popcorn at the 1904 St. Louis World's Fair at age twenty-five. He formed a partnership with renowned St. Louisan, Marion Lambert, who served as his mentor. They made millions with a St. Louis auto distribution company for Pierce-Arrow and Ford.[209] Known as Lucky Sam because of his fortune in life, or Singing Sam to others because of his barbershop vocals, Breadon was a likeable fellow with the "gift of gab."[210]

Breadon originally invested in the Cardinals when Jones owned the team. He had never seen a big-league game until he moved to St. Louis. He liked the game but had no real interest in the sport. A friend and fellow automobile associate, Fuzzy Anderson, persuaded Sam to invest in the community venture. At first, he only purchased four shares but before long Breadon was hooked. He met some of the players, got baseball fever, immersed himself in the game, and acquired large blocks of shares.

In 1918, before investing much more in stock, Breadon lent the troubled club $5,000 to stay afloat and then shortly after that an additional $18,000.[211] The Cardinals' ownership never seemed to have enough money to do what they wanted with the club and Jones, noticing Breadon's financial success and interest in the game, pulled him into the business. In early 1920, he took over as team president, a successful position he held until 1947.

In May 1922, Breadon recognized the community ownership did not work as "every fellow who had a few shares of stock felt he should tell you how to run the team...It was a case of too many cooks making a stew out of a ball club." It was not long before he "realized being president wasn't enough—to really run the club I had to own a majority of the stock." He acquired his buddy Fuzzy Anderson's shares and went on to purchase James Jones' stock. That acquisition allowed him to hold majority stock in the franchise, 67 percent ownership.[212] Finally, he held power to run the club the way he wanted to.

That same year the Cardinals introduced a new club uniform that featured "two redbirds perched on a sloping bat that passed through the letter 'C' in the word Cardinals." It served as the emblem of the team for both the home and road jerseys and continues to this day.[213] The following year the Cardinals became the first team to use player numbers on the uniforms.[214]

With players Rogers Hornsby (Cardinals) and George Sisler (Browns), both St. Louis teams played competitive and exciting baseball in the early 1920s and allowed Ball to rack in huge profits. Sportsman's Park remained virtually unchanged from its 1908 renovation until a major makeover that eliminated wooden structures and permanently brought a more solidly built concrete steel structure. With profits from his club, and the Cardinals rent, Ball revamped Sportsman's Park before the 1926 season. Osborn Engineering of Cleveland reconstructed Sportsman's Park. With good prospects from both organizations, Ball added seating to the park and renovations. The capacity increased from 18,000 to 34,000. The remodeling, though, added nothing to the facade of the park which was "nondescript, lacking the architectural grandeur of Philadelphia's Shibe Park or the distinctiveness of Pittsburgh's Forbes Field."[215] It was a serviceable building that sat just north of midtown St. Louis, served by a solid streetcar connection.

The overhaul of the park brought drastic changes to the structure but continued the tradition of blending the park with the neighborhood. A simple design was chosen in lieu of some ornate architectural edifice.[216] The overall look of the two-tiered seating arrangement remained for the next 40 years. A gravel track bordered the natural grass playing field. A dugout situated on the third base side housed the home team players and a matching one for the visiting team lined the first base side. Bullpen sections for warming up pitchers and catchers sat down the track parallel to the right and left fields. The upper deck was extended to the foul poles and bleachers added to the outfield. This was a hitter's park designed to bring out the fans in the era of home run king, Babe Ruth. Dimensions of the playing field measured: left field, 360 feet; center field, 429 feet; right field, 310 feet; 75 feet from home plate to the backstop. Seating included 128 deluxe boxes, 3,617 boxes, 19,552 grandstand reserved, 2,203 general admission, 2,400 right field pavilion, and 2,600 left field bleachers.[217] In addition, they allowed for about 3,000 standing-room-only tickets.

Right field became a home run hitter's paradise which would be okay if the home team always benefited, but that was not the case. In July 1929, the Detroit Tigers racked up eight homers during a Browns' home stand. That prompted Ball to install a "33-foot screen that extended 156 feet toward center field…from mid-1929 through the life of the park, with only a one-year respite in 1955"[218] over the right field pavilion bleachers. J. G. Taylor Spink, publisher of the *Sporting News* called it "the only outfield place with seating where you couldn't catch a homer."[219] The renovations included more seating. When the park's seating extended, some believed fans lost out because it depersonalized the game, separating players further from the fans to destroy much of the informal aspects of the intimacy of going to the game; but the improvements assured more fans a seat the day of a game.

The overhaul encouraged segregation by social class as ticket prices varied according to the proximity to the field. With the spruced-up park, attendance soared along with profits. Owners found that commanding higher prices for certain seats increased profits while isolating lower-class patrons to distant, less expensive parts of the park. Prime tickets were box seats, simple green wood folding seats anchored to the stands and located close to the infield playing area. The reserved seats, next in price, resembled box seats except not as close to the playing action. A few of these seats became problem seats if they were stuck behind one of the numerous steel girded posts supporting the roof of the park. Reserved seats not sold by the day of the game became general admission seats and this lowered the cost of the ticket. The pavilion backless seats sat under a roofed section in right field. The left field bleachers, cheapest seats in the house, were backless benches without a roof and were the farthest from home plate.

St. Louis, a city divided by geographic location, centers on a north/south grid; it is not a sprawling city. The city limits are roughly fifteen miles long by seven miles wide. It was closely connected with a streetcar transportation system that ran north and south and served the crowds attending the baseball games. Parking spots close to the park were scarce, so public transportation served the team and the fans well.

Bob Broeg noted that the 3 p.m. starting times for games during the late 1920s and early 1930s drew diverse crowds. Starting time was conducive to various groups of fans. White-collar executives headed to the ballpark on their way home from work, and factory workers stopped off after their shifts. School kids, some who could just walk over or hop on the streetcar for a nickel, could be there in no time. Summers, too, allowed kids to head to the park since school was not in session. They could view batting practice, catch a game, and still be home by supper. It worked great for the Knot Hole Gang.[220]

Aesthetically, Sportsman's Park blended with the rest of the neighborhood. By the mid-twenties, the area developed into a mixed German industrial-residential neighborhood. The space available and the arrangement of the adjacent thoroughfares basically determined the rectangular shape of the park. The simple facade served to define the streets and the outdoor spaces fit into the strict and traditional urban streetscape.

Businesses and residents around the park could complain about the increased traffic, or they could accept the enterprise and profit from the results. Grand Avenue, the major thoroughfare bordering the park, was lined by unassuming three-to-four story apartment buildings. The ground floors housed a pawn shop, a cleaner, a shoe repair, a short order restaurant, a barber shop, or a loan office. Above these establishments sat simple apartment dwellings. Air conditioning, a luxury item until the second half of the twentieth century, did not exist in this working-class environment. On the day of a game shopkeepers rested on stools outside their shops, conversed with folks who passed by, and tuned their radios to the play by play. From the twenties to the late sixties this area was a friendly, safe place. Carter Carburetor's factory operated across the street from the park and a YMCA sat on another corner. The residential side streets had many corner bars and all vacant lots, as well as front yards, immediately became parking slots the day of a ball game. Game day could prove quite profitable for the neighborhood regardless of the outcome of the game.

Continuing to recognize the importance of increasing revenues park owners utilized all available resources to promote the game. They opened the game to sports reporting, identified players over a public address system, kept up the grounds somewhat, supported American patriotism, and sold space to advertisers eager to pitch their messages.[221]

In 1929, sportswriter Red Smith reported that Sportsman's Park had "a garish, county fair sort of layout." The press box hung from the roof over the second deck gave a "bird's eye" view, and the announcement of the starting lineup came from the voice of Jim Kelly through a raised megaphone. A goat assisted the groundskeepers in maintaining the grass.

In case of rain a huge tarpaulin sat rolled up aside the field ready to offer protection. Outfield walls featured large advertisements for cigarettes, soap, beer, and other products and the enormous hand-operated scoreboard that sat above the bleachers noted the balls, strikes, hits and runs of the game, as well as the scores of the other teams in the league playing that day. It also featured advertisements for the radio broadcast of the game, for razor blades, beer, and cigarettes. During each game a recording attached to Johnny the Bellhop's billboard on the lower right-hand corner of the scoreboard announced his famous cry "Call for Philip Morris." A large clock sat perched atop the scoreboard as an American flag flew from a pole high above dead center field. It was a typical big-league park seen throughout the league in the mid-twentieth century but the Browns, the Cards and their fans found it a special place they called home.

Though the Browns financed a 1925 park improvement, the Cardinals emerged as the real beneficiaries of the renovated complex. The winning, and overly popular Cardinals, drew more fans than the American League team that usually held down last place.[222]

Breadon, always cautious about finances, initiated a moneymaking strategy that attracted fans by the droves with the use of Sunday doubleheaders that gave fans a full day of entertainment. Originally the practice was criticized but eventually the custom became the accepted norm in baseball throughout the middle years of the twentieth century.[223] Two games in one day taxed the players but for the most part, fans loved spending all day at the ballpark.

A heated pennant race eventually led to the Cardinals winning their first pennant and World Series Championship and on June 27, 1926, they drew the largest crowd to date. A crowd of 37,196 settled in for a doubleheader against the Cubs. The Cards topped that on October 6th with 38,825 in a World Series loss against the New York Yankees when Babe Ruth and his boys hit town. The next day, in another defeat, they bested that attendance record with 39,552.[224] That first year of the revamp of Sportsman's Park the Cardinals packed in 668,428 fans.[225] Clearly this was a good move for the Redbirds. They had found a home.

The popularity of radio changed the world as it ushered in a new era and helped to produce a shared national culture. In 1927, following Charles Lindberg's transatlantic flight broadcast over the airwaves many were inspired, and it brought him international acclaim aboard his flight on the *Spirit of St. Louis*. Yet, a year before radio spotlighted St. Louis and forever changed the world of baseball. This communication allowed fans to follow the game without being in the ballpark. Radio made instant heroes out of unknowns and brought additional fans to the St. Louis team. The new medium transformed a single moment into a spectacular event. With instant communication, the fans became a part of the drama without ever leaving home.

It was clear, though, that not all supported this new coverage. The *Sporting News* noted "Mr. Radio is going to butt into the business of telling the world all about the ball game without the world having to come to the ballpark to find out…Baseball is more an inspiration to the brain through the eye than it is by the ear." Over time, the sport captured more followers via this new medium that sparked national interest in baseball, and attendance increased. Interest in the game spread beyond the local confines to rural areas, before long folks began to organize pilgrimages to nearby cities to take in the games. The combination of radio communication, improved roads, and mass-produced automobiles expanded the reach of the fan base to more distant areas.[226]

Interestingly, the Midwest latched onto more frequent radio broadcasts than the east coast teams, except for Boston. The first Cardinals World Series against the New York Yankees was broadcast nationally with play-by-play announced by Graham McNamee. The following year KMOX picked up the rights to broadcast games at Sportsman's Park. Radio and the newsreels shown in movie theaters brought the sport attention and allowed fans to get more up-to-date accounts of the game. With newsreels, they could see the game in motion. Fans who might never be able to attend a game felt a part of the entertainment.[227]

These early days of baseball, before night baseball and television, were easy to follow and to keep up with other teams in the league as well. Each league only had eight teams. It was simple to follow the standings as well as the day-to-day play. With all the games being played in the afternoon the late edition of the paper brought the results of the day. Folks could talk about it that evening and into the next morning. Without distractions to include television, computers, texting, and other professional sports, baseball was a common topic that all could become enthralled with and discuss.[228] Early and mid-twentieth century were the heyday of baseball as the all-American sport.

Meanwhile, in 1926, pennant fever galvanized the city of St. Louis. The Cardinals clinched their first National League pennant with a 6-4 win over the Giants in New York. Loudspeakers were set up in the downtown business area to broadcast the action.[229] Thousands of fans flanked the downtown streets to listen to the play-by-play of their first National League pennant win. The fans burst into excited elation. Jazz-age fans reached an excited pitch in their enthusiasm. The *Sporting News* reported "Great cheers went up…Factory whistles shrieked, automobilists tooted their horns, trucks went about with cutouts open and the drivers backfiring their engines, impromptu bands and parades were organized…tying up traffic in general. From office buildings, great wads of paper, ticker tape and confetti were released, falling like the snow of a Dakota blizzard on the pavement below."[230] When the World Series against the New York Yankees ended, the St. Louis Cardinals returned home sporting the 1926 World Series Championship crown.[231] That first World Series win earned new fans and solidified the base.

Fans have never been able to predict what owners will do during the season or even once it ends. Certainly 1926 was no different. Job security was nonexistent. Even though player/manager Rogers Hornsby owned 12.5 percent of Cardinal stock he was not a protected commodity. A megastar and fan favorite Hornsby, Cards manager/second baseman, lived baseball all year long. When asked what he did in the winter when the season ended, he replied, "I stare out the window and wait for spring."[232] Baseball was everything to him. Hornsby and owner Sam Breadon never minced words, many times publicly disagreeing. The manager had some tense moments with Rickey, too. During the winning season, Hornsby questioned a lot of the front office decisions. The owner took the side of administration, telling the manager "You manage your end—the ball club. I'll take care of the other end." They had all worked together in the past, even if not in an amicable way, and one would think that the first World Championship would cause bygones to be bygones. That would not be the case.

Breadon had enough of constant disagreements and came to the "decision that if I was president, my chief must work with me. If he didn't, either he or I must get out, and I wasn't ready to leave the club." Hornsby had a decent year in 1926, hitting .317. Still, he had dropped his average from .403 the year before. He balked at Breadon's offer at the end of the season even though it presented a $20,000 a year increase. The one-year contract presented Hornsby the opportunity to make $50,000. That was only second to superstar Babe Ruth, but the Cards star would not budge. Hornsby held out for a three-year contract.

Breadon set out to prove he made the decisions. He looked for more control over his player's antics on and off the field. Hornsby, noted for betting the horses, became a challenge for the owner who sought to end the gambling. The Giants had been after Hornsby for a long time, offering huge sums for the star player, but Breadon always turned them down. This time, at the winter meetings in New York, when they came back knocking for a trade, Breadon exclaimed he was not interested in more money; he wanted to swap players. He shipped Hornsby to New York and the Cardinals acquired Frankie Frisch. The deal was not settled that easily though as Hornsby had Cardinals stock and a player could not own stock in one team and play for another. The value placed on his shares came to $116,000. An agreement was reached where Breadon covered $80,000, the National League and the Giants covered $18,000 each.[233] Owners united to control the players and show who commanded the sport.

Fans were irate. The whole city exploded in outrage. In fact, "Mayor Victor Miller and the St. Louis Chamber of Commerce contacted baseball Commissioner Kenesaw Mountain Landis and National League president John Heydler to see if the trade could be cancelled. Mark Steinberg, a member of the Cardinals board of directors, called the trade 'an insult' to the St. Louis fans."[234]

Fans showed their displeasure with Breadon by shouting insults to him, draping his home and office with black mourning paper, and phoning him with their vile diatribes. The harassment became so annoying Breadon disconnected his phone. "One sportswriter vowed he would never cover another Cardinals game and kept the pledge for 10 years." Breadon defended the move stating that "flattering friends" allowed Hornsby to develop "too big of an opinion of himself." He supported his theory, pronouncing that the team was "a good team with Hornsby and they will be a great team without him." Hard as that was for the St. Louis fans to hear, eventually Breadon would be proven right.

Not readily accepted by the fans, Frisch convinced them of his value, "putting up solid offensive and defensive numbers." Attendance the following year shot up to 749,340, convincing Breadon "that what the fans want is a winner, and that a popular player is quickly forgotten by one who is equally popular." Even popular players are dispensable.[235] Cardinal owners throughout the history of the team have followed that philosophy.

Rickey and Breadon found a profitable investment in their brainchild, the farm system. The World Series win in 1926 was the beginning of a squad that would take four pennants in the next six years. Attendance doubled. With an excess of players through development "Rickey supplemented the team's profits by selling off his surplus—players who did not make the Cardinals—to other teams...Despite the limited size of its market, the Cardinals became the most profitable franchise in the major leagues." Breadon dealt away youngsters and Cardinal idols in the years that followed.[236]

Rickey and Breadon faced wide criticism over many of their trades "for seeming lack of baseball sentiment in selling crack stars to rival clubs...Yet, the policy of the club...dispose of stars while they still have considerable sales or trading value" usually held merit. As Breadon had proven, for the most part his trades over the years benefited the team. In the case of the Hornsby/Frisch swap, Frisch saw the Cards win four more pennants over the next eight years and he went on to manage the 1934 pennant winning team. He continued to manage the club until 1938.[237] On balance the Hornsby/Frisch swap was a good trade.[238]

The 1930s hosted the Great Depression. In St. Louis factories closed and for close to twenty-five per cent of the city times were rough. Without a safety net of federal programs, the financial disaster bowled folks over. They did not know where to turn as they fought hunger and homelessness. Early in the decade, St. Louis neighborhoods saw evidence of the financial disaster firsthand with Hooverville's that sprang up all over the city. It was estimated that close to 3,000 people lived in shacks that lined the downtown riverfront. In 1932, blacks and whites marched together on city hall demanding attention to the problems and they brought violent confrontation with them. They found the police warding off their bricks with tear gas and guns. Times were rough all around.

With a Democrat in the White House, the city of St. Louis, seventh largest in the nation, helped its chances to garner Washington attention when they elected Democrat, Bernard Dickman as mayor. Dickman used his party influence to get things done and to ease the economic hard times.

A good move for St. Louis came when Congress repealed Prohibition in spring 1933. At the time, St. Louis unemployment across the area was over 30 percent, while nationally it had peaked at 25 percent. With the repeal in April, Budweiser, Columbia, Falstaff, Hyde Park, and a handful of other local breweries reopened for business, thus putting a lot of people to work. Franklin D. Roosevelt's New Deal programs, especially the Works Progress Administration, also brought construction jobs and changed the architectural landscape of the city. The influx of money allowed for the completion of programs started with the 1923 bond issue to improve the city. The city received funds that would begin decades of a long journey to overhaul the downtown riverfront. Demolition of forty blocks of nineteenth-century brick buildings, as well as many of the Hooverville shacks, began in 1939. Eventually this area would be the site of the renowned St. Louis Gateway Arch and an estimated $503 million renaissance of the city but that would take another twenty-five years.[239]

The magic of place mattered especially to those living through the Great Depression as folks looked for diversions from the depressing times. Many found comfort and fun following the colorful St. Louis Cardinals. The ballpark was a gathering place for fans, and they carried fond memories of the place.

Sportswriter Bob Burnes covered the Cardinals for the *Globe-Democrat*. He grew up in St. Louis and reflected on the importance of seats with proximity to the field. Fans wanted to feel part of the action and familiarity with the players. One afternoon Burnes saw Babe Ruth "leaning over a box before the game, conversing with spectators, waving to the fans who cheered him and pointing his finger at those who jeered him." The intimacy of the park came through as Burnes recalled Buzzy Wares coaching at first base and "gesturing the crowd to step up the tempo of the staccato applause as the Cardinals rallied...He had fun. So did the fans. Even in the depression days of the thirties, it was fun to go to the ballpark on a lazy afternoon."

The fans felt a part of the games' activities. It was easy to approach the players on and off the field. Some of the players lived close to the park in boarding houses or hotels. Burnes recollected, "What a thrill it was too, of an evening to walk past the old Hamilton Hotel...for a glimpse of the athletes relaxing." Some of the other players in the early part of the twentieth century stayed in the neighborhood too, boarding at Mother

Doran's on Grand Avenue.[240] It has been said that many a night she had to put her "baseball boys" to bed.[241]

Fans recalled that the seating allowed them to sit close to the field and that one could see the facial expressions of the players and officials. Not only did they overhear field conversations, but they talked with the players, too. Another fond memory of the old park was the clubhouse walkway that took the players from the home dugout to the clubhouse. They passed through an inside corridor open to the fans and players were physically accessible to the fans. Eventually the walkway was covered by a chain-link fence, but that still allowed fans to see the players and converse with them.

The 1930s saw Jim Kelly at Sportsman's Park using a "giant microphone so large he needed two hands to steady it." He announced the lineup and changes throughout the game. He would stand by home plate and give out the batting order for the benefit of those in the press box and those in the lower and upper deck seats, then would move down a little to the left and right and simply announce the batteries. When the lineup changed for a pinch hitter, pinch runner, or reliever he would do the same. In the 1931 World Series, the Cardinals placed official and consistent numbers on the player's uniforms.[242] The players became recognizable heroes who fans cheered.

Breadon saw the benefit of installing lights for night games. He presented this idea to league officials, Commissioner Judge Landis, and other owners as early as 1930. His financial argument stated, "It makes every day a Sunday." In 1932 the National League granted permission for night games and Breadon offered to cover half of the expenses, yet Ball argued that the American League was against night games. It would be ten years before the Cardinals convinced Phil Ball to install lights at Sportsman's Park.[243]

Many memorable teams played at the park to include the Gas House Gang of the 1930s, and St. Louis Swifties of the 1940s. A character fans could not forget, either on or off the field, was the Cardinals pitcher, Dizzy Dean. He was a great pitcher who believed brains did not make the player. His theory of pitching was "The dumber a pitcher is the better. When he gets smart and begins to experiment with a lot of different pitches, he's in trouble. All I ever had was a fastball, a curve, and a change-up. And I did pretty good."[244]

Dean's homespun humor translated well to broadcasting in 1941 once his playing days ended. He called the games for the Browns, as well as the Cardinals. The *Sporting News* referred to him as "baseball's announcer with the worst diction;" but within three years the same publication named Dean "Announcer of the Year." The St. Louis Board of Education gave a vote of no confidence to Dean and wanted him yanked off the air for his atrocious English, especially his made-up past tense. He was known to say runners "slud" into the base, pitchers "throwed" the ball and when a hitter seemed quite confident at home plate Dean remarked the batter "is standing confidentially" at the plate. Dean replied to the board that he was simply "trying to learn 'em English." He was quite a character and eventually left the Cardinal organization for a national position with CBS.[245] He became part of the place memories of Grand and Dodier.

Team salaries produced battles throughout the history of the team. As time progressed, more established rules came in line such as paying players for post-season play, so they did not get ripped off like Von der Ahe's teams. During the era of the Great Depression, close to 25 percent of Americans were without a job, while the average salary for a congressman was $8,000. In the early 1930s there seemed to be some improvement in player salaries over the earlier years, but nothing compared to the introduction of the baseball unions and negotiators in the 1970s, certainly nothing analogous to the twenty-first century multimillion-dollar deals. The 1930s found salaries around $18,500 for player/manager Frank Frisch, $6,500 for Leo Durocher, $7,500 for star pitcher Dizzy Dean and $3,000 for his sidekick, rookie brother Paul Dean.[246] While that seems paltry by the standards of the twenty-first century it was more than a decent living during the Great Depression.

Players found ways to supplement their income in the off-season. Cardinals' national hero of the 1931 World Series, Pepper Martin took to the vaudeville circuit making $1,500 a week. That lasted about a month when the colorful character walked away from a five-week commitment that would have brought him $7,500. He remarked, "I ain't an actor; I'm a ballplayer. I'm cheating the public…Besides, the hunting season's on in Oklahoma, and that's more important business."[247] Martin's sideline appeared inconsequential when compared to the deals that the Dean brothers worked out in the off-seasons of '34–'36. They received "$86,000 in those three years, in side pick-ups…with $70,000" of that going to Diz.[248]

Baseball cards were around since the 1860s. The early cards were associated with tobacco and appealed to adults. In 1933, a new focus came to attract young fans who continued to have an interest in the game with the bubblegum cards sold by the Goudey Gum Company. For a penny, one could buy three sticks of gum and receive a baseball card. Sportswriter Robert W. Creamer recollected that as a kid he and his buddies carried these around "in our pockets, used them to play games with…They stimulated our interest in baseball and we loved them."

The cards were collectables the kids used to learn about the sport and to trade with others. They were not the cherished commodity of the card collectors for the money they would bring in, but for the fun they brought.[249] These cards served to interest the fans and they would come to the ballpark to see the live version of their collection.

St. Louis baseball during the 1930s entertained through the colorful antics of the "Gas House Gang" that Rickey described as "a high-class team with nine heavy drinkers" that consisted of Dizzy Dean, Leo Durocher, Frankie Frisch, Pepper Martin, and Joe Medwick. Their playing antics drew attention throughout the 1930s. They took the field and brought excitement; they played to win and made it a rule not to let anyone get in their way. Durocher once remarked, "If I was playing third base, and my mother was rounding third with the winning run, I'd trip her. Oh, I'd pick her up, dust her off, and say 'Sorry, Mom,' but nobody beats me."[250] Fans liked that commitment at all costs.

Winning was important, and players did what they could to lift spirits. Martin, from Temple, Oklahoma, was a feisty guy. Branch Rickey praised his playing ability with the comment that Pepper played with a "spirit of adventure."[251] Martin was noted for his speed.[252] Nothing stopped him. He was admired for his toughness. Pepper Martin knew he was not the whole team though. He appreciated other players on the team acknowledging, "When Ol' Diz was out there pitching it was more than just another ballgame. It was a regular three-ring circus, and everybody was wide awake and enjoying being alive."[253] The Gas House Gang went on to win National League pennants in 1930, 1931 (with 101 victories) and 1934, taking the World Series in 1931 and 1934.[254]

Young Bob Broeg attended those series games beginning in 1930 when as a twelve-year-old he skipped school and sat in the bleachers for a dollar. The Gas House Gang took its antics off the field as well. A group led by Pepper Martin on harmonica and guitar, with others playing fiddle, washboard, and jug, formed a hillbilly band they called the Mudcat Band. They performed some on the radio with the most popular tune being "Possum Up a Gum Stump."[255]

The financial strains of the '30s took a toll on the organization even though the team produced winning seasons. Attendance went down from a high in 1931 of 608,535 to a miserable 256,171 in 1933. In 1934, Breadon's team took the best of seven from the Detroit Tigers to win the World Series and the owners cut amounted to $143,811. Without that extra dividend, the team would not have shown a profit as attendance only hit 325,056. This colorful, winning team posted a low attendance in 1934, fifth in the league for attendance figures and tenth overall.

When the season closed Breadon thought it might be a good time to sell the team while they were on top as World Champions. Rickey knew an oil millionaire, Lewis Haines Wentz, from Ponca City, Oklahoma, who came close to owning the team but "negotiations…broke down over Breadon's high valuation of the Cardinal farm properties."[256] When the deal fell through Sam talked of moving the team to Detroit. That did not happen. Fans got the message and attendance increased the next year to 506,084.[257] They did not want to lose the community spirit the team gave the city.

The city of St. Louis survived the Great Depression of the 1930s but "the census of 1940 was a shocker…For the first time in 120 years the population had declined, though by less than 1 percent to 816,048… The county [received] a 12-percent increase." It fell to eighth place. The city faced a downturn in the Depression years but then thrived during the 1940s as they retooled their factories for the defense industry. They accommodated the manufacturing of airplanes, electronics, clothing, food processing, and ammunition; at the same time, local universities serviced the government with their research labs. New opportunities opened for women and blacks with the shortage of male labor caused by World War II enlistments. The city and the county gained population.[258]

Night baseball came to St. Louis with the installation of lights before the 1940 season. Browns and Cardinals shared the $150,000 cost. Browns hosted their first home night game on May 24th, and on June 4, 1940, the Cardinals played under the lights.[259]

America entered World War II on December 7, 1941 with the bombing at Pearl Harbor. On January 16, 1942, President Franklin D. Roosevelt sent a letter to Kenesaw Mountain Landis, the Baseball Commissioner, stating "it would be best for the country to keep baseball going" but he expected players of military age to enter the armed services "even if the actual quality of the teams is lowered by the greater use of older players, this will not dampen the popularity of the sport."

Baseball was important to the home front and to the armed forces during these war years "but no one has ever argued that it was essential;" the essential aspects of those years were those in the uniform of their country. Hundreds of major league players enlisted in record numbers as did thousands of minor league players, including hundreds from Rickey's farm system.[260]

During the war years, the Cardinals ruled the National League even though scores of their own players served in the armed services. One of the Cardinals to make it to the big leagues and manage to stick around was rookie Stan Musial. The stash of ready players in the Cardinals farm system, developed by Branch Rickey, helped to sustain any losses to the war effort.

The 1942 St. Louis team, under the leadership of manager Billy Southworth, won one hundred six games, and swept twenty-one of their last twenty-six to meet the New York Yankees in the World Series.[261] The winners included twenty-one year old rookie Stan Musial who earned $4,250 for the season.[262] The 1942 daredevil team, youngest ever to win a major league championship, consisted mainly of high school and college age guys that Rickey had scouted for years.

Teams throughout the leagues simply could not make up for the loss of veteran players, but the farm system built by Rickey proved successful in easily replacing the men off to war. His philosophy spoke to "out of quantity comes quality." Seasons 1942, 1943, and 1944 the parent club won over 100 games. The team carried the best percentage in baseball for the '40s at .623 with 960-580 record. Throughout the decade they fielded very competitive teams, hosted two All-Star games and won the pennant in 1942, 1943, 1944, and 1946 while winning three World Series. The Cardinals took either first or second "fifteen times in twenty seasons between 1930 and 1949." Musial noted that the 1942 team "played together and fought together...had that Cardinal spirit. We thought we could beat anybody, and we did."[263] The team attitude inspired fans who looked for ways to help them forget the drudgery and fears of war.

The winning spirit started in 1942 when the team livened up with a little musical relaxation. The clubhouse became a joyful place with the team belting out a rendition of the novelty song, "Pass the Biscuits, Mirandy." Instruments added to the levity with trainer Dr. Harrison J. Weaver on the mandolin and Musial on the slide whistle or knocking out the beat with coat-hanger drumsticks.[264]

The 1942 World Series "was the first to be broadcast to American armed forces around the world by shortwave radio, and it was the first since 1918 where proceeds went in part to the Army's Emergency Relief Fund." The Yankees were favored to win, but the Cardinals outplayed them. It was a major upset, the first defeat for the Yankees in the World Series since they lost it in 1926—to the Cardinals.

Cardinals were ecstatic with their victory. New York did not take the defeat well as seen by Joe Williams' column the following day in the *World Telegram* where he stated, "The capitalistic system took another kick in the pants today when the aristocratic and well-fed Yankees were forced to bend the knee to the Oakies of baseball, the underprivileged St. Louis Cardinals...The Yankees were blown up by their own special brand of dynamite. The poor man's team from the Missouri Metropolis, little fellows who relied on little hits and their great speed, knocked the bombers out cold with home runs."

Dan Daniel, who covered the New York team added further insult to the mid-west team's victory when he wrote in the *Sporting News* that "many of the Bombers went in to the classic fighting the war and not the Cardinals…The Cardinals conceivably were not bothered as yet by the wartime considerations." Walker Cooper, catcher of the World Series winning team, responded that this was a good Cardinal team with confidence. "We could beat anybody…We hardly ever lost two in a row. The Yankees were a good ball club, but we were just much better." Ah, sour grapes for the New Yorkers, but as the decade rolled on the Cards fielded great teams that entertained and won even more pennants for their fans. The Yankees won four World Series in the Forties, but the Cards took three (1942, 1944, 1946) and they "finished either first or second every season from 1941 through 1949." There was no denying this young team put on a good show and deserved the accolades and honors of their championships.[265]

By the start of the 1944 season the Cardinals lost at least eight men to include "four key pitchers, a starting second baseman, and a center fielder."[266] Still, Southworth and his team went on to win the National League pennant, clinching in a double-header in Boston on September 21st. They ended the season with 105 victories.

Surprisingly, their opponents were the St. Louis Browns with 81 victories out of 154 games. Manager Luke Sewell fielded a group of misfits, some physically unfit for military service, yet they became the favorites of St. Louis because of their loser reputation. Another shocking detail was that the Browns took in 508,644 spectators, more in attendance that year than the Cards who recorded 461,968. That was a record that had held since 1926 when the Redbirds had won their first World Championship and captured the hearts of the St. Louis fans. The 1944 season seemed like a sure thing for the champion Cardinals, but this was phenomenal for the underdogs and folks wanted to see what all the news was about.[267]

Sportsman's Park came alive and St. Louis buzzed with excitement in the 1944 Fall Classic. The Cardinals faced the Browns in the streetcar series. Fans were divided on who to root for, the favorite champion Cardinals or the team that showed up for their first World Series. The tickets for the games were limited to those living in the St. Louis metropolitan area as a federal order from the Office of Defense curtailed civilian travel on trains, planes, and buses for military use.

While the city was happy to have an all St. Louis series, the games themselves garnered little excitement as fewer people (206,708) attended the World Series that year than attended the minor-league championship series in Baltimore. War took a toll on quality professional players. This could be seen when one looks at the Browns. They won the American League title with the lowest winning percentage [.579] since 1928. They had never won a pennant and customarily rested in the cellar. Michael D'Antonio reported, "Sportswriters were so aghast they refused to name a member of the team the league's Most Valuable Player."[268] Yet this event, too, helped to show the importance of place for the St. Louis fans would carry the Grand and Dodier series in their hearts.

Meanwhile, Cardinal fans had the pleasure of listening to Harry Caray for 24 years (1945-1969) before he became a fixture in Chicago. The "Holy Cow" and "it might be, it could be, it is a home run" began in St. Louis. He brought the excitement of the game into the homes of Cardinal fans that relied on Harry to tell them what they were missing, even if at times the account was a bit exaggerated. The radio fans also heard native St. Louisan, former Cards catcher and humorist Joe Garagiola before he moved on to television fame as a co-host of the *Today Show*. A longstanding fixture behind the microphone that fans associated with the Cardinals was announcer Jack Buck. He sat next to Caray for fourteen years, mentored numerous sportscasters to include his son, Joe Buck, and former player, Mike Shannon. Jack was the voice of the Cardinals for close to fifty years. His "that's a winner" was etched in the memory of Cardinal fans throughout the country as well as his famous 1985 cry of "Go crazy folks, go crazy" when Ozzie Smith ignited a frenzy with his right field homer in a playoff game against the Dodgers.

The war years brought success to the team on the field while it proved the farm system an excellent training ground. By the beginning of 1945 among those Cards missing were Walker Cooper, Murray Dickson, Max Lanier, Marty Marion, Terry Moore, Stan Musial, Howie Pollet, and Enos Slaughter. Things were so bad because of tighter restrictions on wartime travel that there was no All-Star Game, the only time in the history of the event that it was cancelled since its inception in 1933. The 1945 season did not garner a pennant for the St. Louis Cardinals.

They came in second behind the Chicago Cubs. In November, Billy Southworth left for the Boston Braves [269] and former Cardinal Eddie Dyer was brought in to manage. He had years of experience managing the minor league system and had "won nine pennants in 15 years from 1928-1942" as well as served as the Cardinals' farm director for two years.[270]

War years proved profitable for Breadon. With most of the top players away his "overall payroll shrunk." Wartime inflation brought federal restrictions on salaries and Breadon did not buck that policy. Times were tough, "There was no night baseball, crowds were small, and the baseball operators had to be shrewd businessmen…The Cardinals didn't pay salaries any lower than were paid in other cities." Only four clubs reported losing money in those years though attendance overall fell. With a winning record the Cards led the National League in profits during the war years with $410,587.[271] Another generation of fans looked to the ballpark to entertain them and allow them to forget their troubles.

Although many of the returning players were not physically up to par, the end of the 1946 season found the Birds tied with Branch Rickey's Brooklyn Dodgers team. In the two-out-of-three playoff series the Cards took the first two and moved onto the Fall Classic against the Boston Red Sox. No Red Sox team in history had ever lost a World Series. The best of seven went to the Cardinals as 36,143 St. Louis fans cheered the 4-3 victory at Sportsman's. Returning vet Stan Musial won his second MVP. This proved to be a banner year financially for Breadon, who before taxes took in over a million dollars.[272]

Breadon planned to build a new park about three miles south at Grand and Chouteau. The plans were to construct a 40,000-seat venue that would be "the last word in baseball construction" for his beloved team. All of that changed the following year. The team simply sucked.

They could do nothing right, even losing in the ninth when the games seemed secure. The team remained mired in the basement until mid-June. Breadon lost hope. He placed a $3 million price tag on the team and gave serious consideration to two offers. Ultimately, he thought better of the idea, saying, "What would I do if I didn't have baseball to worry about?" He called a team meeting where he told his players, "I think you fellows can win." He stuck it out, and so did they. From June 12 to 21, they went on a winning rampage, taking nine in a row, including four straight from Brooklyn. The city once again had faith in its team. The Cards finished second to the Dodgers and attendance soared past the 1946 mark to 1,247,913. Business was so successful that Breadon, the guy who invented Sunday doubleheaders, discontinued them.[273]

Money dictated the policies of the owners and not much kept them from racking in all the profits they could, but some social customs refused to budge, even if it meant losing a target audience. During the first fifty years or so of the twentieth century Cardinals baseball did not attract many black fans. The competition of great baseball that played throughout the Negro National League meant that blacks supported their own. The St. Louis Stars, a black team, played in St. Louis at Stars Park (seating capacity of 10,000) located at Compton Avenue and Market Streets from 1922-1931 but the financial stress of the Great Depression caused the team to disband. Black fans did not immediately gravitate to Sportsman's Park to cheer for all white teams.[274]

In 1944, Judge Kenesaw Mountain Landis, the first Commissioner of Baseball, died. The following spring major league owners met and named former Kentucky governor and United States Senator Happy Chandler to replace him. The death of Landis opened a window for possible changes in baseball.

In 1947, a tremendous transformation hit the baseball scene. The Brooklyn Dodgers, with the assistance of their General Manager, Branch Rickey, broke the color line when they introduced African American, Jackie Robinson to their lineup. Landis had been an ardent opponent to integrating baseball as had most of the owners. In fact, when the owners voted on the issue of admitting blacks to major league baseball the only one to vote for it was Walter O'Malley of the Dodgers. Chandler met with Rickey and arbitrarily made the decision to allow blacks to enter the game. World War II helped him reach his conclusion arguing, "If black men could fight and die for their country, they could play major league baseball." Much publicity surrounded this shift. Not all supported the controversial move. Post-war America in many regions supported strict racial segregation that followed Jim Crow policies. Racism was prevalent.[275]

Many players, both those on other clubs and even Robinson's own Dodgers, had concerns about playing on the field with an African American. It seemed that older players, especially those with southern ties, moved to the front of the controversy. There had been talk of an overall strike in the National League on opening day and although many deny that a strike vote occurred, it was clear that this change would not come easily.

Most of the press rejected the idea of integration, but in 1942 the St. Louis-based *Sporting News* published an editorial that "argued that both whites and blacks favored segregation" and in 1947 they reprinted the story but stated, "The presence of Negroes in the major leagues is an accomplished fact."[276] On May 6th, while on a road trip to Brooklyn, the Cardinals "threatened to strike over the presence of Robinson on the Dodgers roster."[277] Breadon and National League President Ford Frick "recommended against integration the year before" but now that it was taking place they had to deal with it and the repercussions. The supposed strike was averted when Frick threatened to suspend anyone who refused to take the field. The game went on with the Dodgers winning 7-6.[278]

Later that month, the Dodgers hit St. Louis. Robinson played his first game at Sportsman's Park. The black newspaper, the *St. Louis Argus*, cautioned its readers "to act like human beings...not like a tribe of cannibals." The public came out to witness this historic moment with the biggest weekday crowd of the season. While boos and racial epithets could be heard, the pavilion section filled with black fans who shouted their cheers of joy and encouragement.

Robinson recalled that as he walked through the Cardinals dugout to take the field, he knew his opponents were staring at him, but he respected the actions of their manager, Eddie Dyer, who was friendly to him. Bob Broeg witnessed the pleasant exchange between the two men.

As Robinson moved toward the visitor's bench, Dyer filled Broeg in on his intentions. "I've got to keep him happy, pal. Jackie's like Frank Frisch. Get him mad, and he'll beat you by himself."[279]

Players who did not like the presence of a black man on the field took out their frustrations by throwing hit pitches and spiking throughout the summer, but Robinson held strong. The Dodgers went on to win the pennant that year and several more in the following years as they continued to field black players. In 1947 the *Sporting News* named Jackie Robinson Rookie of the Year.

Integration was slow coming to St. Louis. Dan Daniel, a New York newspaperman wrote, "In St. Louis they say that fans would never stand for Negroes on the Cardinals or Browns." Both teams pulled their crowds from the south and southwestern regions of the United States where the custom was at the end of the workweek white men would take off for St. Louis to catch a weekend series. Teams did not want to lose this fan base. Those Alabama, Arkansas, Mississippi, and Tennessee crowds might well boycott the games, not to mention the local crowd might as well. The Browns experimented with a few black players but not for much duration. Bill Veeck, who had signed black players with the Cleveland Indians, hired the aging Satchel Paige in the early fifties. It did not do much to increase their attendance. It would be another seven years until the Cardinals added a black player.[280]

Owners of Sportsman's Park looked to capture the almighty dollar but thought better than tread on the sacred ground of racial practice. Even years after the official integration of the game sections of the park were segregated by class as well as race. St. Louis, a midwestern city, had been a southern city in many ways, including its racial policies.

Blacks and whites "knew their place" in this city that saw segregated schools, hotels, and restaurants. Progressive ideas of diversity were not welcome. African Americans who attended Sportsman's Park sat either in the bleachers or mainly in the roofed and screened right field pavilion that was officially segregated until May 1944. Sportsman's Park was "the only major-league park to practice segregation" based on race.[281] In the 1940s and 1950s, even after Jackie Robinson broke into major league baseball, Sportsman's Park remained the only big-league park with an unofficial Jim Crow section.[282]

Integration of the game produced results, including an opening for Latin Americans; with the color barrier broken, the number of Cuban players increased. Some light skinned Cuban players had passed and played during the war years but most quickly fled home when the Selective Service ruled that they had to register for the draft. Post-war baseball opened to colored players, yet the numbers from Cuba were drastically reduced after the Cuban revolution in 1959, and then virtually dried up with the United States policies of blockade and embargo. With that tie severed, baseball scouts turned their attention to other Latin American countries, to include the Dominican Republic, Mexico, Nicaragua, Panama, Puerto Rico, and Venezuela.[283]

The Cardinals appeared on television for the first time on April 12, 1947 in an exhibition game against the Browns. Changes to radio coverage took place that year, too. For the first time, St. Louis radio stations began to broadcast away games for both teams. At first the announcers did not travel with the teams. They stayed based in St. Louis and re-created the road games with background sound effects of crowd noises and updates from the Western Union ticker. Cardinals began road coverage live in the 1950s.[284]

Breadon learned early that fans came to the ballpark if he fielded winning teams. Throughout his association with the Cardinals they won nine National League pennants and six World Series. The farm system paid big dividends throughout Breadon's ownership and the team increased in value. The ballpark, players, owner, and fans had found a way to adjust to the social changes that emerged during the middle of the twentieth century and Grand and Dodier continued to matter as an important venue to St. Louis.

At the end of the 1947 season, one that brought out a "record 1,247,931 crowd," Breadon, still in love with his team and the excitement they brought him, decided to sell. Bob Broeg speculated that perhaps the success of Robinson, and the rumor that Rickey had more black talent to come, might have helped Breadon to step aside after twenty-seven years as club owner.

The racially divided city of St. Louis was not ready for integration and it appeared that Breadon did not want to take up that issue. He did not discuss his health but stated that at his age anything could happen. Breadon had no direct male heir and noted that he did not want to leave the team in the hands of a woman.[285] In addition, on the event of his death he did not want to pass onto his family huge inheritance taxes as had happened when the Yankees had sold. Many also believed that he wanted to pick his successor.

The Cardinals were a valuable commodity. "Breadon owned 78 percent of the team and had about $2.6 million in undeclared cash reserves, a million earmarked for a stadium." The asking price of the team was reported to be between three and four million. It was "the highest in baseball history up to that point." Robert Hannegan, the United States postmaster general, and Fred Saigh, a St. Louis attorney, purchased 75% interest in the Cardinals. When the finality of the sale hit, Breadon attempted to back out of the $3+ million sale. Hannegan told Breadon he could not back out as he had already stepped down from his federal position. So Breadon honored the deal.[286]

On November 25, 1947, an emotional Breadon proclaimed the sale of the team and twenty minor league farm clubs. He made the formal announcement himself, acknowledging it was a very difficult decision. He also expressed gratitude to "the fans of St. Louis whose loyalty has helped make the Cardinals the greatest organization in baseball." Breadon agreed to continue with the team as an advisor but that was short-lived. In May 1949, Sam Breadon died from cancer at the age of seventy-one.[287]

Hannegan, age forty-four, held 24% interest in the club and Saigh, age forty-two, held 51%, but it was the former that stepped forward to run the team. As a past chairman of the Democratic National Committee and part of President Harry Truman's administration, Hannegan was used to the attention he would gain now as a Cardinal executive and owner.

Space and place mattered to this son of a police captain. Hannegan, a native St. Louisan, former Knot Hole Gang member and one-time peanut vendor at Robison Field loved the game, but more importantly he loved the Cardinals. He was elated with this dream come true, an opportunity to own his Cardinals. He admitted the reason he sold concessions was "to get into the park and see my beloved Cardinals—for nothing...The ball club concessions man could have had all the money, just so long as I could get in to see the Cardinals play."[288]

Hannegan took an active leadership role in the public arena and in personal negotiations with his players. He became a cheerleader for the team even in times of defeat. Hannegan cheerfully boosted the team's spirits through his inspirational rhetoric. After a loss he would tell the team "Snap out of it fellows! This isn't a funeral parlor. You'll win tomorrow and the next day and the next day after that."[289] He was the voice of the fan in the locker room.

Hannegan had a good rapport with his manager, Eddie Dyer, and they planned great strategy for the future of the club. Those plans evaporated quickly when, only in his forties, Hannegan developed serious health problems with a history of hypertension. His doctors advised him to sell his shares of the team. Reluctantly, he agreed. It had been rumored that Joseph Kennedy, the patriarch of the Kennedy clan, had offered to buy his shares for $1.1 million, but Hannegan sold his stock to his partner Fred Saigh in January 1949 for $1 million and within the year Hannegan, age 46, suffered a fatal heart attack.[290]

Saigh, an attorney, grew up in Kewanee, Illinois, a Chicago Cub fan, but in 1947, when first offered the opportunity to be a part of the

Cardinals, he was hooked by the spell of the Cardinals and simply could not turn down the opportunity. He was a civic leader and a successful businessman. As a city booster he understood the attention the team brought and how it helped to put St. Louis on the map.

Saigh was not knowledgeable on the aspects of baseball business. At first, he did not think he had the experience to run the club, so he was more than happy to turn those duties over to Hannegan. Now just two years later, he was the major owner with close to 90 percent of the stock. He decided to try his hand at leading the team and do a few things his own way. He kept Eddie Dyer as manager. He formed a relationship with newsmen to act as sources and channels for news leaks. Soon he realized that he liked the business and people in baseball as well as the "glamour" of it all.[291]

In May 1949, Saigh released plans to build a new stadium at a cost of $4 million. Architect Syl G. Schmidt drew up plans for a modern stadium that would contain no posts to block fans view of the game. The owner did not disclose the location but claimed it would rest on eighteen acres of land he already owned and that he was looking into purchasing an additional eight to nine acres adjacent to that plot.

No new baseball stadium had been built in the United States since 1932 when Municipal Stadium in Cleveland opened. Saigh's plans for a new stadium never got off the ground. It was unclear why this dream did not materialize, but it took another owner and seventeen years before the Cardinals got a new home.

That first year of Saigh's sole ownership proved to be quite exciting for the Cardinals. They went down to the last day before being eliminated from the pennant race. Saigh took the loss hard. "We lost it in Chicago; I was pretty depressed that train ride back and a long time later." The team broke the Cards attendance record, drawing 1.4 million spectators. It proved the zenith until 1966 when the Cardinals moved to a new downtown stadium.[292]

Saigh became a real leader among club owners and good for the team. He had a mission of success as a Cardinal owner. "I tried to be very close to the players and take care of their little problems and I tried to cater to the fans."[293] He paid the players fairly, more than Breadon had. He made St. Louis superstar and favorite Stan Musial one of the highest players in the game with a $50,000 contract, second at the time only to Ted Williams. Saigh played it safe and that did nothing to bring St. Louis a championship season. He resisted integrating the team because he thought it would hurt ticket sales yet the new talent that helped win championships in the 1950s were men of color.[294]

Television changed things in baseball. Between 1950 and 1951 close to ten million Americans, a quarter of the nation, owned a set. At first owners were skeptical of presenting their games free on TV for fear that it would serve to keep fans from coming to the ballpark; but the broadcasts spurred an interest in the game and eventually brought more out of town viewers to the park.[295]

Nationally, the 1950s ushered in problems with the Cold War, a budding Civil Rights Movement, school integration, and a burgeoning economy brought on by suburbanization. St. Louis, still eighth in U.S. population of cities, was an integral part of all those events. Some brought trying episodes, but others brought success to the city. Part of that change came from the formation of a new group of powerful city businessmen who created Civic Progress. They were proud to call St. Louis their home. Members of Civic Progress had confidence in St. Louis and were committed to the downtown area. They espoused a determination to move the city forward with progressive ideas. St. Louis had a new spirit of commitment from those who could financially bring about change.

As far as championships and World Series wins, the 1950s harbored less successful seasons than the 1940s when the Cards owned the league, though these were the greatest years for Musial. Other Cardinal players included Don Blasingame, Kenny Boyer, Joe Cunningham, Red Schoendienst, and Enos Slaughter. They all brought exciting times to the field, yet the team only posted a .504 percentage during the 1950s and never finished first. In fact, for the 1955 season they ended in seventh place with a 68-86 record that proved to be the worst percentage of any Cardinal team since 1924.[296]

Problems plagued Fred Saigh in fall 1952 when he faced federal charges of income-tax evasion for unpaid funds amounting to over $500,000. He received a fine of $15,000 and a fifteen-month prison sentence. Years later Saigh reflected on the incident and noted that he was a victim of some things going on in St. Louis.[297] Saigh claimed innocence. He could have turned the team over to a trustee group and fought to retain ownership, but he elected to attend the owners' meeting and step aside to avoid embarrassing baseball.[298]

By the end of 1952, the Cardinals had not won a pennant in seven seasons, yet they continued to be one of the more successful franchises in baseball, usually landing second or third place in the league. In the past 27 years they had racked up nine National League pennants and six World Series championships. Groups outside of St. Louis showed substantial interest in purchasing the club for a considerable profit but they wanted to move the Cardinals to either Houston or Milwaukee.

Determined to keep the team in St. Louis, on February 20, 1953, Saigh accepted an offer of about a half-million less than outsiders presented. The club passed locally to Anheuser-Busch for $3.75 million. Publicity releases under the entire dynasty of the brewery ownership promoted

August A. Busch, Jr. as the savior of the team, but Saigh said, "it was a sort of mutual thing" to assure the team stayed in St. Louis. Busch noted that once the deal was finalized, "Saigh was sitting alone at the table, hands over his face, sobbing."[299]

Recognizing that the sale would be a huge financial boost to the brewery, Saigh "invested heavily and became the largest non-Busch family stockholder" in Anheuser-Busch.[300] Stock in the brewery brought him millions, but the sale of the team and the way he was treated hurt Saigh. For whatever reason, Busch did not extend a welcome or invite Saigh to team events.

Close to forty years after the sale Saigh, a financially successful tax and corporate lawyer with large holdings of stocks and real estate, was still bitter and hurt. It would be almost fifty years later, and under new ownership, that Saigh would return to witness firsthand a game played by his beloved Cardinals. He fondly reminisced, "The time I owned the Cardinals was a very important part of my life."[301] At age 94, Saigh died on December 29, 1999, noted for his kindness and his charitable endeavors throughout the St. Louis area.

Loyal St. Louis fans rooted for both teams throughout the first half of the twentieth century but that would soon change. The year after the Cardinals changed owners the Browns left for Baltimore. Brown's owner Ball died in 1936 and the team was sold several times over the next few years; then in 1946 Richard Muckerman purchased the ball club and park for close to $450,000. He promptly spent $750,000 to improve the park. The cost of refurbishing and of running the club placed Muckerman in a financial bind that caused him to sell the club to Bill and Charley DeWitt in 1949 for $1 million. These brothers had sold peanuts and sodas at Sportsman's Park when they were youngsters and they loved the game. They first attempted to raise the Cardinals $35,000 rent but the Cardinals owner pointed out that they held a contractual agreement that fixed the price until 1952. The DeWitt's tried to remove the Cardinals from Sportsman's Park, leading to a long legal battle.

Meanwhile, the Browns continued to have trouble producing a winning team. In 1951, the DeWitts sold the team to Bill Veeck. The Cardinals maintained their lease of the ballpark from the Browns until 1953 when the Browns moved to Baltimore. Veeck sold the park to the Cardinals at that time.[302] Yet, for thirty-three years National League and American League schedules accommodated the home and away games to avoid conflict; therefore, games played almost every day of the season as both the National League Cardinals and the American League Browns shared Sportsman's Park. Cardinal shortstop Marty Marion noted, "We used to play at old Sportsman's Park and there wasn't even any grass, it would be worn so much…It was like playing in a brickyard."[303] Though many die-hard Brownie fans would miss their American League team, now at last the field would get some rest. The Cardinals secured their home and took over as the sole team of St. Louis. Place as a mattered space would at least be a little easier to keep beautiful with rest periods between home stands and no arguments on how the park was to be maintained.

The ownership of Breadon and his successors saw a lot of changes to the culture of the United States and to baseball. Transportation moved into an automobile society and the technology of radio helped to promote the game. Numerous examples in the 1930s and 1940s showed that the owners still controlled the lives of the players and while trades upset the fans they always came out for winning baseball. The time period showed a dip in attendance during the Depression, but when faced with losing the team the fans anteed up and attendance returned. The war years proved trying on the franchise, but the strength of the farm system carried the team with rich rewards.

While baseball was integrated with the signing of Jackie Robinson and other black stars, the southern connections to the Cardinals organization kept the team from moving forward on the racial issue. This clearly showed the connections of the owners and the perceived concerns of the fans over what players took to the field. Place mattered as fans witnessed changes that ushered in announcers, numbers on uniforms, and night baseball. It mattered even more in the memory of fans who used the ballpark to escape the monotonous 1930s and the fears of the 1940s. The decade of the 1950s and new ownership brought profound changes to congeal the interconnectedness of the triad as the new ownership found ways to bring the fans out to the ballpark and support the sport. Long needed changes to St. Louis baseball emerged with the new owner of this space as the team moved into a new era in Cardinal history.

SPORTSMAN'S PARK, THE FIRST BUSCH STADIUM

August A. Busch, Jr., owner of Anheuser-Busch Brewery (A-B), bought the Cardinals for $3.75 million in 1953 mainly as a business venture; he also appealed to civic pride. The day he purchased the team Busch noted, "During its 100 years of existence, Anheuser-Busch has shared in all St. Louis civic activity. The Cardinals, like ourselves, are a St. Louis institution. We hope to make the Cardinals one of the greatest baseball teams of all time."[304] Fans saw progress in that statement; one of commitment and hope, but again change would not come over night.

The ownership proved quite beneficial for the brewery. At the time of the sale, "Budweiser trailed Schlitz nationally and was third in the St. Louis market to Stag and Falstaff." The rival brewery Griesedieck Brothers brewed Stag. They held exclusive rights for broadcasting the Cardinals and when they lost those rights the company went under. A-B "stock rose $2 a share the day after the sale." Before long the company rivaled the number one and two national brewers, Schlitz and Miller, both located in Milwaukee.[305]

Gussie Busch, age 53, president of the brewery since 1946, was not much of a baseball enthusiast early on. He favored horsemanship and hunting, noting, "I've been a baseball fan all of my life. But I've been too busy to get out to the park in recent years—unfortunately."[306]

Public relations guru Al Fleishman helped clean up Busch's image, for when he purchased the team, he had a loose reputation for chasing women. "He was a heavy, two-fisted drinker and was disliked by more polite society…People just put up with him." With Fleishman's magic touch a new image emerged. He began to be a community leader and humanitarian.[307]

Owning the team brought a human quality to the executive. Busch was gregarious, and baseball presented an inroad to talking with people. In the beginning he was quite accessible, fans talked with him, and sportswriters would ring him up at his Grant's Farm residence for his opinions.

Busch embraced the team. He became more involved daily and even donned a uniform at spring training. He was a noted presence at the games, especially on the occasions where he led a team of A-B Clydesdales onto the field to the melodic cadence of the A-B advertising jingle. St. Louisans readily recognize that melody and to this day associate it with Busch and the Cardinals.

In 1953, A-B bought Sportsman's Park from Bill Veeck for $800,000.[308] Veeck's team only garnered 297,238 in attendance that year. He was losing money, wanted out of St. Louis, and searched for a path to profit. Escape seemed his only alternative.

Veeck desired to break into a west coast market. He conducted preliminary studies and knew that Union Oil would pay him for television rights. He planned to convert the massive Los Angeles Memorial Coliseum for baseball; after an exhausting ten-hour sales pitch at a league meeting the vote was called. The American League owners blocked Veeck's move. His next interest was to move the team to Milwaukee, but Lou Perini blocked that market. With the approval of the National League, Perini moved his Boston Braves into a new County Stadium in Milwaukee.[309]

The power of the owners solidified over the century as they looked more to programs that were beneficial to most of their group. The American League successfully blocked Veeck in, forcing him to stay another year in St. Louis. Fans lost complete interest in the cellar team and saw no reason to support them.

On September 27th, with 3,174 fans present, the Browns played their last game in St. Louis. They lost in 11 innings to the White Sox 2-1. Veeck, hung in effigy at the last game and nearly bankrupt, sold the franchise to the Baltimore Baseball Club Inc. and the team became the Orioles.[310] After 52 years of St. Louis baseball represented by both major leagues, the American League team pulled up stakes and left the Cardinals as the sole major league team.[311]

Once the Browns left town the playing field would receive needed rest and care. Busch thought Sportsman's Park was in deplorable conditions, and it was. The park had been rebuilt in 1908, and other improvements had been made throughout the century but especially over the past several years the Browns had not kept up with even normal maintenance. The field, in the scorching heat of St. Louis, was regarded as the worst field in the majors. Because it was in constant use with the two teams it never rested; there was insufficient time to work on it during the season. The flimsy tarp used to cover the field left puddles throughout the infield, and "mounds of dirt and debris littered public areas under the lower grandstand." Over the next two years Busch initiated refurbishing at a cost of $1.5 million and it became "one of the finest stadia in America in the mid-1950s."[312]

Busch pulled out the centerfield bleachers to improve the batter's view, covered the area with attractive shrubs, and installed a flagpole in centerfield. He removed the advertisements from the outfield walls and added touches of his own company to select sites throughout the park. Neon and animation enhanced the scoreboard to show a large Redbird swinging a bat and hitting a ball that then would indicate whether the official scorer had ruled a hit or an error on the play. When a Cardinal hit a homer the Redbird "would hit a ball and fly back and forth across the board."[313] Busch installed an electrical red and blue sign of the Anheuser-Busch "A" symbol that lit up a flying American eagle each time a Cardinal hit a homer. The memory of the flying Eagle remained with fans long after they left the ballpark. In addition, every seat was either removed or repaired and brighter colors of red and green paint sparked the place up. Busch put in new dugouts and clubhouses.[314] He adopted the motto, "Customer comfort is second only to winning in importance and a close second at that." A high priority was presenting a clean establishment that people wanted to frequent with their families. Consequently, new restrooms were installed, and lighting improved.[315]

Busch sought to rename the park Budweiser to advertise his beer, but the powerful National League officials stopped that as too commercial. Commissioner Frick, concerned that naming a ballpark after an alcoholic beverage sent the wrong message, vetoed the name change.[316] Instead, the name of Sportsman's Park changed to Busch Stadium and shortly thereafter A-B introduced a new beer, Busch Bavarian Beer.[317] Busch found a way to win his point.

Major league owners knew that to keep fans coming to the ballpark they had to reach beyond local concerns and involve the fans in national competition. If they could build a rivalry, get fans interested in league standings and the pennant race, they could increase revenues. The league standings often changed daily, but St. Louis fans knew the order at a glance with the display of team flags flying over the park lined up in standing order. On the right side of home plate above the stands flew the eight American League team flags and to the left of the plate flew the eight National League flags.

Mass patronage could only come about if baseball was a respectable enterprise, one that could attract the right crowds, including all of society. Therefore, the organization promoted rules of proper decorum to clean up the sport. Baseball was originally a man's sport associated with foul language, drinking, and gambling. League rules attempted to clean up the game with fines for "inappropriate behavior" on the field, and over the years betting on the game was officially banned. Alcohol proved harder to curtail as saloon keepers or breweries owned a few of the teams, including St. Louis, and they used the game to advertise and sell their products. Drinking was more difficult to handle, at least with the fans. As a solution to problem drinkers, rough kids, unruly fans, and to keep overall order at the ballpark, Sportsman's Park hired uniformed "Andy Frain" ushers and policemen to work the game. Fans learned the space would be monitored for proper behavior and it helped get more families to the venue.

Attracting the right mix of fans worked to present baseball as a "proper" middle-class entertainment. If owners expanded the audience to a respectable group that included women and children, they could possibly fill the stands, promote the outing as a proper place to be seen, and assure future generations to the game. Promotional efforts began to lure a more diverse audience into the park.

Pictures of the first fifty years or so of baseball audiences show a sea of businessmen dressed in their white shirts and ties. As previously noted, Von der Ahe and other team owners attempted to woo females to the games with hosting Ladies Day games; this became a successful marketing tool for getting women interested in the game, or at least interested in the players. Kids, too, were a market for the game. They were wooed through special promotions of the Knot Hole Gang, and YMCA events. Servicemen in uniform and the clergy received free or reduced admission, too. With all this promotion, by the mid-1950s the ballpark crowds were quite diverse. The young and old, rich and poor, men, women, and children flocked to the games though it was still more of a predominantly white crowd. Busch wanted to go further to reach a family crowd. Evidently it was a successful endeavor.

Cards fan Tom Schneider recalled he fell in love with baseball when his dad took him to Sportsman's. He noted that he came from a typical single income, post-World War II family with limited funds. Going to the game was a luxury. Usually they would sit in the left field bleachers, to him the best place in the world. On special occasions, like when Gibson or Koufax pitched and the bleachers were sold out, they upped the ante for reserve seats. He fondly remembered one-time spotting "the greatest assembly of sports announcers...Harry Caray, Jack Buck, and Joe Garagiola...All together walking on a catwalk above us." To him those days were special. Special times to be alone with his dad, but also magical in the drive to the game itself, finding a place to park, the lights of the park looming overhead as the sun set, the sound of the organ, the smell of the hot dogs, beer and peanuts, the thousands of strangers there, yes, it made those Friday nights a sacred utopia.[318]

Judy Clarke Dwyer reminisced that her mom, Mary, was quite a fan and would listen to the games as she ironed her husband's white shirts. She knew all the players' names and averages, though she went to only a few games she followed them as a true radio fan. Judy noted that when she attended the games at Sportsman's after Busch first bought the team a lot of men and boys were in attendance and that the dress was more formal. She remembered going to the games with her dad, Johnny. They would take either the bus or streetcar. In those days the neighborhood was safe with the crowd polite. Her husband, Fran Dwyer, recalled the playing days of Stan Musial and seeing the Browns play where he witnessed a Mickey Mantle home run. They both reminisced that when not many people were at the game they could move down to better seats without any problems or hassles.[319] For them, too, this was a special space and one they tied to fond memories of the place to be in St. Louis.

Once women entered more seriously into the equation of baseball the game became the place to be seen. Fans began to pay more attention in the 1950s and 1960s to the private lives of the players, whether they were married and had kids. Fans liked to see the players' families at the game and enjoyed the annual game where the ballplayers and their families paraded around the stadium in convertibles and after the regulation game brought their kids onto the field for a game of baseball. Many of the players brought the families to town during the season and quite a few decided to permanently settle in St. Louis.

In the years following World War II society harkened to a time of "family values" and the separate spheres philosophy where women were associated with the home and charitable activities. Baseball wives began to socialize more with each other and decided that they would give something back to the community. Some Browns' families still lived in the St. Louis area, as well as wives whose husbands played for other major league teams. Along with Cardinal wives, the women established a charitable group known as the Pinch Hitters Club. Three of the founders were Mary Schoendienst, wife of Red; Taffy Wilbur, wife of Del; and Isabelle Lenhardt, wife of Don. They received enthusiastic support from the other wives and before long they were meeting and planning an annual activity to benefit needy children in the St. Louis area; the beneficiary changed each year.

The club involved a lot of work, but they were up to the challenge and enjoyed the planning stages as well as the event itself. The Cardinals helped with the publicity and Harry Caray and Jack Buck gave radio time to discuss the event. The first few years the fund-raising project was a fashion show/luncheon where the wives and children of the players modeled fashions and sometimes a few of the players participated. These events proved successful. After a couple of years, the wives changed the program to bring in more fans and to tie the event closer to the game. They introduced the Ball-B-Que. They sold tickets to an afternoon Cardinal game and afterwards the women hosted a barbecue at the Busch compound, Grant's Farm. Most of the players from the Cardinals and the opposing team came to the dinner and mingled with the fans. For some patrons the overall event was too expensive, but others looked forward to attending every year. The player's wives also produced and sold cookbooks with their favorite recipes and the proceeds went to charity.[320]

As far as fashion went, owners did not have a strict dress code, except on the field where players wore team uniforms. The fans took control over the proper fashion attire. American society had a stricter dress code in the first half of the twentieth century compared to the latter half. In the early years people in all sections of the park dressed in what became known as "church-going clothes." Men wore white shirts, ties, dark trousers, and some sported a fedora or straw hat. Women wore nice dresses with slips, silk stockings, high-heeled shoes, jewelry, and many wore dressy hats. Even those sitting in the bleachers did not dress down. A day at the ballpark was considered an outing to be seen at as well as to see. The sea of red and more casual attire so prominent in recent years at the St. Louis ballpark did not take hold until after they team moved downtown and the more relaxed fashions and lifestyle of the 1970s took over.

Baseball owners, entrepreneurs ready to cash in on the profits, had company at the ballpark. Independent vendors invented ways to make a day at the park seem incomplete without the all-American hot dog or a box of popcorn. Some of the most colorful people in attendance were the vendors in the stands. They would canvass the park selling hot dogs, peanuts, popcorn, crackerjacks, lemonade, soda, and beer. The popcorn sold in paper megaphones, when emptied they were used by the fans to shout cheers to their favorites on the field. The friendly beer vendors chanted colorful banter to sell their product. The park filled with the smells of these foods as the merchants weaved their way through the crowds. Memories of the game conjure up these characters, too.

Keeping score became a way to make folks feel part of the game and offered another way for owners to grab advertising dollars. The scorecards originally were free, paid for by the advertisers, but ten cents became the common price for most of the years at Sportsman's Park/ Busch Stadium with an additional nickel for a pencil. What a value for a dime! Fresh cards were printed daily. They listed league standings, the name and number of all the players, and a box score for ten innings of play with a section to the right listing the stats for each player in the lineup. It presented the starting lineup with uniform number, position, and the up-to-date batting average of the players. For the pitchers it showed their year-to-date won-loss record. Rules for special plays were listed, as well as numbers for officiating umpires. The cards advertised products as well as upcoming home games and became a great place to collect player's autographs.

Throughout the century baseball continued as a popular form of entertainment. At a time of simple pleasures, the game provided an escape from the drudgery of the everyday industrial life and reminded

Americans of "a vanished and mythical simple rural past."[321] Even though baseball had become big business, most fans did not see it that way until television revenues and the player's union brought the mega salaries of more modern times. This was a game that adults remembered playing as children. They knew it well. Fathers took their sons to the game as a rite of passage that served to unite the generations. Fans at Sportsman's saw it as chummy, small and cozy, where they felt a part of the excitement. Many heard conversations emanate from the field. Those in box seats leaned over the dugout roof and talked to the players, some in general admission sat directly behind the bullpen and chatted with the players; bleacher bums yelled to outfield players. It was not a difficult task to coax an autograph from a player before the game or as they walked over the ramp from the dugout to the clubhouse. Some even carried on conversations with players as they headed to the clubhouse. In the decades before million-dollar contracts the players seemed one of them, not interested in projecting an "image." Guards did not hold back fans.

Before the 1970s, some of the players lived in working-class neighborhoods. Many of the players worked odd jobs around St. Louis in the off-season. They "sold cars, drove deliveries, worked in warehouses, or restaurants. You could see them, touch them, [and] relate to them."[322] In the 1950s and 1960s it was not unusual to find players living in St. Ann and Florissant, newer suburban areas that catered to the working/middle class. Fans saw Ernie Broglio, Ken Boyer, or Dal Maxvill out in public with their families. One fan, Mary Rackers, from Florissant babysat for Lindy McDaniel's children in the 1950s. Some of the girls going to local high schools knew players' families and helped them with babysitting. Players did not make the mega salaries in those days and therefore they fit in more with the fans living in working-class neighborhoods.[323]

Owners used the park to garner revenues, while fans used it to relax, unwind, and escape boredom. For the most part, everyone saw a day at the ballpark as a cheap form of entertainment that offered value. Nostalgic fans remember the innocence and simplicity of the atmosphere of the five decades at Sportsman's Park. George Fields remembered "one could go out for a good time simply on the spur of the moment. For a nominal fee you could hop on a streetcar or bus and head for the ballpark." Admission was reasonable. Many fondly recalled that the doubleheaders were the best buy of all, two games for the price of one. Going to the ballpark was a safe, cheap evening of fun that as Fields recollected, "Didn't need all the advanced planning and the bucks that the games of today involve."[324] Moe Knepper, known as an institution in the old Sportsman's Park area, evoked that in the old days, "You were up close to the players, you could see them and recognize them...I don't enjoy the game as much [at new

Busch Stadium], you are so far away from the players, you can't see what a guy looks like…and the tickets cost so much."[325]

Judie Campana reminisced about her teenage years in St. Louis and the fun of attending Cardinal games. "The best bargains were Ladies Day games. My sister, Connie, and I went to a lot of those games. As teenagers we didn't have much money. We babysat for fifty cents an hour but could afford the games because admission on Ladies Day was only fifty cents." Campana knew the entertainment value. "You always went to the ballpark early to get a good seat either in general admission or the bleachers and to watch the players practice; we always hoped to get an autograph or to coax a player to throw us a baseball. Our favorite seats were the ones right behind the bullpen because we could talk with the players."[326] Mary Anne Hagedorn remembered the ease of getting players to sign autographs after the game. "They all came out a single door that opened onto the sidewalk where fans congregated, and they had to pass us to get out the door. Most of the players willingly signed our scorecards. Musial never refused."[327]

General Manager (GM) Bing Devine's youngest daughter Jane had fond memories of Sportsman's Park with her Dad. She remembered the great burgers at the concessions, the best in town. She also recalled that they always stayed late after the game, then walked the flat roof of the stadium and collected baseballs.[328] Bing used to sit on the roof "during Cardinals games so he could keep up with games and players in other cities on his transistor radio."[329] To each of these fans the stadium was a magical place that stayed with them throughout their lives. The first half of the twentieth century was a simpler time and had much more of "a community feel," even in a park that held thousands of people.

Changes in following the Cardinals came in 1954 when Jack Buck joined Harry Caray in broadcasting the games. The team left KSD-TV where they had been since 1947 for WTVI and all 77 of their road games were carried. The following year they began broadcasting regularly over KMOX. Buck, a Hall-of-Fame broadcaster and fan favorite, announced the games until 2001. His son Joe joined the broadcasting team in 1991 and moved on as a sports analyst/commentator for FOX network nationwide.

When Busch took the reins, one of the first things he tackled was to bring winning baseball to the city. For the first six years, he went through five managers to include Eddie Stanky, Harry Walker, Fred Hutchinson, Stan Hack, and Solly Hemus and several general managers beginning with Richard Meyer, a brewery vice president, moving onto Frank Lane, and then Bing Devine.

When Busch first took over the team he called in manager, Eddie

Stanky and asked what was required for the team to win. Stanky's simply replied, "Better players." Busch did not hold back. He set out to buy the best players in the league though he did not realize some players were not for sale, even for a million dollars.

Busch decided to foster young talent and to lure them with a hefty bonus. The Cards acquired Dick Schofield, a high school graduate from Springfield, Illinois, with a $65,000 bonus; and throughout the years there were many more bonus babies, to include Tim McCarver, Von and Lindsay McDaniel, as well as Bob Miller. Fans came out to watch these youngsters play.

Busch was astonished when he showed up to his first spring training. The team consisted of all white players. Gussie questioned how it could be the great American game if blacks did not play. He believed it "was morally wrong to exclude blacks" plus he worried blacks, who bought a lot of Budweiser, may well boycott his product. He remarked, "Hell we sell beer to everyone."[330] He set about to change the previous ban on blacks playing in St. Louis.

Finally, in 1954 the first African American player for the franchise took the field. Tom Alston, 23-years old, ushered in integration for the Cardinals. The rookie first baseman came from the Pacific Coast League for $100,000. Cards public relations man, Fleishman cautioned Alston of race problems and bigotry that he might well face in St. Louis. Alston calmly assured him, "I know I'm a Negro, and I know that there are going to be some people who hate me for nothing more than that. But that's not my problem, that's their problem." Though the Cardinals did not take the lead in breaking the color line, Busch proved willing to bring the talent to the plate. Black players who came to St. Louis during the late 1940s and early 1950s faced discrimination off the field, too. In this racially divided city, they could not stay in the same hotels or eat in the same restaurants with their white teammates. While some white players stayed in the posh, air-conditioned Chase Hotel, blacks suffered through St. Louis summer heat in black hotels without air conditioning.

Brooks Lawrence, a black pitcher also played during the mid-fifties for the Cardinals had played in the minor league system under Johnny Keane. He came to the majors in June 1954 to play for manager Eddie Stanky. He served as a starter and reliever. Other players accepted him, but he had no friends on the club. Stanky played him hard. In fact, in the first month he pitched in nine ball games, winning seven and losing two. There were times he pitched three and four days in a row, starting and in relief. He had nothing negative to say about the manager but noted that Bob Broeg questioned Stanky about using him like that and the retort was, "I didn't know you could hurt one of them."[331]

Lawrence roomed with Alston in a black section of town. He recalled, "We never went more than five blocks from the house…We almost never went downtown…There wasn't anything downtown for me." When the team went to the train station Brooks could not sit with the white players, he would have to "sit in the colored waiting room." One day he did sit in the white waiting room and visited with the pitching coach, Bill Posedel. A waitress approached to see if the coach wanted to order a drink and he said "Yes, a beer and a Coke." She replied, "I can serve you, but I can't serve him." Posedel told her to bring the drinks, and then he gave Brooks the Coke. Lawrence noted, "Strange as it may sound, that was the only incident I ever had in St. Louis. I never was in any place to be causing an incident." It was clear St. Louis "for a time was the most segregated city in the big leagues, the city that visiting black players liked to visit the least."[332]

Busch lifted the Cardinal race ban. The team continued to add black players and fans came to respect the abilities of Lou Brock, George Crowe, Curt Flood, Bob Gibson, Ozzie Smith, Bill White, and others who have since worn the Cardinal uniform. Early black players helped expose the racism of the day as they brought fun, excitement and championships to St. Louis.[333] Fans found the sacred space opened and while not all were happy about the infusion of this new talent, fans continued to attend the games and support the team.

Once more black players made the team they started to speak up for equality. After prompting from their major black players, Cards' management took an open stand on the racial issue in 1962 in St. Petersburg, Florida, where they held spring training. Florida had strict segregation "entrenched by both law and custom for decades." Since 1954, when they hired their first black player, Florida law banned blacks from staying in the same hotel as the white players. Blacks "lived and ate at private homes and rooming houses during spring training."

Bob Gibson wrote of his first trip to the big-league spring training camp in 1958. He took the train to Florida "sitting solemnly in a seat assigned to black passengers…that didn't stop three yahoos from trying to rough me up, assuming, I guess, that I need to be taught a lesson for having the gall to ride on their train instead of the Greyhound bus." When he arrived at the Bainbridge Hotel, where the team stayed, "the clerk advised me that there would be a room for me in a private home on the other side of town." There was a cab in the back waiting to drop him off along with the other black players. Gibson recalled the humiliation a few years later of driving south in the days of segregation and the degrading experience of the restrooms for blacks that were "filthy, stinking room[s] back there with no lighting or sink." It was horrible "pulling into gas stations and watching Charline and our daughters walk into Colored Only bathrooms…we slept in the car because the motels wouldn't take us in[334]

Gibson, White, and Flood let the Cardinals know they did not feel part of the team. One thing that bothered them was the St. Petersburg Yacht Club's tradition of hosting a breakfast for the Yankees and Cardinals. The African American players noticed they were never invited, even though white minor league players received a welcome.

White, college educated from Ohio, had been raised in a primarily white community and was a quintessential gentleman. He had played in the racist south in the minors, "where he sometimes carried a bat in order to get through the hostile crowds." He became upset with the rebuff from the Yacht Club and made sure to leak the information to a reporter of the *St. Louis Argus*. Duly offended by this incident the paper called "for a public boycott of Anheuser-Busch." Soon, other black players spoke out against the Jim Crow policies of Florida cities and establishments.

Busch took up the cause. Before the 1961 season, General Manager Devine contacted the Vinoy Park Hotel in St. Petersburg and requested rooms for all the players, black and white. The reply came that African American players would not be welcome and if the Cardinals had to have all their personnel in the same hotel they should go elsewhere. That year Devine caved, stating, "We don't make the rules and regulations for the various localities." By the following year a solution was found. Busch arranged for some local "friends of the team" to purchase two adjacent hotels in St. Petersburg, the Skyway and the Outrigger. One was used for the black and white players alike and the other opened to the public.

Musial and Boyer took the lead for the white players. They traditionally had private accommodations with their families at spring training, but they too moved into the hotel. The Cardinals broke local custom. White saw this as pivotal in forging a bond between the entire Cardinals organization. He noted, "There were a lot of unsung heroes. Stan Musial, Ken Boyer, and their families gave up their personal comforts off-site to move in with black players." As well, White hailed the efforts of the front office "because as long as the ballclub accepted segregation, there would be no change…it was our own little civil rights movement." Visitors to the south were given an example of camaraderie that crossed racial divide as the team had cookouts, and they all swam in the hotel pool. Close friendships developed between the black and white players, and that helped with play on the field and the atmosphere of the clubhouse. White and Gibson became the "self-appointed guardians of racial respect…if word of a racial indiscretion arose," they would confront it and "made it clear that there would be none of that on the St.

Louis Cardinals."[335] The team set an example to fans how to handle such problems and to become one team regardless of race.

The decade of the 1960s was one of change and cultural upheaval from involvement in the Civil Rights Movement, riots in the streets, assassinations of important United States leaders, participation in the Vietnam War, and anti-war demonstrations. Some of this affected St. Louis, but not as harshly as other parts of the nation, dropping the city to tenth most populous city in the country.

Monumental change came for St. Louis in the 1960s as makeover plans of the late 1930s came to fruition at the downtown riverfront. Blight and decay existed in pockets of the city. Completion of the federal highway system, school integration, white flight and higher crimes rates were evident in the drastic changes in population figures that showed 622,236 residents in the city, while the county counted 951,671.

Downtown St. Louis as a commercial and tourist site saw life return with the unveiling of the Gateway Arch and a new downtown stadium for the Cardinals. The city once again became an international tourist stop. In addition, championship baseball returned both at Grand and Dodier and then twice at the new downtown venue.[336] All of this helped solidify the connection of the organization and the community, and of course brought fans to the ballpark.

The 1950s and early 1960s did not result in pennant winning years for St. Louis but for several years they brought pennant fever to the city. Baseball was fun to watch with the playing of the Ken Boyer, Joe Cunningham, the McDaniel brothers, Stan the Man, Vinegar Bend Mizell, Wally Moon, Bill White, and others. The Cardinals fielded teams under the management of Eddie Stanky, Harry Walker, Fred Hutchinson, Solly Hemus, Johnny Keane, and Red Schoendienst. General Manager Devine came to be seen by many as one of the greatest minds in baseball. In 1963 and 1964 he was named National League Executive of the Year in a *Sporting News* poll.[337]

While Busch and Devine supported black players, others believed the thirty-six-year old player/manager Solly Hemus, who steered the team from late 1958 to 1961, did not relate to blacks."[338] Broeg remembered Hemus "as friendly, amusing, polite…an aggressive player." But Gibson saw it differently. He did not see Hemus up to managing. His decisions never seemed to be very logical, and it was difficult to read where he was headed with the plays he made.

Hemus had no rapport with the players; in fact, he could not deal even with Musial. Musial? Everyone got along with the mild-mannered superstar. There was talk of trading Musial but that never materialized. Broeg pointed out to Hemus that Stan was popular with the press and the community. He brought the fans to the park. Perhaps it helped that Musial "voluntarily proposed a twenty-thousand-dollar pay cut in January 1960," which still left him the highest-paid National Leaguer at eighty thousand dollars. Stan had a lot to offer and perhaps with another manager, one who knew how to use him (and the rest of the team) Musial would have come around.[339]

Gibson presented many stories in his book *Stranger to the Game* that back up his allegations. Hemus really could not handle White, Flood, or Gibson. "Either he disliked us deeply or he genuinely believed that the way to motivate us was with insults...He would goad us, ridicule us, bench us-anything...to make us feel inept." Hemus had no confidence in his players and tried to intimidate them. Flood concurred that Hemus could not manage blacks. "We were at the stage of our careers where we still questioned ourselves...we'd make strides, and then we'd be sent back to Omaha...up and down, up and down." Gibson grew up in Omaha and had family there, but it was not the big leagues. There were two bright sides of reporting to the minor leagues in Omaha, one was the manager Johnny Keane, and two, and he could play, stay in the game, and win. Gibson noted, "Keane had no prejudices concerning the way I played... He had no prejudices concerning my color, either."[340]

Busch gave up on Hemus the Fourth of July weekend 1961 and turned to third base coach Johnny Keane who had over thirty years of experience in the Cardinal organization. He was "a reflective, gentle voiced Texan...[with] character." Under his leadership things turned around. Many of the younger players had been with him in the minors, and the players knew him as their coach. Keane instilled confidence in all his players. Even though the Cards finished in fifth place, thirteen games out, the last eighty games of the season they won forty-seven, and things looked promising for the next season.[341]

In 1962, the season expanded from one hundred fifty-four games to one hundred sixty-two and the first of expansion occurred with the addition of the New York Mets and the Houston Colt 45s.[342] Musial had a few records he wanted to break. He believed one more season would do that. Keane wanted him to play more than Hemus had allowed, stating if this "is going to be your last one, make it one to be remembered." Musial broke both records he had set his sights on and more. He remarked that this "proves we modern ball players are as good as the old-timers say they were."[343]

On March 12, 1963, with a secured twenty million from St. Louis businessmen, including five million pledged from Busch, the Cards held a news conference to discuss the planned redevelopment area south and west of the riverfront project, the Gateway Arch, and presented a model of the new Busch Stadium to be completed in 1965. The complex set in downtown St. Louis included office buildings, ample parking garages, and a large hotel. It was hoped that this fresh infusion of capital would bring the downtown area alive and start a complete rehabilitation of the St. Louis streetscape.

The same year Busch placed players' names on the back of their uniforms and padded the outfield walls of the park. Keane and Busch sought ways to strengthen positions at short, catching, and pitching. The Cardinals brought in eighty-one-year old Branch Rickey as a consultant to help shake up the roster and bring the long-awaited winner to the city.[344]

Fans, players, and owners know that sometimes trades make all the difference in a season's outcome. June 15, 1964, entered the history books as a remarkable day in the history of the Cardinals. It marked the Devine trade for Lou Brock. For the most part, fans in St. Louis did not welcome the trade for a favorite St. Louis pitcher, Ernie Broglio. The *St. Louis Post-Dispatch* questioned the trade noting, "Why didn't the Cardinals get more than Brock, a flashy outfielder who could become a star, for Broglio, an 18-game winner last season and still regarded as a top pitcher?"[345] The trade was not popular in the clubhouse. Broglio, a known commodity, could win games. Gibson remarked, "I thought it was a dumb trade. I didn't know how good Lou would be. No one knew. I didn't even remember facing him." No one seemed to know much about the .250 hitter Brock except he could steal bases.[346]

Johnny Keane and his coaches knew what they wanted from Brock, his speed. For the remainder of the season he hit .348 and swiped thirty-three stolen bases. He proved to be a great asset. With his acquisition the '64 team, under the helm of thirty-five-year veteran of the Cardinal organization Keane, won the NL pennant and the World Championship.[347]

Keane had some problems that season in the clubhouse, especially with shortstop Dick Groat who had joined the team at the beginning of the 1963 season. Rumors were aflutter that by the end of the season Keane would be replaced by Leo Durocher. Keane's honest approach stunned some of the players and hit home for Groat who approached Keane, offered an apology, and admitted that he had been responsible for some of the bad behavior. Soon after that the "ballclub caught fire." The season was far from over, and failure was not in the cards.[348]

The pennant race was not easy, and even Auggie Busch did not see promise for the team. Busch did not like the way the Groat-Keane incident had been handled. He thought he should have been informed of locker room hostility and that Devine kept the information from him. To Devine, that was his job as GM, to keep things under control and not to bother the owner "with all the little details." Busch began to have his doubts, "If that's going on, what else is going on?"

On August 16th, with the team 9.5 games out and holding down third place, Busch took the advice of his special consultant Branch Rickey. He fired Devine. It looked like the 1964 season was over; it would be time to plan for next year. On the recommendation of Rickey, Busch hired Bob Howsam as the new GM and Devine accepted a position with the New York Mets.

A relaxed Cardinal team overcame a 6.5 deficit over the last two weeks of the season. They were six games out with eleven to play. The Cards battled down to the last game to win their first pennant in eighteen years, their first pennant for Busch. Fans mobbed the field and players scurried to safety. The site was bedlam.[349] Memories of this ballpark and the historical pennant would live forever in the hearts of the fans. The season was not over.

Fans from near and far flocked to get coveted World Series tickets. American essayist, Roger Angell captured the neighborhood of the park at Grand and Dodier as a "seamed, rusty, steep-side box" that hosted the event. He noted that the site "reminded me of an old down-on-her-luck dowager who has been given a surprise party by the local settlement house; she was startled by the occasion but still able to accept it as no less than her due." Many locals camped outside the park for two days to capture their pavilion or bleacher tickets.[350]

The looseness of the team continued even during the World Series against the New York Yankees that pitted brothers Kenny and Clete Boyer, against each other, both playing third base for their respective teams. The Cardinals defeated the Yankees in seven games for one of the most exciting World Series in the history of the game. Gibson wrote, "There was a deep satisfaction of winning for Bing Devine and Johnny Keane...our triumph was not a product of hitting and fielding and pitching skills alone, but...the mental, social, and spiritual qualities that made the Cardinals unique."[351]

The 1964 championship was memorable. It would be the last World Series in the original Sportsman's Park. Keane would go on to have the last laugh on Busch. The day after his team nailed down the series Keane announced his resignation and moved to take over as the new skipper for the Yankees.[352] Busch fired senior consultant Rickey and named Red Schoendienst the new manager.

By the decade of the sixties, the neighborhood surrounding the ballpark had changed. It still housed a "neighborhood feel" and industry, but the district was becoming increasingly a poor run-down ghetto with deteriorating properties. The action, the place to be, was with the revitalization going on in the downtown area. Economic resources had virtually fled the district. Busch was not interested in gentrification. He wanted to be a part of the redevelopment in the downtown area around the new St. Louis Arch, a move was inevitable.

At the time, baseball owners with a motivation of profit, politically and economically, united with government funding to control the public space of the baseball playing field. Federal funds were there; "between 1950 and 1970 the U. S. Congress appropriated more than $10 million to support urban renewal," and, by the latter years, cities across the United States had initiated the planning of, began to implement, or had completed, over two thousand urban renewal projects. For St. Louis this meant a chance to "arrest urban decline and shape a new kind of city."[353]

Vast changes to the riverfront and the new ballpark benefited from this investment. With the influx of federal grants, slum areas cleared from the decaying waterfront, and a modern city emerged to draw attention to and highlight St. Louis as a place on the map. The beautification project set out to bring about revitalization in architecture as well as provide jobs for the city. With the multiuse structures of entertainment, hotels, retail establishments, residential condos, offices, and a national park, St. Louis moved into a modern era and hoped to leave behind the old traditions that kept it from being a major player in the competition of city importance.

Even the terminology to describe the scene of play changed from the pastoral setting of "park" to "stadium," which signified a huge arena of tiers of seats to house thousands of spectators. The closeness and intimacy of Sportsman's Park ended with the Cardinals' move to the downtown Civic Center Busch Memorial Stadium in May 1966. Former player Gene Oliver reflected on Sportsman's as a "good spectator's park… much nicer because the stands were so much closer. The fans and players had more contact…The old ballpark had a lot more charisma."[354]

Busch was in search of modern charisma. The move downtown, wrapped in civic pride and progress, continued to fool some, but continually more fans began to see the true force behind the change of scenery, the need to put money into August Busch's pockets. Fans had mixed feelings about leaving the old site, but the deteriorating Sportsman's Park needed major repairs. Old meant obsolete, new meant progress.

Some supported the move as a positive force for the city and because they recognized the need to vacate a dilapidated building in a changing neighborhood; but not all fans supported the decision to leave Grand and Dodier. Some die-hard fans attended the last game at the old stadium but then refused to attend the ceremonies honoring the move. For some, it would be years before they felt the urge to check out the new site. It was not clear if fans truly realized the changes that moving to the new stadium would bring about or if they understood the sweet financial deal Busch arranged, but many devoted fans felt torn by the decision to vacate a place that had housed baseball for 100 years.

Mixed messages and diverse feelings settled on those left behind. Residents may have considered it a blessing to finally reclaim the area from the crass business of baseball and the disturbances a game presented, especially that of having strangers roam their streets, noise disturb their solitude, and bright lights interrupt their vision. Some would miss the revenue the game brought or the excitement surrounding the park. Businessmen would miss the extra income a game brought their way, but they could also reclaim parking spots and return to a less hectic pace. Life would not be the same around Grand and Dodier, or downtown St. Louis. Fan loyalty was challenged, but winning baseball helped lure them to a new location and spark the economy.

On May 8, 1966, professional baseball ended at the St. Louis north side location with the Cards' loss to the Giants 10-5. At the game's end, a helicopter swooped in and transported home plate to the new Busch Stadium at Seventh and Spruce. Baseball would continue to be played at Grand and Dodier after the Cardinals left as Busch donated the land to the Herbert Hoover Boys Club. They built a new building on the site and installed a new ballfield.[355]

She was a grand ole park in the traditional sense. She had hosted 10 World Series, 3 All-Star Games, and for 33 years running had shared her space with two major league teams simultaneously. Marching bands, and stately Clydesdales paraded in her home. Stan the Man honored her with five homers in one doubleheader. She witnessed striking pitching duels, stolen bases, and great fielding. She put up with the crazy antics of Bill Veeck. Forty-eight of her sons had gone on to Cooperstown. She tolerated tobacco juice, empty beer cups, hot dog wrappers, popcorn megaphones, and paper confetti, then cheerfully cleaned up to start again. She had been an integral part of the "Golden Age" of baseball, but now her time had passed.

Dan O'Neill summed up the unique qualities of Sportsman's Park in comparison to future Cardinal stadiums that emerged: "It was a provincial palace. It never stood alone, separated by white space and parking garages, convenient to major highways. It was a baseball church comfortably ensconced in its blue-collar parish...The ball yard was a neighborhood joint."[356] The team moved on, but for those who knew and loved the old place, somehow nothing would ever be able to match that special feeling of place and the warmth of feeling one had come home.

This move marked the end of an era. For St. Louis this was the end of baseball situated in a residential and industrial neighborhood. It was the end of "old-fashioned" ballparks where fans were closer to the field of play. Everything at the new address would be "modern," from the cityscape of the new arch, to the expressways, office buildings, hotels, and the circular coliseum stadium. New was in and old was out.

CHAPTER SIX

A MOVE TO DOWNTOWN

The actual move downtown took over a decade. In 1953, August Busch took a group of civic leaders to observe the Allegheny Conference on Community Development where city, state, and federal funds supported redevelopment in Pittsburgh.[357] The leaders returned to St. Louis and spearheaded an effort to eliminate downtown slums and bring a massive redevelopment project for the riverfront area. The new modern look to an old industrial city would be a tourist attraction, but this urban renewal also stripped away much of the nineteenth-century architectural context of the business district.

An entire section of downtown was destroyed to allow room for the clean and simple designs of the modern era. Included in the new structures were a multiuse stadium, new office buildings, a shopping mall, hotels, parking garages, restaurants, and the Spanish Pavilion Cultural Center. These additions would accent the centerpiece of the civic center project—the ultra-modern Gateway Memorial Arch located at the Mississippi Riverfront. The entire area was designed to garner the national spotlight as well as international attention, to stress the cultural importance of the city, promote the tourist industry, increase tax revenues, and promote local business. The Cardinals recognized the redevelopment as one to benefit their investment.

Busch presented himself as a true baseball fan; that fact has not been disputed, but it was also true that since 1953, when Busch bought the Cardinals, he longed to make them a profitable venture. During dealings at that time, Busch convinced the other civic planners that Busch Memorial Stadium could serve as a focal point of the main project, and he arranged to transfer costs of parking garages, new streets, lighting, and costs of stadium construction outward. Busch decided to cash in on the availability of public money in the fifties and sixties for his private profit-making venture. He set up the Civic Center Corporation, one of the Anheuser-Busch Companies, to oversee the operations of the stadium. With financial backing secured, he shaped the stadium to his specifications and placed it in a choice area of the redevelopment project just north of the Anheuser-Busch Companies, Inc.

The downtown neighborhood at Seventh and Spruce was drastically different from that at Grand and Dodier. The facility, to service both football and baseball, was specifically designed to be a great city symbol to demonstrate the progress of the era, show that St. Louis was culturally elite, attract tourists as well as local attention, and revitalize the downtown area. The new freestanding building sat in an island surrounded by parking garages and skyscrapers that blended stylistically with the modern skyscape. This was a stark business and tourist district, not a blue-collar residential area that welcomed local pedestrian traffic. A trip to this new stadium would be a planned event.

The stadium was not close to residential properties. The middle of the twentieth century was one guided by automobile transportation. The stadium was flanked by parking garages that each accommodated 1,000 cars and there were nearby parking lots. There was a large parking lot for 160 chartered buses. Public bus transportation, including the Red Bird Express, continued, but it was assumed most would arrive by car from the residential suburbs or far-reaching destinations via the new major interstate highway system. All the major highways had multiple exits at the stadium site.

As owner of the team and a member of the Civic Center for Progress, Busch pushed for the new $24,000,000 classical-designed stadium and promoted creature comforts at the new edifice. With the redevelopment plan funded by federal dollars and bond issues, it could be said that Busch spared no expense of taxpayer dollars in supplying the most up-to-date technologies and amenities. Fans would benefit from the comfort enhancement at the new stadium, but these improvements would not come cheaply if one considered the fans in the role of taxpayer. Ownership of the club reaped the bulk of the improvements as the value of the franchise increased with the promise of more attendance and an increase in revenues. Busch worked out a steal of a tax-incentive package that protected his $5 million investment. Under Missouri's 353 Redevelopment Law, businesses active in the redevelopment of blighted areas did not pay taxes on that property for ten years and were required to pay only half of those taxes for the next fifteen years.[358]

On opening day, May 12, 1966, 46,048 fans entered a modern facility that hardly compared to Sportsman's Park.[359] Stadium enhancements included ample parking, cushy seats, luxury suites, a Stadium Club restaurant, unobstructed views, 40 public rest rooms, 19 public drinking fountains, wider passageways leading to 30 modern concession stands, circulation ramps that blended with the building's facade and facilitated entering and leaving the seating areas, a $1.5 million fully-automated scoreboard along with a multi-million-dollar sound system. A motorized infield tarpaulin unrolled automatically when rainfall came. The raised press boxes sat directly behind home plate to provide an excellent view of the game. Spaces were provided for television cameras to offer the view from the "best seat in the house." This civic monument was a state-of-the-art sports complex that could be used for baseball and football games, soccer matches, circus performances, rodeos, and rock concerts.

By the 1960s, the art of planning, building, and financing a stadium was not the sole decision of the team owner, though Busch wanted to make sure the structure would be one he and his family would be proud to place their name on. The architect had to please the owner, the tenants, city planners, league authorities, civic progress officials, the taxpayers, and the fans. In addition, the designer had to conform to the city building codes and league restrictions that applied to baseball and football. The structure of the stadium, designed by internationally renowned architect Edward Durell Stone for the St. Louis firms Sverdrup and Parcel, Inc., and Schwarz and Van Hoefen, covered 12 acres of land.

The coliseum shape, reminiscent of Roman arenas, was almost perfectly circular. The architectural style followed the cookie-cutter shape of numerous other ballparks built in the 1960s.[360] Busch Stadium was easy to pick out from the rest because around the top there were little "archways to the west" that complimented the mammoth Gateway Arch that was partially visible from many of the seats in the stadium. It was a double-deck stadium that, because of its deep power alleys, was considered a pitchers' park that relied on sequential hitting and speed to win. The playing field sat 10 to 30 feet below street level. The dimensions of the playing field measured: left field, 330 feet; center field, 383 feet; right field 330 feet.

The stadium, a planned space, organized society with physical separations of class division within the stadium and all sorts of distinctions. With the special seating arrangements, the owner took control of the spaces. Tickets marked the proper gate one was to enter which curtailed fans from entering the park at will and roaming around.

The smallest percentage of seats was set aside as cheap bleacher seats. Field boxes were usher-guarded to admit only ticket holders, thereby eliminating the opportunity for those without box seat tickets to get close enough to the field to seek a player's autograph. By out-pricing many of the working/middle class patrons, they found a way to create a privileged society for the well-to-do patrons. The higher-priced seats in the deluxe rooms supplied a status symbol. Fans in the suites had air-conditioned rooms equipped with television sets, stocked refrigerators, telephones, and complimentary snacks. The Stadium Club allowed patrons to view the game inside a plush restaurant overlooking the field. The upper class possessed the power to overlook those in the cheaper seats as they sat in the luxury of air-conditioned comfort away from the sweltering St. Louis heat. The general admission seats were so far from the field that fans referred to them as the "nose-bleed section."

For the first few years, the bleachers were fenced off from the rest of the stadium seats so that those in the lower-priced areas could not mix with the rest of the customers. The cantilevered roof, an engineering feat, provided the support necessary to eliminate the steel girders that obstructed the view in Sportsman's Park, but all seats were farther from the playing field. Seating capacity increased to 50,126 with 312 deluxe rooms; 11,985 lower boxes; 10,046 lower reserved; 2,646 upper boxes; 12,973 upper reserved; 8,082 general admission; and 4,082 bleachers.[361]

Photos of the 1966 crowd arriving the evening of the opening game demonstrated that the fans did not look any different than those who attended the final game at Sportsman's Park the previous Sunday. They were a group of conservative-looking citizens dressed for a "special occasion" in their business or church-going attire. They appeared well-behaved and expected to be guided in their behavior. The design of the stadium came to direct their movements and for the first few years those who chose to attend the game would fall into line. Change did come about overall with the rebellious years of a cultural revolution; baseball fans changed their style of dress as American society faced a crisis of identity in the 1970s when proper decorum fell by the wayside and casual attire took hold.

The new place was fun. Judy Clarke Dwyer and her dad Johnny Clarke marched in the first game parade. She did not think the new place had the atmosphere of the old stadium, but she grew to love the winning ambience. She noted the Cardinal tradition, the great players; the birds on the bat were there as well as more women attending the games. She felt that the games became more of a family outing. Judy recalled that drinking to an excess seemed more common in those days. Though restricted at first, as time went on, freedom to walk around the entire stadium became the norm, and her husband, Fran, thought the architectural style of the arch theme's cutout of 96 open arches that circled the field on the top of the stadium fit well with the St. Louis Arch. Judy noted that with the distinctive design, everyone could recognize where the game was being played.[362]

Cards fan Tom Schneider hated this stadium from the start. It was too modern and cold. He really detested the Astroturf installed in 1970. His love for the team was still there, something he had inherited from his dad and a love he passed on to his own children, but this stadium, compared to Sportsman's, did not strike his fancy. Tom came to like it over the years however, especially after a trip to Rome where he visited the Coliseum and drew comparisons. He attended many games there, including World Series games, and over time memories moved to the downtown location.[363]

On opening day, the Cardinals beat the Milwaukee Braves 4-3, with a 12th inning single by Lou Brock. They finished the season in sixth place, 12 games out. It was a memorable year with 21 victories for Gibson and 74 stolen bases for Brock. The team hosted the All-Star Game on July 12th in front of a capacity crowd of 49,936. Cards catcher Tim McCarver assured the National League victory by sliding in with the winning run in the bottom of the 10th. The heat, though, was unbearable, reaching 103 degrees. Baseball legend and Mets manager Casey Stengel exclaimed, "It sure holds the heat well."[364]

Later that summer the sizzle continued. Under summer rain, the Beatles arrived for a song fest in front of 23,143 screaming fans. Then in September, with the moveable grandstand in place, the football Cardinals took the field to defeat the Eagles 16-13.

General Manager Bob Howsam spent two years with the Cardinals and introduced the "Straight-A" ticket honoring topnotch students with free tickets, a reward for scholarship that promoted students and helped to bring in younger fans.[365] Howsam went on to the Cincinnati Reds in 1967 and put together the Big Red Machine of the 1970s, and Stan Musial was named GM.[366] Fans came out to this new space with enthusiastic curiosity. They wanted to christen the new space and get back to the World Series. To many die-hard fans, Stan was the ticket to accomplishing that.

The Cards felt right at home the following season. Nationally, the Civil Rights Movement took center stage, but for the St. Louis team those changes had already taken place. Gibson called the ethnically diverse team the "Rainbow Coalition." Under the leadership of GM Stan Musial, Manager Schoendienst, Orlando "Cha Cha" Cepeda, Bob Gibson, Julian Javier, Tim McCarver, Mike Shannon, and other El Birdos, the 1967 team garnered 101 victories and the National League pennant, 10.5 games ahead. They faced the Boston Red Sox in the Fall Classic. Roger Angell noted the Cardinals that year were "in many ways the most admirable team I can remember in recent years." The guys had "long-ball power...{knew} the subtleties of opposite-field hitting, base-running, and defense" to not only win but to entertain.[367] Cardinal attendance soared with over two million fans for the first time, and they led the majors in attendance.[368] Fans embraced those with talent regardless of race or ethnicity.

Die-hard fans in St. Louis circled the stadium and camped out all night for tickets to the first World Series at this location. The team came back from the east coast having split the first two games. More than 54,000 spectators showed up for the third game and saw the home team win 5-2. Play returned to Fenway Park and went to seven. For the last game, both teams' best hurlers were pitted against each other. Jim Lonborg, with only two days' rest, for Boston, and Gibson for the Cards;

the former even managed to hit a homer in the fifth, as did Javier in the sixth. St. Louis took the title.[369]

The following season Musial resigned as General Manager but stayed on as a senior vice president. Busch saw the error of his ways and brought back Bing Devine.[370] Busch supported his players economically. They led the majors with a payroll of over $1 million, with $607,000 of that going to the Cardinals' nine starters and manager Red Schoendienst. The Cards, especially pitcher Bob Gibson, owned that season too, taking the lead on June 2nd and never relinquishing it. They finished 97-65 with a 9-game lead. On his path to be the best pitcher, Gibby had perfected his game.[371] He racked up 22 victories with 13 shutouts and posted a remarkable 1.12 ERA, winning the Cy Young and MVP.[372]

Game One of the '68 World Series in St. Louis saw 54,692 fans witness a Cardinal victory 4-0 over the Detroit Tigers. Gibson awed his opponents and struck out seventeen. The second game went to the Tigers 8-1 and play resumed Saturday in the Motor City. Visitors took Game Three 7-3. Game Four saw Brock hit a homer, triple, double, and steal his seventh base of the Series; even Gibson hit a homer. The chants of the Detroit bleacher fans to bring on more rain and the antics of the Tigers to delay the chilly, rain-drenched game came to no avail. The World Series went on and the Cards posted another victory, 10-1. The home team pulled out a victory in Game Five to keep their hopes alive. They headed to St. Louis.

In the River City, after waiting outside the stadium all night, even battling the line rush in the middle of the night, George Fields and his sister Connie purchased coveted standing-room-only tickets. These weary, dedicated Cardinal fans headed home by the third inning when the Tigers managed to rack-up ten runs in one inning off three Cards pitchers. By the end of the game, that included a long rain delay, it was estimated that only about 10,000 of the 54,692 fans were there to witness the 13-1 defeat.

Most fans drove home to watch the dismal defeat on television and placed their hopes in another seventh game victory. For Fields and his sister, this was their third World Series in five years. They knew the Cards would take the seventh game and remain World Champions. But the Tigers were unstoppable. They took the final three games, the last one 4-1. The Cards lost the championship. Gibby was outstanding in that final game. He retired 20 of the first 21 batters. The final blow came in the seventh when outfielder Curt Flood slipped on wet grass trying to catch a rather routine line drive hit by Jim Northrup; it turned into a triple to score two runs. Then on a hit by Bill Freehan, Northrup scored. The Tigers scored again in the ninth, and Cards lost 4-1. Gibson expressed the sentiment of all of St. Louis that day: "It's hard to put into words your feelings when you have just lost the seventh game of the World Series…I feel terrible."[373] Fans took to this new space, though, as they racked up memories to bind them to this special place.

Many pitchers would feel terrible for a long time to come after that 1968 year, the one noted as the Year of the Pitcher. The pitchers managed to keep hitters in check with "a batting average of .236 (the worst in history)." There were "only five National League batters" who finished over .300 and in the American League only the batting title winner, Carl Yastrzemski, hit .301.[374] There was a lot of speculation about what had occurred and even more about what should be done to bring back a hitting game. The pitching game improved and benefited from the larger physique of the players who threw harder than those of other generations, as well as the "technical and strategic innovations" over the years. The new ballparks with bigger outfields, the larger infield gloves, more night games, the mastered control of the slider pitch, the banishment of the spitball, and the increased use of the bullpen seemed to shift the advantage to the mound.[375] The rules of play changed to reflect these more modern conditions of the game.

Meanwhile, at the winter meetings the owners fired Baseball Commissioner, General William D. Eckert, who had held that position since 1965. Players were threatening with a strike "over the renewal of their pension fund, centering on the allocation of funds from a new fifty-million-dollar television package." The Players Association rejected the owners' first offer and the owners were not eager to return to the negotiating table. Perhaps they would flex their strength with a new leader. They appointed National League attorney and fan of the game Bowie Kuhn as Commissioner. Rather than the pension fund garnering most of the attention though, it was the "Year of the Pitcher" and the demise of hitting that brought changes to baseball.[376]

Pitchers seemed to be punished for their great season. Rules changed in 1969. The mound was lowered from 15 inches to 10. This benefited the offense as did similar changes within the next few years. In 1971, mandatory batting helmets became the rule. While it certainly was a protection for the batter, some saw it also made for a more aggressive batter as it lessened his fear. Then in 1973 the American League installed another measure to support the offense, the designated hitter rule as an experiment that has stayed.

Additionally, major changes came to baseball with expansion. For close to sixty years there were sixteen teams in Major League Baseball, eight teams in the National League and eight in the American League. The schedules were rather simple and straightforward as was the championship series. There were no division playoffs. Over the years that all changed.[377] Additional big-league cities showed geographical changes that took place in post-World War II America. Baseball expanded not only to other cities, but as well to further outposts that showed modern technological advances in transportation that allowed for speedier travel.

The 1970s, throughout the nation, was a time of decline for industrial cities of the Rust Belt, and St. Louis was no exception. In fact, St. Louis was "a model of urban decline." Hope languished that the city could ever reach the wonder of by-gone days. The Arch, the new stadium, new hotels, vast parking garages, all held promise of a revived city life in the 1960s, but surrounding areas were not faring well. Old neighborhoods were run down and in need of sprucing up, yet it was easier and cheaper to simply abandon them; except for ball game traffic the downtown area shut down at the close of a business day. Post-war improvements in transportation, technology, and energy meant that most of the downtown economy had moved with the people out to the suburbs.

St. Louis was no longer seen as one of the big cities of the nation. In fact, the metropolitan area was not even in the top ten, it fell to eighteenth. The standing of the city further reduced with the push to develop the Sun Belt regions. A study by the Rand Corporation noted St. Louis as "the worst-case scenario come true." The report noted the city had "no way out" of this decline. Civic Progress leaders invested in building new downtown offices that brought some life back to the area and helped improve the architecture to compliment the riverfront area, but it was not enough to turn the city around.

What helped to bring the city back was the 1972 demolition of the Pruitt-Igoe housing development, a 1950s eye-sore that showed how wrong that project had been. In addition, massive rehabilitation and renewal programs in neighborhoods like Lafayette Square, Soulard, Hyde Park, and the Shaw neighborhood brought new blood to the city and hope for revival. Urban renewal federal assistance as well as the Landmarks Corporation played key roles to help save the city and bring life back. The city was recognized as a national leader in restoration. By the end of the decade plans were underway to restore Union Station for a hotel and shopping complex. This acknowledgement of historic importance, as well as the new downtown Convention Center and riverfront attractions, brought tourism to the city by the carloads. The city kept its standing as the Gateway to the West. It became a place on the map to visit.[378]

March 1970 saw the installation of Astroturf at Busch. It helped to spruce up the look of the field in a climate that tended to burn up the grass, and the "water-proof pad made rain checks a thing of the past," but it did not bring winning seasons.[379] Playing on the artificial surface intensified the temperatures on the field and in the stands. Baseball did not seem as exciting to watch without the grass stains. The Cardinal dynasty of the late 1960s had ended.

The team continued to look for ways to involve their fans in the excitement of the game. They had an organ installed in 1971 and hired keyboardist Ernie Hays to belt out tunes to excite and energize the fans as well as the players. Hays served as the official Cards musician until his retirement in 2010 when Dwayne Hilton took over the reins. Music helped to bring a spirit to the festivities on the field, especially in the lackluster days of the 1970s.[380]

Then, one of the worst trades in St. Louis Cardinals history occurred in February 1972 when left-handed pitcher Steve Carlton, who finished the 1971 season with twenty victories, went to Philadelphia for Rick Wise. Carlton and Busch never could see eye-to-eye over salary disputes. Before Carlton agreed to a two-year contract in 1970, Busch remarked, "I don't give a damn if Carlton ever pitches another baseball game for the Cardinals." That was not a wise move. The year after the trade the Phillies ended in last place, but Carlton won twenty-seven and went on to a fabulous pitching career, winning the Cy Young four times.[381]

The late sixties and the seventies were nationally a time of rebellion in the form of anti-establishment activities on college campuses and throughout America. The era became a rallying call for civil rights for blacks, women, hippies, Native Americans, Mexicans, the elderly, gays, and any group that felt threatened. To some it was a breakdown of order, but to others it became time to evaluate the status quo and speak out for justice and equity. This rebellion also played out in the world of baseball. As with society at large, major changes took place and things would never be the same.

Modern change in baseball came slowly, but eventually players began to find ways to take on the autocratic control of the owners. The 1972 season opened with a one-week players' strike. The Cards' opener on April 15th drew only 8,808 fans. The same day Busch dealt 22-year-old Jerry Reuss to Houston. The owner would not pay the lefty the salary Reuss wanted, and Busch also demanded the youngster shave his beard. Reuss refused. This has gone down in history as a bad move for the Cardinals.

Changes came in the radio booth in 1972, too, as Mike Shannon, a former Cardinal, joined Jack Buck in broadcasting the games.[382] That season flannel uniforms were discarded for a double-knit, lighter-weight fabric. None of that seemed to make a difference to play on the field as the Cards finished in 4th place, 21.5 games behind, and attendance dropped to 1,196,894.[383] Brock noted he felt the responsibility of leading the team and bringing in the fans. "To be respectable became critical to me during the 1970s…Sometimes I was it, and I knew I had to be it."[384] Baseball attendance fell overall that decade. The sport did not rule or dominate as it did for the first half of the twentieth century. There were many other sports venues to garner fan attention to include pro football, soccer, basketball, hockey, tennis, and golf.

For three seasons Cardinals football took the focus under the leadership of head coach Don Coryell. Cards pitcher Bob Forsch, who pitched his first no-hitter in April 1978, in front of only 11,495 fans, remarked, "A lot of it [low attendance] had to do with the football Cardinals doing so well…We were a pretty boring team at the end of the '70s."[385] Forsch recalled the play was so bad even Busch "very rarely came around the ballpark."[386]

On January 1, 1979, the Cardinals introduced a mascot, Fredbird, to help lighten the atmosphere. Brock picked up his 3,000[th] hit in August and finished the year with a .304 batting average. Keith Hernandez finished the season as co-winner of the MVP award with Willie Stargell of the Pittsburg Pirates. Again, not much motivated the team that finished in third, 12 games behind first.[387]

Traditional baseball excitement returned to St. Louis in the 1980s with Whitey Ball. Manager Ken Boyer was fired, and on June 9, 1980, Whitey Herzog took over the last place team. He agreed to a three-year, $100,000-a-year contract and promised the Cardinals "would hustle and bust our tails, or else I'd find people who would."

Herzog remembered, "It wasn't easy to get to Gussie." Whitey sensed Gussie wanted to be more involved, and he turned to his friend, Bing Devine, for advice. Devine showed him the path. It helped that Herzog drank, and of course, so did Busch. Devine thought that would be a huge advantage. Whitey initiated spur-of-the-moment drop-by visits at Grant's Farm, Busch's compound, where he and Gussie would "sit and eat sandwiches, play gin, and drink beer." Whitey believed that "your players have to respect your knowledge."[388] He knew what to do and needed to have the power to carry through. Within a few weeks 81-year-old Gussie Busch met with Herzog for an evaluation of the team. Always outspoken, Herzog told him "Well, Chief, you've got a bunch of prima donnas, overpaid SOBs who ain't ever going to win a goddamned thing…mean people, some sorry human beings. It's the first time I've ever been scared to walk through my own clubhouse." He backed up his assessment with, "I've never seen such a bunch of misfits. Nobody would run out a ball. Nobody in the bullpen wanted the ball."

Herzog showed complete disgust with the lack of self-discipline and motivation, but even more so with the drug and alcohol abuse. In no uncertain terms, he told Busch that if they wanted to win, they would have "to do some housecleaning." Herzog received full authority to bring winning baseball to St. Louis. Whitey Ball, speed over power, arrived.[389]

Herzog realized, if he did not have someone in the front office he could work with, he would never be able to produce a winning combination. Therefore, he served the dual role of manager and general manager without the dual pay. He volunteered to do both stints since the team was "losing money." The only condition he made was, "if I ever want to give up one of the jobs" Busch would agree to let him.

Herzog was the most powerful man in baseball. He had the supremacy to reshape the team and guide it along his way of thinking. He drew up a master plan of the team he wanted to field and based it a lot on geography. He knew, except for Chicago and Atlanta, most of the ballparks in the National League were not conducive to strong hitting, and six of those parks, including Busch, had artificial turf.

The trick was to field a team with "speed on the bases to take advantage of groundballs hit on the turf, and speed in the outfield to cut off balls before they skip through on the turf to the wall." Herzog's overall strategy was to "take your runs one at a time and hope for more. Hit the ball on the ground and run like hell. Steal a base, sacrifice, push the runner along, first-to-third them to death." Herzog also valued a strong bullpen "who can come in with a one-run lead and get you six outs" and a catcher "who can throw."

During the 1980 off-season Herzog produced the same headline throughout the sports world, "Whitey Shuffles the Cards."[390] St. Louis was not happy with this crazy guy shaking up its traditional team. Whitey justified the breakup of the team noting that "they hadn't won a damned thing since 1968, so I figured what the hell? We might as well shake things up and see what happens."[391]

Tradition holds that fans want to keep their favorite players and yet, the bottom line was winning. One player traded away was popular St. Louis catcher, Ted Simmons. After Herzog brought in his old buddy Darrell Porter from Kansas City, he restructured the other players and their positions. St. Louis fans were not impressed with this move. Porter had been battling drug and alcohol addiction. The common St. Louis complaint against Whitey was that he was "going back to Kansas City and signing…fishing buddies."[392] Herzog noted, "The fans there [in St. Louis] are some of the best in baseball, conditioned by the Cardinal heritage… fans in St. Louis tend to become very attached to their players." He stated that the city really is "like a small town…with hometown heroes and traditions. The trouble is that baseball isn't played that way anymore."[393]

Ted Simmons had spent his twelve-year career with the Cardinals, and fans would have more willingly given up other players, such as Keith Hernandez. Whitey recalled the fans were so upset "you'd have thought we'd traded the Gateway Arch."[394] Simmons had a right to veto the trade to the Brewers. Herzog's point was Simmons did not fit as his catcher because he had Porter who could throw, and he had offered the first-base position to the strong hitter, but Simmons would not try it. So, per the manager, Simmons "traded himself."[395] The Brewers negotiated to pay Simmons $750,000.[396]

Herzog defended trades he made throughout his career. He claimed, "You make a deal based on your best judgment at the time, on your needs at the time, and on your best guess about what will happen down the road. If the trade works you are a hero, if it doesn't you are a jerk that cost your team the pennant and gave away home heroes."[397]

George Will summed up the 1980s Cardinals as track teams set up to "scamper across the carpet of cavernous Busch Stadium." Herzog's style of managing flew in the face of the myth that the thrill of the game and the way to win is the long ball. In 1982 the championship pitted the Cards, who hit 67 homers, against the 216 homer-hitting Milwaukee Brewers. The Cards took the World Series.

Many St. Louis fans believed that the Cardinals were robbed of a postseason 1981 slot because of the midseason 52-day baseball strike from mid-June to mid-August. When the 103-game season ended, the Cardinals had the best record in the NL East with 59 wins, 43 losses, and one tie. But the split-season brought in new rules from the Commissioner Bowie Kuhn that changed the outcome for the St. Louis team. In August, play resumed, the club owners had agreed "to split the 1981 pennant race, with the winners of the two halves of the season competing in an extra round of playoffs for the division title."[398] The first part of the season the Cards finished one game behind Philadelphia and for the second half of the season they finished one-half game behind Montreal, so even with the best overall record for the season the Cards were denied a place in the postseason play. Fans could not believe the results and threatened to boycott future games if this was the way things were determined.[399]

One of the most controversial moves by Cards manager Herzog occurred on August 26, 1981, when Garry Templeton was ejected in the fourth inning for making an obscene gesture to the crowd, the third time that day he had signaled his disgust with the booing fans who thought his heart was not in the game. Busch saw Templeton's gesturing and disrespect as uncalled for. Templeton requested a trade. In the off-season, he was dealt to the San Diego Padres for back-flipper Ozzie Smith—The Wizard.

Ozzie became a legend in St. Louis and a most beloved man off and on the field. At first, he was not sure he wanted to go. Herzog promised if Smith came "there is no reason we can't win it all. Better than that, if you come...we can agree to go to arbitration...if you don't like St. Louis after one year, you can become a free agent." For Smith, it became "a no-brainer." Sure enough, that first year with Ozzie the Cards won it all, and he came to love St. Louis. For the 1983 season, he signed for $1.1 million, "the fastest contract" he ever signed. He reminisced that Herzog was great to work for, "everybody knew his role; we didn't have any players worrying about playing time, because Whitey utilized everyone…He'd tell you what he thought, because he was ruthlessly honest…He had just two rules: Be on time and give 100 percent."

Herzog named Ozzie the best shortstop of all time. No one could "do the things on a baseball field that he can do." The acquisition, before the 1982 season, assured St. Louis a quality Hall of Fame shortstop and that, plus other trades of acquiring Willie McGee and Lonnie Smith, solidified a championship team. In February 1982, Herzog visited with Busch and told him he wanted to step down as the GM. The "two years of negotiating contracts" had become too much. He did not want "to be sitting around the office listening to bullshitters anymore." Herzog's assistant general manager, Joe McDonald, took over and the two worked closely together. Busch showed his gratitude and confidence by giving Herzog a $75,000 a year raise and extended his contract another two years.[400] The 1982 season would be the first time in fourteen years that the team would make the playoffs and go on to take it all.

To draw over three million fans in a small market like St. Louis is phenomenal. The Cardinals have done that regularly since the late eighties. Things changed on the field and in the stands. "Whitey Ball" stressed decisive pitching backed with a strong closer, strong defense, and speed. It was exciting to watch. Roger Drake worked for the Cardinals in the late '80s and the first part of the '90s as the coordinator of the scoreboard programming for all the video pieces that played pre-game, during, and post-game. He noted that during this era more up-to-date modern, piped-in music played to rev up the crowd and "get players in the mood." Ernie Hays, maestro of the organ music for twelve years, "was the only music in the stadium." Around the mid-1980s, though, things changed; organ music by Hays still announced some players, like "'The Wizard of Oz' to introduce Ozzie Smith" and some tunes that highlighted activities, especially pre-game and the seventh inning stretch, but more and more attention was paid to contemporary music that appealed to a younger crowd. Signature pieces were used for players as they came to bat or in the case of pitchers as they took to the mound. The upbeat tunes seemed to match up with the fast pace of "Whitey Ball" and the introduction of the diamond-vision scoreboards with colored videos.[401]

Whitey's teams brought the thrill of speed and defense with two hundred or more stolen bases over seven consecutive seasons. Willie McGee noted "We all knew what our roles were. If you didn't run, Whitey was mad. It's a fun-type of game."[402] Along the way the teams also racked up pennant-winning years in 1982, 1985 and 1987. The organization averaged more than 2.5 million fans from 1982 through 1989 and topped 3 million in 1987 and 1989.

World Series tickets sold to season ticket holders, but also to the common fan willing to line up blocks away from the stadium, waiting all night to get to the ticket windows. Parents brought their kids to camp out on St. Louis streets surrounding the ballpark. Even if it meant the kids would be late for school the next day, this was a good cause. It is St. Louis where opening day, play-offs, and World Series are viewed as unofficial holidays, sacred days.

The wait for tickets was worth it. One fan noted he did not have tickets but decided to just hang out around the stadium the day of the seventh game for the ambience. Gary Vollmer from Wildwood, Missouri, got to Busch about an hour before the game and saw scalpers getting about $100 for a ticket but he held back. He heard someone ask if he had tickets and then this guy, "an angel dressed in a suit with an NBC 'peacock' pin on the lapel," offered him four tickets for free. He was there for an historical Cardinal moment.

In 1982, the team and their "One Tough Dominican," Joaquin Andujar won the best of seven against the American League Milwaukee Brewers at home. Jack Buck shouted, "That's a winner!" as catcher Darrell Porter leaped into the arms of closer Bruce Sutter to mark the Cardinals taking their ninth world championship before 53,723 fans. Fireworks exploded overhead; the crowd ignored the warnings to stay off the field as they spilled over the walls to celebrate. Players escaped to the clubhouse and champagne flowed. Whitey Ball was infectious and fun. Gussie Busch spoke for all Cardinal fans when he stated, "I've never been happier in my whole life."[403]

The following April the name of the stadium changed from Civic Center Busch Memorial Stadium to Busch Stadium and some changes occurred. New Astroturf was laid, and a more modern scoreboard was installed to include video replay. The season showed promise. Though they lost first place standing in mid-July, by mid-September playoffs seemed possible. Then the Cards lost nine out of ten and were out of contention. The team finished in fourth, eleven games behind and posted a losing season of 79-83, they drew 2,317,914 fans for a club record.[404]

The Cardinals appeared on pay cable television in 1984. They played 52 games on cable and 37 on the local KSDK-TV. They continued to broadcast their games on KMOX radio.

Not many outsiders held out hopes for Cardinal contention in 1985. Die-hard fans believed their team would finish first every season. They were not disappointed that year.[405] Shades of 1981 appeared on August 6th when the players threatened with a strike. Two games were postponed, and the strike ended on the 8th; both missed games were made up with doubleheaders. The Cardinals took over first place on September 16th and clinched on October 5th at Busch Stadium. They won 101 games, held a .353 team batting average, and had the MVP winner in Willie McGee and the Rookie-of-the-Year in Vince Coleman who stole 110 bases.[406] Andujar and Tudor both picked up 21 victories.[407]

Clinching the NL championship was not easy against the LA Dodgers who posted a 95-67 season and took the NL west with a 5.5-game lead. Victory required some extraordinary plays and the Cardinals delivered. Bad luck for a fast, running club came before Game 4 of the NL championship series in St. Louis when Vince Coleman had a freak accident on the field. The nearly one-ton automatic tarp rolled over his left leg and took him out of postseason play. His buddy Ozzie Smith would come to the rescue, though, in a most unexpected way.

October 14, 1985, a beautiful, sunny baseball day in St. Louis saw the series split 2-2 for Game Five. The score was tied 2-2 in the bottom of the ninth when Ozzie came up to bat. As a switch-hitter, he had never hit a home run left-handed in more than 3,000 at-bats, but that day his walk off homer soared over the right-field wall, barely fair, to give the home team a 3-2 victory. Jack Buck issued the cry for everyone to "Go crazy, folks! Go crazy!" And they did. Pandemonium broke out. Two days later play returned to Los Angeles and Jack Clark hit a walk-off homer in the ninth to give the Cards a 7-5 victory and the NLCS championship.

The I-70 Series matchup had two Missouri teams vying for the World Championship as the Cards faced the Kansas City Royals. The Cards seemed to have the title in the bag on October 26th; the score going into the ninth had the Cards leading 1-0. The 1985 season showed that the Cardinals had a 91-0 record of winning decisions when leading after the eighth inning. But then along came umpire Don Denkinger and his controversial decision.

Jorge Orta led off the ninth with a bouncer to first-baseman Jack Clark. Clark fielded the ball and tossed it to Todd Worrell covering the bag. Denkinger called Orta safe. Replays clearly showed that "not only did Worrell beat Orta to the base, but Orta also stepped on the pitcher's foot." That bad call seemed to jinx the team. The rest was history—horrible, nightmarish history that lives forever in the hearts of Cardinal fans. They went on to lose that game. The team and the fans felt robbed.

The next night was freakish. They could not shake the horrors of the previous night. They took to the field in Kansas City, and it appeared the game was over before it began. The Royals posted two runs in the second, three in the third, and six in the fifth. The Cards were on edge; when John Tudor was relieved in the third, he "angrily smashed an electric fan in the dugout and opened a nasty gash in his left hand that required stitches." In the dreadful fifth inning, Herzog went through five pitchers. He and Andujar were thrown out for arguing the strike zone with Denkinger, the home plate umpire. The Royals took the game 11-0 and the World Series.

It was a long and painful off-season for St. Louis players and fans, and the following year did not fare well. Vince Coleman came back in fine shape after his fall injury, racking up 107 stolen bases, and pitcher Todd Worrell won the Rookie-of-the-Year Award with 36 saves and a 2.08 ERA, but overall the players did not produce their productive years of the past, especially from the 1985 season. The team posted a losing season with 79-82, ending up in third and 28.5 games behind first.[408]

Despite injuries to Tony Peña and John Tudor in the beginning of the 1987 season, the team took over first place on May 20th and stayed there all season, clinching the pennant at home in the final week and racking up 95 victories. With the running game, they "scored four or more runs in 16 consecutive games…the longest such streak since 1950." They were last in homeruns with only 94, "and one man—Jack Clark—hit 35 of them."[409]

The Cards set a club record that year for attendance with 3,072,122 fans as they returned to playoffs and reached the World Series for the third time in six years.[410] The successful defeat of the San Francisco Giants in a seven-game series brought the team face-to-face with the Minnesota Twins.

In examining the importance of place, visiting other teams' stadiums matter too. Playing games on "enemy" territory can have disastrous affects to the outcome of games and those memories of place fit into the minds of fans. The Twins played in the Metrodome, an indoor stadium. The first game saw the Cards defeated 10-1. They lost the next game in Minneapolis 8-4 and then moved on to St. Louis where 55,347 saw the home team win 3-1. The next day the Cards took Game Four 7-2 with a home run from Tom Lawless. The following day it looked like the Cards were well on their way to a World Series victory when they defeated the Twins 4-2. The series moved back to the deafening Metrodome that rattled opposing teams and their fans. The Twins claimed an 11-5 victory, and then, on October 25th, the Twins took the final game 4-2 for the championship. Home field advantage made the difference.[411]

Victory in the 1980s was in the cards for St. Louis. It was their decade with none of the bleakness of the 1970s when football seemed to rule. The football team complained in the mid-1980s that they needed more seating, so Busch added 3,000 seats and 14 luxury boxes. They also installed new seats throughout the entire park increasing the baseball seating to 53,138 and football to 54,392. But after twenty-eight years and believing they needed a new stadium if they were to stay in St. Louis, the football Cardinals moved to Phoenix, Arizona in 1988.

Beginning the decade of the 1980s, family attendance was strongly supported at Busch Stadium; places were set aside where children could play and not have to watch the game. Mascot Fredbird frequented the area to entertain. Women attended the game in equal numbers to men. The politically incorrect "Ladies Day" games changed to "discount days" where all fans received a discount for certain areas.

African Americans still did not appear to be a real presence at the ball games, perhaps because they did not feel welcome, they did not want to financially support the baseball ownership, or maybe they were not that into baseball. From the latter part of the twentieth century no specific ethnic presence could be observed except for what has become the all American Anglo-Saxon look. The dress code relaxed over the years. Jeans, shorts, and casual-styled clothing became the norm. Spectators attempted to take control of their space by forging individualism in style, but it came across as a copy-cat look. On most day games, one could find some male fans sans shirts, particularly in the bleacher section. The crowds appeared to be a sea of red Cardinal T-shirts with everyone hoping to fit in with this look that usually sports the name of the team as well as a favored player.

Profits for the owners remained an important issue. Though many remarked that baseball was still the cheapest-priced sporting event to watch, tickets could be costly. In the 1960s through the 1990s the prices of the seats reflected the increase in the cost of living, not including the special deluxe sections that seemed to out-price most spectators at $25,000 a season.[412] Continuing to push for the almighty dollar, the team presented commercialism around the stadium. The electronic scoreboard sold space for advertisements. Independent vendors were replaced with stadium employees. Closed-circuit television played in the concession stands to display the play-by-play of the game, so fans did not miss a play as they waited in line for food that consisted of the typical ballpark spread as well as pizza, nachos, and cotton candy. The commercial enterprise was more intense as the century ended. The gift shop did a booming business as did the small souvenir stands. All in all, the true spirit of the game succumbed to agree with the consumer culture of commercialization.

The heart and soul of the Cardinals emerged under the tutelage of Gussie Busch. He rescued the Cardinals in 1953 and he loved the team. He built a beautiful, modern home for them by the riverfront. As a devoted fan, he lived and died for the team. Whitey Herzog, manager of the Cardinals during the mighty 1980s, had a close relationship with the owner. Fans became familiar with Busch's presence at the games in his "Cardinal red blazer, scarlet cowboy hat, and black string tie," not just when he held the reins of the Clydesdales but at other times as he paraded around the stadium directing his team.[413]

Throughout his long association with the team, Busch became an official power broker in the annals of baseball. Cardinal direction with Busch at the helm officially ended September 29, 1989, with the death of 90-year-old August A. Busch, Jr. Hoping to pull off one final championship in memory of Busch, the team came close to a division title that year but could not bring it home. His teams served him well in the 37 seasons he guided them, winning six NL pennants and three World Series. Busch's burial at Sunset Cemetery was a private affair; a few days later there was a public memorial mass at the St. Louis Cathedral where "shuttle buses brought employees from the brewery and loudspeakers were installed outside the church for the overflow crowd. Six priests celebrated the Mass."[414]

During the decades that Gussie Busch guided the Cardinals, the owners gained more control over each other and, for a while, their players. Early on, the stadium took on the Busch family name, and it became a place of rule and order. He brought a more family-oriented atmosphere with promotional offers to woo spectators, including children. Players' private lives came into play more and that saw more female fans. Busch also broke the color line and supported his players' requests to fight southern segregation. Modernization and change took hold of American culture and that played out in the move from mid-town to downtown. Fans continued to support the team throughout the 1960s, especially with winning baseball and a new home.

The 1970s were troublesome for the United States as a cultural of individualism took hold to include the first strikes in baseball. Players, fans, and owners became disillusioned with the status quo. Competition for the almighty dollar and how to spend leisure time surfaced as it had not done in a long time. That showed at the box office with low attendance and in the lack of enthusiasm from Busch.

Busch shook things up in the decade of the 1980s when Herzog introduced Whitey Ball. It was the fix to re-cement the triple alliance that brought back the significance of place and the fans back to the diamond. The exciting play, with the support of the owner, players, and fans, reignited the St. Louis spirit of baseball frenzy. At the same time, Busch and Herzog demonstrated, as owners before showed, that fans adjusted to giving up their team favorites if it meant bringing championships back.

This powerful connection of the three entities proved strong enough to garner over three million in attendance, which showed the support of Cardinal Nation for those who put the team on the field. Happy times returned during the 1960s and the 1980s when Busch worked to find ways to solidify his support of the players and the fans.

The early 1990s challenged the triad. It would take new owners to bring back that strong interconnection. With the loss of Gussie, August A. Busch III, chairman of the brewery, inherited the team. Seen as "moody, arrogant, virtually friendless," he seemed to resent the time and money his father spent on the Cardinals. He did not display love of the team. The sport had never been a game to him, it was business and with his father gone he could end the "loose rein" he had extended to the old man. August knew, over the more than three decades the brewery owned the team, that ownership had been good for business. In fact, on the twenty-fifth anniversary of Busch's reign, Gussie stated "Let's face it, we not only made money most of the years, but the ballclub ownership was good for the brewery's image and mine, too. We went from under 6,000,000 barrels a year to 35,000,000 now [1978]." Over the next ten years "those barrels had more than doubled, due in part to the fact that every Cardinals' broadcast was a nine-inning advertisement for Busch and Budweiser." As well, there were signs all over Busch Stadium that constantly pushed the products and "when the Clydesdales were flashed on the mammoth instant replay screen and the fans started clapping and stomping to the Bud theme during the seventh-inning stretch, it was the ritual's high moment."

August Busch was an astute businessman. In the early 1980s he maneuvered a steal of a deal for an estimated $53 million when the brewery bought "in addition to the stadium...four parking garages, a hotel on the riverfront, two undeveloped parcels of land and $15 million in investments" from Civic Center. The entire area covered thirty-four acres in downtown St. Louis. Once that deal was accomplished the brewery got the city's Board of Aldermen to pass "an ordinance that banned the independents [vendors] unless they had a contract with Civic Center." August III knew the value of this business venture though he did not want to be involved with it personally. His first decision, on the death of his father, was to keep the team; but he turned control over to Fred Kuhlmann, Stuart Meyer, and Mark Lamping, all executives of the Anheuser-Busch brewery.[415]

THE DEATH OF GUSSIE BUSCH BRINGS CHANGES

The Busch family kept the team for the next five years. Clearly, though, the ownership did not give the support or involvement of Gussie's years. The sparkle of the 1980s, the excitement of "Whitey Ball" blurred to a memory. Whitey Herzog missed his close relationship with Gussie. He became frustrated and fed up with lack of front office support. On July 6, 1990, with his team resting in last place, Whitey managed his final game. He still had a commitment of two-and-a-half years to the team; but Whitey was quite disillusioned and embarrassed with the team. Joe Magrane recalled the team was in San Diego when, at a press conference, Whitey said, "Fuck it." He just upped and quit. He took full responsibility for not being able to get the guys to play. After 17 years of managing, it was over. The Whitey Era had ended.[416]

Red Schoendienst filled in for a couple of weeks until GM Maxvill hired 50-year-old former MVP Cardinal Joe Torre. The Cardinals finished with a 70-92 record in last place, a feat they had not accomplished since 1918.[417] Though the attendance ranked third in the National League with 2,573,225, disillusionment and despair set in.[418] Fans longed to field a winning team and they believed that this Busch did not have the drive to win, certainly not at any cost.

Over the next five years the Cardinals posted a losing record of 369-374. In late August 1991, they lost nine out of eleven games. They finished the season second, third for the next three seasons, and then dropped to fourth with a 62-81 record in 1995.[419]

Changes could be seen, if not so much on the field, certainly throughout the park. Jack Buck's 21-yearold son Joe joined the broadcasting booth in 1991. That same year, with continued problems of excessive drinking by spectators, the club decided to stop the sale of alcoholic beverages at the end of the seventh inning. They promoted the new policy with the caveat that it would "ensure a positive experience for all fans."[420] Some patrons, especially those who attended games with their family, appreciated the straightforward course of action and hoped it would curtail drunken behavior. Yes, in some cases there had been problems with drinking at the games, but many thought they had been treated as children unable to control their own behavior. Not everyone owned the problem and resented the Cardinals.

Relationships with the organization did not improve the next year. Even before the 1992 tickets went on sale, the Cardinals declared a ticket price increase. Fans wondered why. The money certainly was not being invested in the players. Fans doubted the movements by the front office or, in some cases, the lack of movement. In the important equation of place, owners, players, and fans, there was an imbalance. By now, the stadium was 25 years old with no major renovations in recent years. The current owner was disengaged, players were disgruntled, and fans even more so.

Fans seethed over what they considered mistreatment of star shortstop 37-year-old Ozzie Smith. He had been offered a $500,000 raise for 1992 and ended negotiations over a contract extension because he was not offered a multi-year contract.[421] *Post-Dispatch* sports columnist Bernie Miklasz addressed this issue in his column, taking on the organization for their "cold attitude" and came out supporting the fan favorite. Smith reached an agreement and ended his career with the Cardinals in 1996.[422]

For the 1992 season, new and improved Astroturf was installed. The dimensions of the field changed to make slightly smaller power alleys while the foul lines remained unchanged.[423] Makeover of the field allowed for an additional 400 seats, 256 in the bleachers. The stadium now held 56,627 patrons, including 1,500 standees. Reaching out to the fans included a new media feature sold at the concession stands, *Cardinals Magazine*. The same year the team celebrated its 100th anniversary as a National League franchise in what they named the "Season of a Century." An off-day celebration in June honored the event. Many past and current Cardinal greats showed up to witness highlights in audio and video presentations of the history of the team, along with 17,673 fans. The Cardinals long-time respected broadcaster, Jack Buck, served as master of ceremonies.

The 1993 season opened with a million-dollar Diamond Vision video screen, measuring 23 feet wide by 31.5 feet high, replacing a video board on the right field scoreboard. Fans noticed the screen vision vastly improved, especially those pictures shown in direct sunlight; images were clearer and larger. The season also ushered in nine new party rooms to accommodate 125 more fans. While seen as an improvement to the property, party rooms were marketed and priced to bring more revenue as they appealed to the high-end scale. These air-conditioned luxury rooms offered concessions with admission to the game. The Cardinals of the 1990s were looking for ways to draw fans to the stadium and bring in more profits. In fact, the cost of attending baseball events by the middle of the '90s had far exceeded past seasons. In June 1993, the club revealed, though, that the Cardinal organization ranked second in the majors for the best value for a family of four to attend a game, at a cost of $78.54.[424] Value for your money or not, the cost of attending the game for a family of four still reached beyond what many fans could afford for the entire family. The audience had changed from the common family coming out for a simple fun time to a planned event for the middle and upper class. Even if not competing for a pennant, the Cards managed to bring in the fans, though the faith in ownership and connections to the players was not what it used to be.

Cost was not the only thing that affected whether fans would support the team, and that proved true when Major League Baseball suffered a work stoppage on August 12, 1994. Player negotiations for a new collective bargaining agreement broke down, and they believed the "actions of the owners" forced their hand.[425] The rest of the season was completely wiped out, including the World Series. To appease angry fans for a lost season, the Cardinals opened Busch Stadium to 50,000 fans on September 25, 1994.[426]

The strike continued into the 1995 season. Opening day did not take place until April 26th. Fans were sickened and quite upset by the stoppage. In fact, they were outraged. The 1994 season cut short and no World Series; many, even die-hard Cardinal fans, vowed never to support the sport again. They were sick of over-priced players calling the shots and controlling the game. Most of them did not care who was at fault; all they wanted was to have a baseball season.

To rekindle interest and show appreciation to the fans, the Cardinals cut prices in half for opening day. Traditionally, the game was a sellout long before the season began but the Wednesday night game hosted a crowd of only 33,539, quite shy of a full house. That same day the organization opened a section outside of the stadium known as the "Plaza of Champions." The display, memorializing the nine Cardinal World Series teams, surrounded the Stan Musial statue at Broadway and Walnut Streets. In addition, renovations to the Stadium Club had taken place in the off-season.

Manager and former Cardinal player Joe Torre got off to a slow start in 1995 and was fired. The season finished with farm director Mike Jorgensen managing and a year-end attendance record of only 1.9 million. On October 23, 1995, well-respected, trained lawyer, and experienced baseball manager, Tony La Russa, from the Oakland A's, came aboard as skipper.[427]

La Russa possessed a fine intellect. Managing was his forte. He proved successful throughout his years with the White Sox and Athletics by following the tactic that baseball is a thinking man's game and that there is no such thing as too much information about one's own team or that of the opposition.

La Russa was noted for playing the "what-if game," to think ahead for all possible plays and not be caught off guard. He looked to his players to be smart, involved in the game, and to hustle.[428] Talent was important, but La Russa said, "I don't care how much talent you have or don't have. If you play the game intelligently, if you execute the fundamentals, you can win." He took chances and many times they paid off.

La Russa's style looked chancy, yet he analyzed things and calculated the best moves. He strategized the game as complex, nuanced, and layered. He knew how to change the game up based on the changes of the day that included certain parks or playing against a specific team. His strategy altered from day to day. No lineup was written in stone. Stats and the study of the game mattered, but mainly he relied on his mantra that the "four important things in baseball, in order of importance, are: play hard, win, make money, and have fun." He was of a breed of managers who truly loved the game and the tradition that accompanied it, and he was always learning.[429]

Things were not necessarily smooth working for Tony, and until he retired, he was not always praised by the fans. Almost every season one could read about the friction between the manager and one of his players because La Russa managed with an autocratic style. La Russa called the shots. In a *Sports Illustrated* poll, La Russa was named as one of the five best managers and one of the five worst.[430]

La Russa brought with him pitching coach Dave Duncan, a modern coach who lived by game tapes and pitching charts. Duncan, a highly active coach, charted all the game pitches to precisely record them and where they landed. He started this extremely painstaking, yet accurate, practice because "I don't trust my memory... I wanted to make sure I had in front of me every ball...hit, not just the ones I remember."[431]

One of the biggest challenges La Russa found in managing was trying to get his high-paid players motivated, "convincing them to make winning their first priority" for the game. He built his players up, convincing them they were worthy. Yet, day in and day out he had decisions to make on how to win the game, and those decisions could collide with the egos of his players. It was not personal. It was the job. He set out to balance the "25 puzzle pieces" to win.[432]

One of the main reasons for La Russa's acceptance of the St. Louis position was his confidence in former Oakland A's assistant GM Walt Jocketty.[433] Jocketty's support for the new $1.5 million manager came through in his statement that "hiring Tony La Russa is a huge step in the rebuilding process of this organization...We have a lot of exciting things in the future."[434]

Throughout the early 1990s, the Cardinals could not match their 1989 attendance record of 3 million fans. Cardinal officials tried to appease fans with aesthetics, if not in acquiring high-priced players.

Cardinals' owner Busch III held firm in his resistance to "escalating salaries and financial parameters of the game, and the product on the field that retreated into mediocrity."[435] He had a difficult time understanding how players, benefiting from free agency and arbitration, demanded and got excessive salaries. Some pulled down more than his $3 million salary as CEO of the world's largest brewery. The bottom line finally surfaced for the Cardinal owner. Faced with sinking attendance, fallen revenues, player demands, and problems with seasons cut short, Busch III decided the "civic duty" of owning the Cardinals was too cost prohibitive. The brewery decided to get out of the game. The franchise, though they would post a loss of about $12 million for 1995, was considered a valuable investment.[436] *Financial World* magazine "estimated the value of the team at $110 million."[437]

St. Louis sportswriter Bernie Miklasz acknowledged that Anheuser-Busch made "millions of dollars in profit off baseball," but that mismanagement of the team by Busch III "pushed the Cardinals into deep mediocrity and boredom." Then in 1995, when the team lost money, "he cashed out."[438] The future rested on the powers that be as to where the Cardinals future and that of their loyal fans would lie.

It was clear that the death of ole man Busch and the indifferent attitude of his successor hurt the deep commitment that the players and fans felt from days gone by. High-paid players appeared not to care if the season played out or not and they certainly felt no affection emanating from the organization. Fans were fed up with over-paid players and an owner whose heart was not in the game. Attendance declined as did overall interest in the game. Championship series did not seem on the horizon, and the bonds that previously tied owner/player/fan severed. That disconnect mattered as well to the site of play as folks did not rally in the same numbers or with the same enthusiasm to Seventh and Spruce.

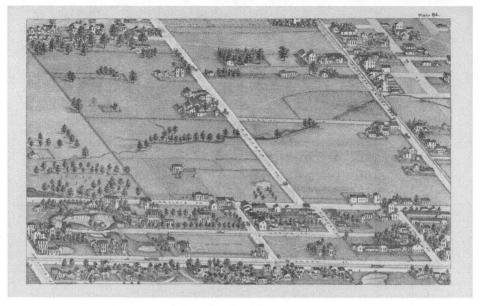

Grand and Dodier site.

Compton, R. J. & Dry, C. N. (1876) *Pictorial St. Louis, the great metropolis of the Mississippi valley; a topographical survey drawn in perspective, A.D. 1875*, St. Louis, Compton & co.
(Retrieved from the Library of Congress, https://www.loc.gov/item/rc01001392/.)

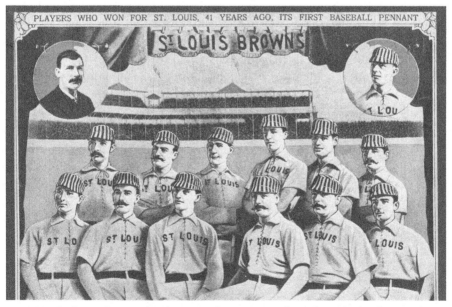

1885 St. Louis Brown Stockings with Sportsman's Park in the background.

(Photo courtesy of Missouri Historical Society)

Ladies' Day Handkerchief from opening day of the 1887 season.

(Courtesy of the St. Louis Cardinals Museum)

Official score book, 1893; Sportsman's Park on the cover.

(Courtesy of Missouri Historical Society)

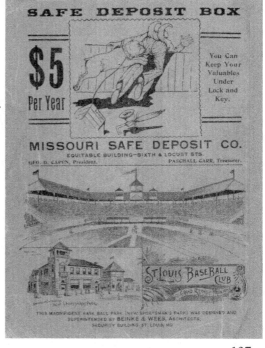

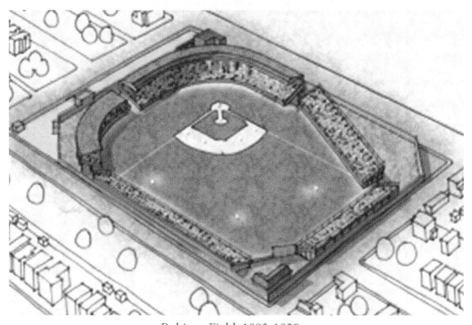

Robison Field, 1893-1920

(Illustration by Jeff Suntala from an original drawing by Marc Okkonen
ThereUsedToBeABallpark.com)*

Fire in the grandstand at Robison Field, May 4th, 1901.

(Photo courtesy of Missouri Historical Society)

Crowd gathered around Cardinals Players during pre-game warm ups at Robison Field (1912).

(Photo courtesy of Missouri Historical Society)

(Bain News Service, P. (1913) *National League team owners including Gary Herrmann, Charles Ebbets and Mrs. Helene Robison Britton*, baseball. 1913.

(Retrieved from the Library of Congress, https://www.loc.gov/item/2014690242/.)

Ladies' Day games in the 1930s.
(Photos courtesy of Missouri Historical Society)

Sportsman's park
(From the collections of the St. Louis Mercantile Library
at the University of Missouri-St. Louis)

Crowd in the stands and on the field at Sportsman's Park
during the 1934 World Series.

(Photo courtesy of Missouri Historical Society)

1946 World Series Crowds at Sportsman's Park

(Courtesy of the National Museum of Transportation. Photo taken by W.C. Runder Photo Co., Inc., Commercial Photographers, 720 Market St., St. Louis, MO.)

Sportsman's Park
(From the collections of the St. Louis Mercantile Library
at the University of Missouri-St. Louis)

Left field at Sportsman's Park, during the 1964 World Series.
(Photo courtesy of Missouri Historical Society)

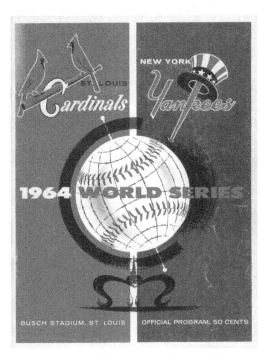

Official program from the 1964 World Series.
(Photos courtesy of Missouri Historical Society)

Busch Memorial Stadium, downtown Saint Louis, MO.

*(From the collections of the St. Louis Mercantile Library
at the University of Missouri-St. Louis)*

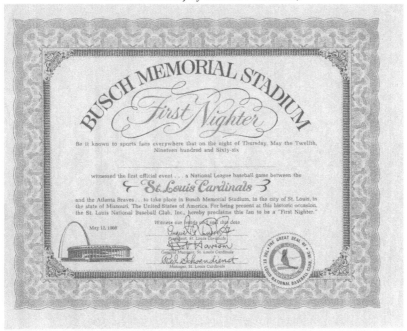

"First Nighter" Certificate given to attendees of the opening of
Busch Memorial Stadium, May 12th, 1966.

(Photo courtesy of Missouri Historical Society)

Crowd at Busch Memorial Stadium, 1960s.

*(From the collections of the St. Louis Mercantile Library
at the University of Missouri-St. Louis)*

Dining room in the club level of Busch II

(Photo courtesy of Missouri Historical Society)

Crowd at Busch Memorial Stadium, 1970s—A sea of red.

*(From the collections of the St. Louis Mercantile Library
at the University of Missouri-St. Louis)*

Busch Stadium III, 2006.

Photo credit: Jim in SC / Shutterstock.com

From C.F. Sexauer's private collection, ticket stubs from a few playoff/World Series games she attended. She has not missed seeing at least one game of a St. Louis Cardinal World Series since 1964.

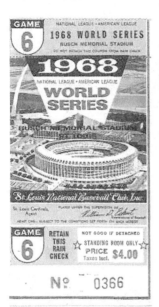

CHAPTER EIGHT

NEW OWNERS RESCUE THE CARDINALS

On Wednesday, October 25, 1995, Anheuser-Busch's chief communications officer John Jacob announced the company decided to sell some of its most identifiable products, the St. Louis Cardinals, Busch Stadium, and its parking garages, in order to improve their cash flow. This severed a 42-year association with St. Louis's favorite team. The company decided to concentrate on the "core businesses of beer, theme parks, and aluminum cans."[439] The brewery hoped the team would remain in St. Louis, but there was no guarantee.

St. Louis media covered the news in detail, as did those across the country and internationally. Speculation formed that if the brewery would sell the team, what else would they do. Fans wondered if the team would be sold to an out-of-state buyer, and others questioned if perhaps the company would pull out of St. Louis entirely[440]

To many, the sale came as no surprise. Former Cards manager Whitey Herzog believed the National League would not allow the team to leave. He pointed out that by selling the stadium and parking garages along with the team Anheuser-Busch assured the fact the team would stay.[441] These typical concerns dominated the conversations on the St. Louis scene for the rest of 1995.

On December 22nd, Anheuser-Busch announced "An agreement to sell the Cardinals for $150 million to a group of investors who say they will keep the team in the city."[442] Brewery executive Mark Lamping agreed to a multi-year contract as club president. He affirmed, "This is, most of all, a great day for Cardinal fans. The Cardinals are in a better shape to win today than they were yesterday." Anheuser-Busch agreed to complete planned stadium improvements of $50 million, including removal of Astroturf with installation of natural grass, and the new owners promised that for the next fifteen years the name of the stadium would continue to be Busch. Deals awaited the approval of Major League Baseball.[443]

New owners met the public on December 22nd. They promised to bring back the great spirit of St. Louis baseball. Fred Hanser, chairman of the group, shared the passion of the investors, "We will make every effort to field great baseball. We will have teams that have talented players who go hard and care about the fans." Hanser did not dismiss the importance of the St. Louis 103-year history with the team or the Anheuser-Busch involvement over the last 43 years. "We plan to operate an effective franchise, just as Anheuser-Busch has. We cannot wait for spring training. We can't wait to get started."

The major investors indicated they would be active in the operations but leave the managing to La Russa. They asserted they wanted to buy the Cardinals because they were "avid baseball fans…They loved the team." Hanser and fellow-owner Drew Baur shared season tickets to the Cardinals for years. Baur announced "You wonder why we want a baseball team. We want to win, and we are going to win." In a celebratory gathering on Friday evening at the Adam's Mark Hotel, Baur continued his fervent remarks: "It's a great Christmas present for the city of St. Louis."[444]

Beloved Hall-of-Famers Stan Musial and Red Schoendienst wholeheartedly supported the effort. Musial called this "a great group… who loves baseball…loves St. Louis." He praised Anheuser-Busch as an asset to baseball overall and in finding these new owners.[445] Schoendienst and Musial knew another new owner, Bill DeWitt Jr. His father, Bill DeWitt Sr. had owned the St. Louis Browns, and Jr. served as a batboy for the team in the 1940s. Schoendienst remarked that Bill Sr. "was a good businessman and a good baseball man. He wanted a good team, as good as he could build it." He agreed with Musial that "it's good that baseball people are back as part of this new group."

Cardinals' player Tom Pagnozzi stressed the importance to a player that the owners expressed a desire to win. Clearly, he did not see those same feelings with the Anheuser-Busch organization. He noted that, while in the cities of franchises in Colorado and Philadelphia, the owners attended "about every game…you feel like it's not just a business with those guys." Cardinals' pitcher Tom Henke concurred. "You like to see hands-on ownership. You don't want to see them interfere with the playing of the game, but you want owners who are interested in what's going on." With A-B it seemed "the interest was not there." Having grown up in St. Louis, Henke knew another A-B story, one when Gussie guided the team and, as a fan, one knew that "Anheuser-Busch and the St. Louis Cardinals went hand in hand." Bing Devine, sports executive for many years with the Cardinals, approved the group and thought they would bring winning baseball back to the city.[446]

St. Louis Post-Dispatch sports editor Bob Broeg praised the new owners, too. With an intense love of the game, and especially the Cardinals, he bubbled over in delight that "nice guys—rich nice guys—have done what many blue-collar or white-shirted stiffs would like to do. They're going to enjoy the joys and pangs of running their ball club." To Broeg, a plus came in that they did not represent a company beholden to stockholders. Their only obligation would be to "their own tidy rah-rah group." Broeg praised Bill DeWitt Sr. who had entered the business of baseball at an early age as a Browns' office boy for Branch Rickey in

1916. He "became one of baseball's most knowledgeable front-office executives. At only 23, he was treasurer of the Cardinals, on route to general manager of the Browns, then co-owner with brother Charley DeWitt and, ultimately, with the revival of the Reds at Cincinnati." Broeg admired him as "an outstanding executive." He could not contain his excitement that the new owners had been "boyhood fans who became club owners, too."[447]

Fans gave enthusiastic support for the prospective owners who were, for the most part, a local group with some familiar names associated with St. Louis baseball. After what they considered a long drought of successful baseball investment, they were ready for winning and fun. Norman Widmer, a 70-year-old St. Louisan, interviewed by the *St. Louis Post-Dispatch*, stated his approval for one of the owners. "I remember this William DeWitt from when his dad used to own the St. Louis Browns. He would come out in a Brownie uniform and shag fly balls in left field." Widmer continued: "I feel safe with him owning the Cardinals. I know he has a love for the game, and I know that I'll be anxious to watch baseball again this spring." Yes, that was the same little Billy DeWitt. In fact, there was a picture of him at age six in a Browns uniform taken with Babe Ruth in 1948 when Ruth took a farewell trip around the circuit. This guy had been around baseball all his life and now, if the deal went through, he would be coming back to his roots.[448]

The paper noted a Cards fan, Gail Johnson, 40, had not been "impressed with the relationship between Anheuser-Busch and Cardinals fans." She stated, "I'm just hoping the new owners can do a better job of getting the enthusiasm of the fans up a little. I think the brewery kind of ignored it for a while." David Busso, 47, had conducted business with Hanser and Baur. He spoke highly of them, "Their business leadership is excellent, and they're avid baseball fans. I'm really glad that they're taking over, and I think they'll do right by the team, the town, and the fans."

Some of the fans, though, were skeptical about what this would mean for St. Louis, the team and especially, the fans. Bill Stoll, 60, of St. Genevieve followed the Cardinals for many years. He used to attend at least six or more games a year but recently was not as enthusiastic and last year only went to one game. "I am waiting to see what they're going to do to get fans back to the ballpark." He recalled that years ago "There was such enthusiasm, such a winning attitude. It was fun."

Linda and Charles Wallace of Belleville, Illinois, agreed with Stoll that they too attended games and it was fun, but now "it just isn't that fun." Robert Joseph Jr., a season ticket holder who described himself as a die-hard fan, repeated the message that baseball lacked the fun of the past. "The spirit of the Cardinals isn't there like it was when I grew up." He believed "it can be like that again if the new owners give the young ballplayers a chance to play." Joseph noted that, if the owners decided to raise the ticket prices to get the big-salary players, he might well cancel his tickets.

Equally important, the new chairman assured everyone that the owners would be accessible. "Fans will see us around the ballpark. We won't be hiding upstairs in a luxury box. We'll be sitting in different areas, talking to the fans. We want to be the fans' owners."[449] The deal was officially approved on March 21, 1996, at the owners meeting in Phoenix.[450] Anheuser-Busch sold the Cardinals for $150 million to the St. Louis/Cincinnati consortium headed by William O. DeWitt Jr. whose family lineage spoke to an interest in baseball.[451]

DeWitt grew up in St. Louis. His father sold the Browns to Bill Veeck in 1951 and continued to work for the club even when they became the Baltimore Orioles. In 1960, the family moved to Detroit for a year and then in 1961 his father accepted a position to run the Cincinnati Reds club. In the meantime, DeWitt Jr. went on to acquire his undergraduate degree from Yale and an advanced degree from Harvard Business School. When his father sold the Reds in 1967, Jr. invested in the team and then sold his interest by 1969. In 1988, he and his business partner, George W. Bush, bought into the Texas Rangers, and later he was with the Baltimore Orioles. Once he heard that the Cardinals might be up for sale, he jumped at the chance to get them.

Sheer excitement met opening day April 8, 1996, against the Montreal Expos, sans the neon flying eagle that let loose around the scoreboard each time a Cardinal hit a home run. It had been a signature of the team since it opened the stadium three decades before.[452] The eagle represented the connection of Anheuser-Busch with the Cardinals. A new era dawned in St. Louis with new Cardinal owners.

Exhilaration and anticipation filled the air, more excitement than had existed for the Cardinals in a long time. Artificial turf had been replaced with genuine grass; a complete overhaul of the stadium had taken place to include new seats, new paint, a host of new players, and of course, new ownership.[453] Weeks before the season opened, the team sold 1.8 million tickets. Group sales increased. Clearly, the fans supported the change of direction for their team as they demonstrated confidence in the new owners being willing to spend money for free agents and retain players.[454] Hanser explained the fan-based philosophy of the new owners. "We increased the payroll by a little bit [an estimated $10 million] to generate some enthusiasm. I'm not sure you'd do this in any city, but St. Louis has the best baseball fans in the country. We feel if we put a good team on the field, they'll come back, and we'll be able to rebound from the strike faster than most cities."[455]

St. Louis waited long enough to get back in the game and the town was ready for this change. The team struggled for a while, coming off a poor start, but 1996 went on to become another memorable year for the St. Louis Cardinals. They won their first division title since 1987. Sale of playoff tickets was different than in the past. Rather than have lines of fans sleeping on the sidewalks of St. Louis waiting for ticket windows to open, the Cardinal organization sold the tickets over the phone. It was believed that selling the tickets in that manner would "give fans in outlying areas such as Arkansas, Tennessee, or Iowa a fair chance to get tickets…[and] reduce the number of scalpers who bought tickets."[456]

Much had been accomplished that first year with GM Walt Jocketty, manager Tony La Russa, and his coaching staff. The team that took the field consisted of older Cardinal veterans, including Ozzie Smith and Willie McGee; some of Tony's Oakland buddies; many new team members—some experienced in both leagues; young players; Hispanics; Blacks; Whites; and costly free agents.

Whatever the key ingredient, the mix worked to bond the team and brought play-off games to St. Louis. The city went wild with excitement and anticipation.[457] The team finished the season with at least 2.65 million spectators, second only to the 3.3 million mark of the Colorado Rockies. The new owners wanted to draw between 2.5 and 2.7 million fans, so they were pleased with the results though disappointed that fans had not turned out stronger in the drive to the pennant. Especially lacking were the spontaneous viewers, those who would decide on the spur of the moment to attend a game. The numbers showed an average of 33,000 per game, down from when the Cards "averaged 41,000 per game in '87." The turnout showed a marked improvement over the 1994 and 1995 seasons with 1.85 and 1.74 million, respectively. A study on attendance numbers by the *St. Louis Post-Dispatch* revealed that the cost of the ticket probably did not keep fans away since one could purchase a bleacher ticket for five dollars and on special admission days a ticket could be had for two dollars.

Reasons for the lower numbers in a race to the pennant were numerous and diverse. Some fans probably harbored a lack of trust and ill feelings from the players' strike that caused the halt of the pennant race and cancellation of the World Series for the 1994 season. Uncertainty of the commitment of the new owners to spend, combined with resentment of the Anheuser-Busch ownership of the past that did not spend money, was a probable factor. Skeptics lacked confidence in the team since the death of Gussie as they did not trust the commitment of his heirs.

After all, those teams had been "so bad and so boring," how could these guys turn it around. Some folks would rather stay home and watch the game in the comfort of their homes as more games were being televised. Competition from other venues, like the Rams and the improved playing by the Blues, as well as the casino boats, played a role in lower attendance at baseball games. In addition, the Cardinals had plenty of new players without the feeling of tradition usually connected with teams of the past. The major reason was perhaps "breaking the habit" of actually attending the games; "the fans fell out of the baseball habit" over the decade of the '90s.[458] As noted by one St. Louis fan, "They tore the heart out of real baseball fans when they did not have the World Series."[459]

Baseball had to find ways to convince the fans to come back; to find a way to trust in the game once again. For the new St. Louis owners, new management, new players, new grass, and renovations to the stadium did not result in bringing all fans back, but a drive for the pennant down the stretch did bring excitement to the city. The Cardinals, for the first time in nine years, clinched the central division, went on to win the first division play-off games against San Diego, but then lost the pennant to Atlanta.

Baseball and the fervent support of the fans returned. For their first year, the owners showed their commitment with the money they spent, the support they gave the players, and the thrill they brought to St. Louis. As *Post-Dispatch* sportswriter Bernie Miklasz remarked, with promise for the future, the new leaders "reminded us that it is possible for wealthy adults to put the game, the joy, back in the business of baseball."[460]

CHAPTER NINE

NEW OWNERS DREAM BIG

As early as Christmas Eve 1995, Bernie Miklasz predicted that the new owners would want a new stadium.[461] DeWitt Jr. and other owners first discussed the possibility of replacing or renovating the 30-year-old Busch Stadium in 1997. They recognized that the cookie-cutter layout presented problems for updating. Specifically, the architecture did not lend itself to the trends in stadium construction of the late twentieth century. The St. Louis stadium, designed in the early 1960s, served as a multipurpose facility to accommodate both baseball and football, though it did not completely satisfy either sport. The outdated structure, like others built in the '60s, lacked a community feel as it removed fans from close play. The newer parks of the league had a post-modern design that harkened to the days of old where fans drew closer to the field to merge more with the game.

The Cards' owners discussed ways to keep up with the appearance and modernity of the newer stadiums to increase revenues. For higher profit margins, they had to have more luxurious areas, such as trendy party rooms, and an upscale atmosphere to attract corporate ticket sales. They also recognized the old structure lacked modern facilities. They needed to upgrade the restrooms, increase concession areas, and provide better access with more elevators and the addition of escalators. While the decision was immediate action for upkeep and cosmetic changes, their dream was a new stadium.

Post-season 1996, the organization surveyed fans and concluded they knew what the fans wanted, winning baseball. The owners invested close to an additional $10 million in their first season to bring quality play back to St. Louis.[462] The beginning of the 1997 season witnessed a 14.9 percent increase in ticket prices. The new prices fell in the medium range nationally; they were neither the most expensive tickets nor the cheapest. Compared to ticket prices of the hockey Blues and the football Rams, they still offered a more reasonably priced form of entertainment. In their acquisitions, the owners demonstrated a willingness to pay high demand salaries. If one could trust the surveys, the fans wanted success. If that were the case, it was decided now was the time for them to share the near $40 million payroll expense.

Raised prices did not sit well with the fans. Management gambled fans would be willing to pay to field a winning team. Team President Lamping remarked, "If you spend more money on player salaries in order to put a good team on the field, fans are willing to help make that investment." The organization knew that if they kept the ticket prices low and did not have money to invest, fans would not turn out. If competitive baseball took the field, it would fill the stadium but that meant raise the prices and use that money to keep the team in the heat of things.[463]

By the middle of the 1997 season, St. Louis was abuzz. Right before the trading deadline, on July 31, the Cardinals obtained slugger Mark McGwire from the Oakland A's. His presence might not bring a team championship that year, but he would add excitement and entertainment. In a time when baseball locally and nationally faced lackadaisical interest, McGwire brought scores of fans out to the ballpark and onto their feet in anticipation of his powerful homers. The Cards finished fourth in their division that year with a 73-89 record. Hope for the future materialized on September 16th when McGwire signed an estimated $28 million, three-year contract with an option for a fourth year.[464]

The 1998 season began with the team moving into its new spring training facility in Jupiter, Florida. That same year, Fred Hanser, the chairman of the Cardinals, commissioned Harry Weber of Bowling Green, Missouri, to sculpt statues of Cardinal Hall-of-Famers. The action-oriented figures included Hornsby, Dean, Slaughter, Musial, Schoendienst, Brock, and Gibson. These were placed at the stadium to honor the heroes of the team.[465]

McGwire carried his electrifying presence into the 1998 season. The Cards finished the year in third place, but fans came out in record numbers. Owners reaped dividends as attendance reached the three million mark for the first time since 1989. Homerun aficionados, as well as loyal Cardinal fans, flocked to the ballpark to witness history. McGwire dramatically battled Cubs Sammy Sosa in hot pursuit of Roger Maris's 1961 record of 61 home runs. The pennant race became secondary. Fans had a significant classic of their own in September against Sosa. That friendly competition managed to "recapture the hearts of the most stubborn fans who had abandoned baseball after the 1994 strike and encourage passion for the grand old game to resurface." Across the nation fans followed the race. Many have come to resent the battle for the homerun record because of the steroid controversy of the 1990s, but during that time fans became enmeshed in the day to day stats of two individual players.[466]

The Cardinal asset paid off handsomely on September 7th and 8th. The first night McGwire tied Maris' achievement with a 430-foot shot to left, off the Stadium Club window. The next day history was made. In the fourth McGwire hit a 341-foot drive that sank over the left field wall. The fans, players, and owners jubilantly celebrated. The last day of the season, Sept. 27th, McGwire hit two more out. He finished the season with 70 longball shots.[467] A permanent fixture to the ballpark (Busch Stadium II) was added, in a corporate sponsorship with McDonald's Restaurant, in the upper deck left field stands where they created a section titled "Big Mac Land" to honor McGwire's homerun ability. Any time a Cardinal player hits a homerun in that section of the ballpark, all fans in attendance can redeem their ticket stub for a free Big Mac sandwich.

With the fans back wholeheartedly, owners began serious discussion with Hellmuth Obata Kassabaum (HOK) Sport on a new St. Louis ballpark. Downtown seemed an ideal spot but the area was fairly closed in by other structures. DeWitt sent advisors to scout sites for a new ballpark. Numerous ideas came up to include moving the team to St. Charles, Missouri, or East St. Louis, Illinois. They also decided to get some calculations on the bus parking lot immediately south of the current stadium. That location appeared a bit too small, but the organization saw the advantage of already owning the land. It seemed a farfetched and almost unfeasible choice as the property sat smack-dab between the old stadium and Interstate 64/Highway 40, yet it kept rising to the top of the list of prime potential sites. One thing enticing DeWitt III was the possibility of the empty eight acres of space produced with the demolishing of the old stadium. Adjacent to the new park, the area could be a jewel in the whole deal if they developed it into Ballpark Village, a complementary commercial development.

DeWitt had fun with the planning and all the possibilities a new venue presented. He stressed the elevation of the entire site as an important consideration, noting that a "submerged field…allows for the service level, which includes the clubhouses, maintenance equipment, and other necessary back-of-the-house spaces, to be underground and out of the way…This frees up space for wider concourses on the first level." Such a setup would eliminate competition between service utilities and amenities for fans and presented a modern solution to many of the problems at the older stadium.

In 1999, the front office team formed to begin the dream design of a potentially new stadium. A first consideration became the design. Research of past ballparks, and trips to newer ones, helped formulate serious discussions on the major decisions of the team. So many things had to be considered to include openness or intimacy, modern or symbolic touches, forward-looking or historical celebration. Others brought up questions of the playability factor that could favor offense or defense, how to convey the concept of a "neighborhood," and how to continue the legacy of the old ballpark. All these concerns were debated. The owners agreed the image they wanted the new home to convey was a memory of "the great history and tradition, but you also can't wait for the next game to start in the Cardinals' new home." Ultimately, the decision focused on a structure to best fit and blend into the area to complement the setting. Important was the consideration to include the three important St. Louis historic landmarks within the vicinity, the Eads Bridge, the Wainwright Building, and the Cupples Station warehouses. Those choices led to a classic brick-and-steel edifice predominate in the St. Louis landscape.[468] Design was the fun part, money the difficult part. That problem came to dominate most decisions. Owners had to convince the naysayers of the necessity of replacing the beloved Busch Stadium, and of course, they needed to find the money.

Meanwhile, in 1999, McGwire continued his knack of smacking the ball where it counted. He hit sixty-five homers and led both leagues for the fourth year in a row. The electrifying star brought fans to the park. Yet another year ended where the Cards did not make the playoffs. They finished with a 75-86 record. Financial concerns bothered the owners. The excitement of a new stadium consoled them, but they knew it would not materialize without the funds to pull it off.

In 2000, the city had plenty to celebrate. The St. Louis Rams won the Super Bowl 23-16 over the Tennessee Titans on February 3rd. Then on March 23rd the Cardinals added 29-year-old Jim Edmonds, center fielder and good friend of McGwire's. The team completed the season 95-67 and finished as central division champs. The team took the National League Division Series over the Atlanta Braves three games to none. They met the New York Mets for the NL Championship Series against and the east coasters took the title four games to one.

By 2000, citizens chimed in with commentary on the possibility of a new stadium and the speculation of who would pay for it. Letters to the editor deluged the offices of the *Post-Dispatch*. They revealed the displeasure of many fans. Prominent concern rested on the elimination of a St. Louis landmark. Even if the stadium had only been around less than forty years, the fans connected it to the history of the city. Some expressed fear over the demolition of the entire historic landscape of the city. They worried about the historical facade of the venerated Old Cathedral, City Hall, the Civil Courts Building, the Old Courthouse, and Union Station. Anxiety surfaced that these landmarks would be shoved aside for "progress." Folks divided about abandoning Busch Stadium. One group supported the new project to progress and saw it as nourishing the city. They spoke to the loyalty of the owners and the need for cooperation. These fans offered support for the good of the community and wanted to dismiss divisive debates that divided the city over issues of class and race.

Agreement materialized on the financial aspects. Consensus supported the idea that the owners should foot the bill. Owners rejected that call. They did not have separate corporate funds to draw on outside their club investment and their proposal had the public financing two thirds of the new venture.

Many voiced oppositions to government's spending public funds for private entities. J. J. Warren, a resident of the loft district of downtown St. Louis, refused to believe the hype that a new $250-million stadium would revitalize the downtown area. He noted that, during the previous season, the current stadium usually packed in crowds; they did not need a new building to do that. He believed that the money could be of better use to the city if it were spent on "housing, retail and clean streets."[469]

Mayor Clarence Harmon strongly supported citizen displeasure and concerns for the use of city tax dollars to help finance a new Cardinals' stadium. He recalled in 1990 the city approved a plan of millions of dollars to help pay for the construction of the football stadium for the Rams which committed the city until 2022. Mayor Harmon called for a vote.[470]

Aldermanic President Francis Slay, who eventually became mayor, showed interest in the project. He felt the city needed more specifics from the Cardinals before decisions could be reached. Missouri Governor Mel Carnahan saw the new proposal as "an intriguing idea with potential benefits for downtown St. Louis, the metro area and the state," but he thought the Cardinals should present a cost-benefit analysis to help move the discussion along. Cards executive Lamping cautioned that any cost benefit analysis coming from the Cardinals might produce skepticism from the public. He recommended an independent study might be a better route.[471]

Though several areas around the metropolitan region demonstrated an interest in the Cardinals moving from the downtown location.[472] Lamping noted that the franchise's first choice was to stay downtown. He did not rule out moving the team to another metro site because he said, "we owe it to our fans to consider all options." to help field a competitive team.[473]

The battle over funding continued for the next few years. The Cardinals "agreed to contribute $120 million to a new stadium and proposed floating a $250 million bond issue to pay for the rest." [474] For the most part, St. Louis preferred keeping the franchise and wanted to see a revitalized downtown, but at what price? Moral support extended to the team, though the feeling overall was if the owners wanted a new stadium it should be financed by the owners, not the public. After numerous discussions, specific financial studies, and a threat to move the team out of state, the owners agreed that the bus lot was the best spot to build. The Cardinal organization decided to private funding with some tax concessions from the city.

On September 11, 2001 the United States faced a horrific surprise attack that leveled the World Trade Center in New York, took out a portion of the Pentagon building in Washington, D. C., and downed a fourth hijacked plane in a rural area of Pennsylvania. The terrorist event killed nearly 3,000 Americans and shocked the nation. Commissioner Bud Selig halted major league games until September 17th. That evening, the Cardinals faced the Milwaukee Brewers in Busch Stadium with a 30,528 crowd. Somber patrons were scrutinized by security forces and a patriotic agenda featured numerous firefighters and policemen who led the pre-game program. The home team took the contest 2-1, but the most memorable part of the evening featured Cardinal broadcaster and World War II veteran, Jack Buck, reciting a poem he had written about the events of 9/11.[475] (See Appendix)

The Cardinals won 93 games that season, but it was not enough to secure first place. They tied with the Houston Astros, and because the Texas team had the better head-to-head record (9-7), they were awarded the NL Central championship and the St. Louis team took the wild card. The Diamondbacks held back the Cardinals to take the Division Series three games to two.

The first misfortune of the 2002 season occurred on June 18th with the death of legendary Cardinal broadcaster and Hall of Fame announcer, 77-year-old Jack Buck. He had been quite ill over the last seven months with Parkinson's, diabetes, and vertigo. Buck was an institution who represented the team both on television and radio since 1954. His passing shook the community. As a tribute to Jack, and to give the fans a chance to grieve and show their respect to his family, the Cardinal organization held a public viewing at Busch Stadium on June 20th.[476]

The second misfortune came in Chicago a few days later. On June 22nd, the team had a scheduled day game at Wrigley. A few hours before the game a couple players noticed that pitcher Darryl Kile had not arrived in the clubhouse. A call was placed to the Westin Hotel to have someone check if he were still in his room. Kile was discovered dead in bed. Medical authorities placed his death sometime in the wee hours of the morning. An autopsy reported the death as a result of blocked coronary arteries, though the 33-year-old had passed a physical during spring training.[477] The game was postponed. Kile's teammates were devastated. The following morning a memorial service was held at the Westin. Kile was scheduled to start that game and it was his wife Flynn who assured the team that her husband would have wanted play to continue.

The Cubs began the game with a moment of silence to pay tribute to Kile's number, 57, throughout the stadium as well as on the ballpark marquee. Flags flew at half-staff. When the Cardinals left the field after batting practice, they received a standing ovation. Not surprisingly, the home team won 8-3.

Kile's teammates returned to Busch Stadium on June 25th, where a memorial service and tribute to the pitcher preceded the game. In addition, Kile's jersey "hung in the tunnel leading to the clubhouse." The Cards lost to the Brewers 2-0. The season continued as a tribute to the pitcher as well as Buck. Players wore small black circular patches with Kile's initials and number on their left sleeve and a patch was also designed to honor Buck.[478]

The team finished the season with over three million in attendance, 97 victories, and for the second year in a row, they faced the Arizona Diamondbacks in the NL Division Series. The Cards swept them in three games, but then lost the next round to the San Francisco Giants.[479]

January 17, 2004, marked the official groundbreaking for the new home of the Cardinals, slated to open in 2006. Not all fans supported the decision, but all were happy that they did not have to foot the bill. Their curiosity peaked with apprehension and anticipation. In February 2004, MLB.com fielded fan questions to President Mark Lamping, the "point man" for the new project. The new ballpark was designed by HOK, a firm noted for building Oriole Park at Camden Yards in Baltimore, Jacobs Field in Cleveland, and numerous international venues. The firm was the "largest design firm in the world specializing in sports stadiums, arenas, convention centers, and amphitheaters."[480]

Lamping revealed the park "will have a total capacity of 46,000. The field dimensions...336 feet down the left-field line, 390...left-field power alley, 400 in centerfield, 390...right-field power alley, and 335 to the right-field foul pole." He guaranteed certain aspects of Cardinals' history would move to the new home. Lamping noted that, though the new stadium abutted the current facility, the team planned to continue their 2004 and 2005 seasons at Busch Stadium without disturbance. He guided fans to the Cardinals' website for construction updates and a cam feature that followed the progress.[481]

In August 2004, the team announced the name Busch Stadium would continue with the team's new home. The naming-rights would remain at least through the 2025 season. Typical Cards fans, steeped in tradition, happily celebrated the custom of keeping a name long associated with the team. Plans for the stadium included a new downtown development project, Ballpark Village, to spruce up the area and gain more of a welcoming presence downtown. The 12-acre site would sit on the spot of the old Busch Stadium between Clark and Walnut streets. It would consist of housing, retail stores, and offices.[482]

Inquisitive fans followed the progress of the new stadium with intense interest through newspaper articles, TV spots, drive-by viewings, and daily updates online. The best way to see the dream unfold was to attend a 2004-5 St. Louis Cards game. One could virtually see the new park taking shape, and excitement came as much by looking southward, out of Busch, as watching the games unfolding inside.

Stimulating conversations focused on the impressive site. One could overhear comments on the design of the park, location of the diamond, height of the stands, layout of the seats, overall architectural structure, as well as the memories left behind and the anticipation of new ones to play out. Throughout the final season no one could ignore the encroaching future. Even Cardinal personnel eagerly commented on the coming of a new era of baseball. Centerfielder, Jim Edmonds, acknowledged that, "It's going to be different. It's going to bring a little bit more excitement and a little bit more fun to the everyday drag. I really think it's going to be exciting for everybody. It's going to bring fans maybe a little closer to the game and give them a little bit more access." Cards manager Tony La Russa had been told that the new stadium would play like the current Busch. He just wanted assurance "it doesn't play any smaller."[483]

Three current Cards broadcasters had been former Redbirds and had their share of fond memories of the old place, but they showed an eagerness for what lay ahead in a new location. Former Cardinals pitcher and broadcaster, Rick Horton observed that the owners had "made a concerted effort to make the experience a good experience.... You're going to have a new stadium, but I think the idea is to transport that [past] experience to a different building." Al Hrabosky, a former St. Louis pitcher and Cards TV announcer, saw the new place as "a better work environment...fan friendly" where folks would "get off at the same exit...[as] it's still right in the neighborhood." Cards radio broadcaster, Mike Shannon remembered both former Busch Stadiums. He celebrated the new site. "It's going to be wonderful. Busch Stadium...had a great run...But it's like that brand-new car that you drove for 20 years. It was fantastic...but now a new one is coming on, and we're going to go to that."

Wayne Hagin, Cards announcer, took time to reminisce about days gone by and noted that things would certainly be different. Hagin wondered what the experience had been like for Harry Caray and Jack Buck to leave fond memories and magical feats behind when Sportsman's Park gave way to the downtown Busch Stadium. He noted this move would be particularly hard for him because he connected the sportscaster's booth with the legendary Jack Buck who had been associated with the team for close to fifty years. "Every time I walk into this booth, I think of Jack...He walked into that door to work in that ballpark, and it's an honor to be there." He acknowledged though that inaugurating the new booth with Shannon would truly be a thrill and an honor.[484]

The 2004 season saw a fantastic team. The Cardinals won 105 games "the most of any St. Louis team since 1944, and [they] reach[ed] the World Series for the first time since 1987." The team took three out of four from the Los Angeles Dodgers and then battled the Houston Astros.

In the National League Championship Series that began at home, the Cards took the first two, and when they returned from Texas, they were down 3-2. Fans did not want to lose the opportunity to play in the World Series, and they certainly did not want to lose to the southern rivals. The heart of Cardinal Nation could be seen in a poem that surfaced. It represented all that the stadium meant to the fans of St. Louis.[485] (See Appendix)

The poem seemed to buy some time as the best of seven went to the Cards, and it seemed they were on their way to attaining a tenth World Series Championship, but the Boston Red Sox, fresh from overcoming a 0-3 deficit and taking four straight from the Yankees, proved they could not lose. Boston conquered an 86-year-old "Curse of the Bambino" as they swept the World Series games 4-0. The Cards and their fans were left in complete dismay, and the sad part was that defeat occurred in St. Louis. Champagne spilt on the carpet of the visiting clubhouse floor.[486]

La Russa, and his team, took the winning impetus of the 2004 regular season with them into the following year as they won the opener 7-3 in Houston and then took the home opener 6-5 over the Philadelphia Phillies. For the past 10 years, the Cardinals attendance had averaged three million. In 2005, the closing season, they "set a new single-season high with 3,538,988."[487] The last weekend in Busch sold out early at premium prices. The Cincinnati Reds came to town to shut the doors of Busch, September 30-October 2, 2005. The end brought mixed emotions for the organization, players, and fans.

Commemoration of the final season had been noted with a Busch Stadium Countdown Clock. Designated honorary people came out before each game to pull down a number counting the days until the final game.[488] The last weekend former Cardinals stars pulled the numbers, including Mark McGwire, Red Schoendienst, and Ozzie Smith. The farewell party weekend had festivities galore to commemorate the end of a 39-year reign.[489] President Lamping observed that the organization wanted "to have one last hurrah at Busch Stadium with the best fans in baseball." He went on to say, "the weekend will be filled with heartfelt tributes to the most memorable athletes, coaches, broadcasters, and plays that have made Cardinals baseball the tradition that it is today."[490]

The last days of Busch played out to the traditional sea of red with record crowds. Fans gathered from across the country and paid premium prices to bid a fond farewell to honor not just the players and the memories, but the edifice itself. They witnessed a tribute to the 20th anniversary of the 1985 National League champions that included Ozzie Smith, Tom Herr, Bob Forsch, Vince Coleman, John Tudor, Jack Clark, and their leader Whitey Herzog. At the Friday evening game, highlights of the Top 10 moments in Busch history, as voted on by the fans, played out on the big screen.[491] The Saturday day game had another sellout crowd that included more than 16,000 employees and family members of Anheuser-Busch for Family Day. In the pregame ceremony, an All-Busch Stadium team, selected by the fans, took the field.[492]

The atmosphere in and around the stadium had an eerie quality. Those in attendance knew they were taking in an experience that closed the place down, but at the same time it was a moving encounter in a depressing, maudlin way. This was it. After Sunday it would all be over. There was no going back again to relive the memories. Some fans took out magic markers and wrote farewell messages on the walls, while others found ways to grab some part of the stadium for a lasting souvenir.

Late Saturday afternoon, when the game ended, ushers did not push folks along to exit for the cleanup crews as usual. They seemed to understand that people wanted to savor the experience. No one hurried away. Groups of fans wandered the familiar turf, taking pictures. They reminisced about the things they had witnessed in this magical place. Michelle Lewis, there with her husband and mother, thought of her deceased Aunt Judie, and her grandparents, folks who had spent many happy days at the stadium over the years. These relatives forged a bond in their visits to Busch. They had celebrated family gatherings, birthdays, Father's Days and Mother's Days, Straight A tickets, gifts for graduations, anniversaries, and just fun trips to the ole ballpark. They had spent the night outside the stadium on more than one occasion to garner play-off and World Series tickets.

Baseball represented an allegiance; a shared pastime and the Cardinal familiarity solidified their relationship. Michelle grew up on '80s Whitey Ball with the likes of Vince Coleman, Joe Magrane, Greg Mathews, Willie McGee, Ozzie Smith, and Andy Van Slyke. As a die-hard fan, she had been there on many of the historic best-of-ten team highlights. She and her husband Rick recalled the fun times they had shared at the games, including McGwire's achievements. Together, they knew they would be back next season, but it would not be there. They observed so many others doing the same thing. There was almost a hushed silence that resembled a wake. They came to honor the passing of something dear and they wanted to savor the moment before its time passed. Fans wanted to say thanks for the memories and to pay their respects. They did not want to leave because then it would be over, never to be experienced again.[493] This space, this place, solidified a bond with the Cardinal organization, and it all mattered.

Sunday's crowd, decked out in red, came early and stayed late. With tickets hard to come by and long sold out, some fans came to the area just to take in the experience and share the historic moment. Paul Pagano, an 82-year-old fan, showed up to bid farewell after 25 years of cheering on his favorites. Stephen A. Norris, a reporter for MLB.com noted that Pagano, wearing red Mardi Gras beads, looked like "a walking bulletin board" sporting a hat that read "Cardinals thanks for the memories" and a sign hung from his neck that stated "Cardinals, it was an exciting year. Thanks for the memories." Pagano knew he would miss the old place; but he also noted that "everything comes to an end sooner or later. It's finally the end of Busch, but we'll get used to the new stadium."

Folks shared sentimental memories of the place and tied it to their own lives. Laura Winkelmann attended her first game when she was six years old and her Dad had tickets from his job. She fondly remembered that first day when she saw Fredbird and even went onto the field. Her friend, Kim Gage, recalled her first game in 1987. The promotional giveaway that evening had been seat cushions, and when Tommy Herr hit a walk-off grand slam, those cushions flew onto the field. Kim said, "I was excited, I was just in sixth grade. To see everyone in the stadium erupt, it was really neat."[494]

The pregame ceremony for the last game, traditionally Fan Appreciation Day, honored the fans that supported the team over the last 40 years. Cards owner Bill DeWitt called the day "The ultimate fan appreciation day—the final regular-season game in the remarkable 40-year history of Busch Stadium. Remarkable for the accomplishments on the field by many talented and gifted players—several who are with us today - division titles, National League Pennants, World Championships, and Hall of Fame players—countless memories. Remarkable for its tremendous support from baseball's best fans, who have made all of this success possible."

Baseball Commissioner Bud Selig's speech highlighted the fan support when he remarked, "to all of you in St. Louis, I am pleased to tell you that all of us in Major League Baseball appreciate your magnificent support of baseball and your devotion to your beloved St. Louis Cardinals." The ceremonial first-pitch honors went to "two men who have watched more Cardinals games at Busch Stadium than anyone: former Cardinals player and manager Red Schoendienst and former player and current broadcaster Mike Shannon." In a film clip, Joe Buck led the crowd of 50,434 in the national anthem. The team went on to win the final game 7-5 for their 100th win of the 2005 season.[495] They made it to the play-off games. The stadium survived demolition for a few more memorable games at Busch.

Cards clinched the NL Central title, and they hosted the Padres on Tuesday, October 4, at Busch. It turned out to be another beautiful October day where a crowd of 52,347 came to see the Cards take the first game. Miracle of miracles it was not over, there was life left within the walls of the stadium. Two days later the team took a two-game lead and headed west where the Cardinals clinched the division championship with a 6-2 victory at Petco Park.

It was back to Busch the following Monday against the Houston Astros. Cards took that game and the Astros the next. Off to Houston, and when it seemed just about over, Albert Pujols homered in the top of the ninth, Jason Isringhausen held the lead. They returned to Busch on the 19th where it all came to an end for the Cardinals. The last game played at Busch Stadium, before a 52,438 crowd, the Astros clinched the NLCS 5-1 over the home team. Now it was over. The Cards were out of it. It was time to wait for the demolition crew.

On November 7th, hundreds came out to view the first swings of a five-ton wrecking ball bring down the beloved home of the Cardinals, the process of the demolition had begun. It was not the planned implosion. Progress on the new stadium had advanced rapidly, and it now set too close to the old park. They could not take the chance of damaging the new home with a mishap, so the destruction took longer than first expected. They moved cautiously through the obliteration. The area was fenced off, but throughout the winter, fans could be seen coming to grieve the loss and gawk at the ruin. The crushed concrete was used to plug up the huge hole left by the old park, the proposed site of Ballpark Village.[496] It was the end of an era, but excitement reigned for what lay ahead.

BASEBALL AS OUGHT TO BE!

April 10, 2006, a beautiful sunny spring day with a *Gameday Program* offering one to "take a stairway to heaven," greeted energetic St. Louis fans that came to celebrate the opening of the new $365 million "pure baseball" structure, the new home to the St. Louis Cardinals.

Die-hard Redbird fans customarily see special baseball days, including Opening Day as an unofficial holiday; they allow their kids to play hooky, and they take the day off work. With the celebration of a new stadium, one would not find too many kids in school or employees at work. Even without tickets, folks flocked downtown for pregame rallies and celebrations. Eagerness of the christening of the stadium filled the air. Opening Day, with a series against the Milwaukee Brewers, was at hand. For the past few years, Cardinal Nation eagerly watched the structure going up. Now they crossed the threshold to paradise and watched history unfold. Fans eagerly awaited the stats to fill the record books.

What changes they encountered! This edifice had no comparison to past Cardinal homes. Robison Field and Sportsman's Park harkened back to a simpler time. Former Busch Stadium (1966-2005) had numerous modern amenities, but one could clearly detect that this new Busch distanced itself remarkably from the freshly demolished multipurpose structure. Bill DeWitt Jr. stated that he wanted a ballpark that would play neutral, in that it would not favor hitters or pitchers, but would be fair overall. He made sure to include everything to please players and fans alike.

Extensive studies went into making an ideal structure; it even allowed reports for game-time conditions to integrate the weather and lighting. The playing field sits below grade and allows the brick masterpiece to lay alongside the existing neighborhood structures. Home plate points toward the Gateway Arch in the southwest corner of the field. Dimensions of the new park have smaller foul territories with plate-to-backstop 52 feet, the right and left field ranges fairly dead-on with 385 range for the field and 336 down left field and 335 for right, center came in at 400 feet.[497]

The architectural style merges with the traditional St. Louis facade of red brick to compliment the numerous Cupples Station warehouses and the historic Wainwright Building. An iron arched pedestrian walkway graces Eighth Street to resemble the nearby historic Eads Bridge. With open spaces strategically placed, vistas of the landmark St. Louis Arch and the Old Courthouse, as well as the skyscape of the city, greet visitors.

As with Sportsman's Park, builders astutely designed the stadium to snugly fit the site precisely, but here the city panorama melds into the park. The diamond, the city, and the people come together allowing the spectators to virtually sit in the landscape of St. Louis. For urban classicists, the scenic observations of the opened structure demonstrate the overpowering feel of the integrity of city living. It delivers a respect for the architecture of St. Louis. Attending a game here allows one to blend with the setting and relate to the city as no previous Cardinals' field. It is part of the cityscape.

Much care has been taken to retain the tradition of the club, but there is no doubt that the fashionable modern structure, with twenty-first century conveniences, delivers what fans across the country have come to expect from new sports complexes. The massive cathedral offers more than just a ball-game experience. It appeals to a new breed of fans, some who do not necessarily come to watch a game as much as to attend an event. Patrons have come to expect the best, and they do not intend to give up modern luxuries just to attend a game; in fact, they expect amenities far surpassing a simplistic dog-and-suds afternoon. This is not the gauche attempt of the entertainment venue presented by Von der Ahe; no, this is class.

The new Busch Stadium is a lavish venue presenting an upscale experience. Seating capacity of 46,000 means 4,000 fewer seats than the previous park. Seats along the third and first base lines sit closer to the action on the field. Fewer corporate luxury boxes are installed, but there are more inclusive "party rooms" that host 40 fans, VIP sections for private seating and lavish amenities offer a more exclusive and inclusive bar (nonalcoholic drinks, mixed drinks, wine, and beer) and they feature food stations or a buffet menu prepared by special chefs, with airconditioned areas for viewing the game, relaxing and visiting, as well as padded outdoor seats. A patio section with numerous open areas invites fans to move about and not be tethered to a specific seat. There are also more standing-room areas that offer great views of the action on the field as well as majestic vistas of the city.

A massive video display board (40 feet high and 120 feet wide) provides up-to-date replays. Thirteen elevators and nine escalators assist movement; a spectacular sound system, with 1,000 speakers, rocks the audio; and 528 television monitors are scattered throughout the park. The two upper-deck levels reach a height of 198 feet compared to just 130 feet at the previous park and offer a magnificent view of the cityscape, neighboring scenes, and the highway traffic that zooms by.

The new venue offers plenty of entertaining aspects with play areas for kids, including video games, and a place to bat the ball around on a kid-sized concrete diamond. Relaxed seating areas all over the park allow folks to just get a drink, grab a bite, or visit. ATM machines are available as well as gift shops to explore. One can recreate Fredbird and clothe him in an array of costumes at the Build-A-Bear workshop. Smoking has been prohibited inside ballparks for at least a decade though there are special designated smoking areas. The new stadium, with close to 1.5 million square feet, is more expansive than that of the former 900,000 square feet. Lighting has improved with the placement of vertical towers as opposed to the horizontal rings of the old park.

The ballpark oozes the history of the St. Louis Cardinals. The spirit of the storied franchise greets guests as they arrive. The sculpture of famed Cardinal broadcaster Jack Buck made the move, as well as Hall of Fame statues, series pennants, the old center field scoreboard, and the distinguished Stan the Man statue which welcomes visitors at the main entrance. They all reassure fans this truly is the home of their beloved St. Louis Cardinals.

Large brick pavers inlaid in the sidewalk surrounding the stadium highlight one hundred of the greatest historical Cardinal moments and 18,000 smaller bricks, purchased by fans, commemorate personal sentiments of what it means to be a Cardinal fan. The outside red brick walls feature stone medallion inserts, designed by St. Louis-area artist Gabe Drueke, that follow "the development of the Cardinal-bird logo as well as related Cardinal insignias and icons from days past."[498]

Some of the anticipated three million fans gracing Busch Stadium each year arrive by Metrolink with a station directly across from the stadium, or by car with plenty of parking available in parking garages and open lots. Some groups come by bus, and numerous hotels sit within walking distance of the park. The stadium area of the city remains as it did with Busch II, largely commercial with few residents.

Nationally, ballpark food at concessions has changed drastically over the last few years, and St. Louis is no exception. With 24 permanent food stands, delivery service, and roving vendors selling popcorn, peanuts, cotton candy, and hot dogs as well, the permanent concession stands sell nachos, pizza, brats, chicken fajitas, BBQ, pasta, meatball subs, portabella fries, and ice cream. The overwhelming variety of tasty treats satisfies even the pickiest customer. Though the menu might well upset the baseball purists, this is the modern twenty-first century experience of attending a sporting event.

The park provides guest services to help with general stadium information, emergency paging, lost children or guests, lost and found items, and the registering of complaints. To help ease familiarity with the stadium, direction signs are posted, and ushers stationed to guide visitors. The park also has restricted smoking areas, drinking fountains, and many restrooms to include the conventional segregated men's and women's, as well as unisex family ones. Security abounds at the park for safety, with St. Louis policemen and park security to make sure stadium rules are followed to the letter. There seems to be a long list of rules that leads one to imagine the violations that have occurred in the past.

Respect for visiting teams and fans rule. Harassment is not tolerated. In addition, the management does not abide indecent clothing, foul or abusive language, or obscene gestures. Alcoholic beverages must be consumed responsibly. In order to retain control of the crowd, the team limited the sale of beer to two per person per transaction and there are no alcohol sales after the seventh inning. There is also a designated driver program. Triple A continues a long-held practice of offering motor assistance during and after each game. If one wishes to leave the stadium and then re-enter, they are required to have their hand stamped prior to exiting. No unauthorized persons are allowed on the playing field and one should be ready to show their ticket when requested. Fans who bring in banners are restricted to what can be displayed, and subject to strict non-abusive language; they cannot obstruct the view of others, and if they are in sight lines, they must be down during playing time.

While all of this sounds great, new parks take time for some fans to adjust to. Judy Clarke Dwyer and her husband Fran, avid Cardinal fans, who have followed the hometown team since the days of Sportsmen's Park, have noted the changes. Judy said it took a while to adjust to the 1966 move to downtown, but she came to love that place. So far, she is not all that fond of the new Busch Stadium (III), at least not as much as she liked Busch II. She and her husband believe the new place was built to bring in more money from corporations and a few individuals. They see the game as more elitist and less affordable for families as prices have increased and there has been more booing over the years. The Dwyer's note that today's nouveau riche expect high-paid players to be perfect, or maybe it is because the fans sense the players do not seem as loyal to the team as those in the past—the players go where the money is.[499] Yet, in reality baseball has always been a business.

Another avid Cardinal fan, Tom Schneider, likes the new venue. He thinks it looks like what a ballpark is supposed to look like. It reminds him of Sportsman's, and Wrigley in Chicago; it puts him in mind of the other new parks designed to resemble those vintage ones. He can see sinking his family roots here, especially with playoff victories, and boasts that this stadium excites him as much today as when he attended his first World Series game in 1967 to see the Cardinals beat the Boston Red Sox.[500]

One Cardinal season ticket holder, who asked to remain anonymous, has shown dissatisfaction with the move. A businessman himself, he noted that the new stadium was built to maximize revenue and that showed with the increase of luxury boxes, premium seats, upscale dining, and such. To accomplish this in the move, some season ticket holders had to be relocated. His tickets were affected by the move and he never seemed to come to grips with that decision. He noted that in the old stadium there were the field boxes, the second level (where his tickets were), and above that, one level of luxury boxes. In the new stadium there are field box seats, two levels of luxury boxes, and then the second level, where his new seats were located. Personally, he was not happy with the results of the move. In addition, ticket prices overall went up. This man still decided to purchase the tickets; after all, he had been a season ticket holder in the previous Busch Stadium for 23 years. He kept his membership for the first five years and then, before the 2011 season, he dropped his ticket package. He continues to attend Cardinal games but buys his tickets on Stub Hub.

While profit has been important throughout the history of the team, marketing seems to play a bigger role in promotion. Ticket sales were brisk for the inaugural season with many programs offered to promote sales and profits. The organization also sponsored a Kids Club to all fans 15 and younger.

The team began increasing ticket prices for "premium games" the final season in Busch and the trend continued with the new park. Ticket prices are subject to increase for games that are considered "premium" to include Opening Day, all Saturday games, and all games against their main rival, the Chicago Cubs. The home schedule also incorporates about 26 promotional dates.

The first few seasons were complete sellouts with those commercial tokens of thanks fans always appreciate. The premier season, and the next few years, brought people from far and wide to see this architectural wonder. Though a new stadium alone reaps fan attendance with the curiosity factor, owners know better than to eliminate promotions that bring out the fans; they also advertise the team in the logo-bearing giveaway merchandise. In addition, the Cardinals have continued support of the active military personnel by offering each a complimentary standing room ticket to each game, subject to availability.

For many, following the team via print media is a local pastime. Full coverage is given by the *St. Louis Post-Dispatch* where Cardinal news can take over the front page and special editions show up with the start of the season and post-season play. Many keep up on news with *Baseball Weekly* and *Sports Illustrated*. Scorecards are sold at the stadium for about $2.50, but other publications abound as well, to include *Gameday Magazine*, *Cardinals Yearbook*, and *Cardinals Media Guide*. Fans also sign up for internet alerts on the news of their favorite team.

The scoreboard in right-center field is 40 feet tall and 120 feet wide with a 32 by 52-foot video screen. It also supplies lineups, statistical information, and the game's line score. There is an additional 16 by 80 feet scoreboard in right field to provide the latest highlights and scores for other major league games. Throughout the stadium there are smaller boards presenting the game's line score and player stats. As well, folks can check out radio and TV broadcasts, text, and try to carry on cell phone conversations. They attempt to keep up with the game at hand as well as those around the country and to share their experiences with friends. The old-fashioned postcard picture pales compared to the instant snapshot inside the stadium and the panorama coverage on websites.

The real way to celebrate the new home came in the Fall Classic. In 2006, the Cardinals christened the new stadium by winning their division, the pennant, and capping it off by taking the World Series. They were the wild card with only 83 victories, the fewest wins by any team to ever win the world title. In the previous six seasons the team made five postseason appearances with a record of 17-4. La Russa acknowledged his irritation of not having been able to take this organization into the World Series; now he had another chance.[501]

The Cards first beat the San Diego Padres to take their division and then the favored New York Mets for the National League Championship. The final triumph came when they took on the Detroit Tigers to clinch it all in style. La Russa remarked, "We played quality baseball and earned that championship." The devoted St. Louis Cardinal fans certainly agreed.[502] The Cardinals waited 24 years to win another world title and hope rang supreme that it would not take that long to bring another championship home. The opening season had been quite an eventful time for St. Louis, and there would surely be many more decades of spectacular baseball fun.

The 2007 season proved newsworthy and troublesome for Cardinal Nation.[503] The theme that year was "the problems with substance abuse." The trouble began in Florida during Spring Training when, around midnight on March 22nd, four-time-manager-of-the-year, 62-year-old Tony La Russa, with "a blood alcohol count of 0.093 percent…was booked into the Palm Beach County jail on the misdemeanor count" for suspicion of drunk driving. The Cardinal organization publicly supported him and announced that he had acquired legal representation.[504] While the episode hit the major networks, and certainly was the gossip of the day, the news soon died down.

For the second time in five years, tragedy struck the Cardinal family. Early Sunday morning, 12:35, April 29, 2007, 29-year-old Josh Hancock's Ford Explorer, going west on Highway 40, rammed into the back of a stopped tow truck. Hancock, traveling alone, was killed instantly. A police report revealed the harsh realities: Josh was texting on his cell phone at the time, did not wear a seat belt, was speeding thirteen miles over the speed limit, had marijuana in his possession, and was intoxicated.[505]

Hancock's death affected fans and players alike. The Cardinals' scheduled home game against the Chicago Cubs was postponed. Shortly after the announcement of his death mourners began to appear outside the stadium to share their grief.[506] The team showed its respect by displaying his jersey in both the dugout and the bullpen and all of the uniforms carried a black memorial patch with the number 32 on the left sleeve for the remainder of the season.[507] Not surprising, the Cards lost all three games in Milwaukee and then proceeded on to Tupelo, Mississippi, for a public memorial service for their fallen teammate.[508]

Hancock's blood toxicology showed a blood alcohol level of 0.157 percent. His drinking took place off stadium property, yet to curtail any future problems, on May 5, 2007, the Cardinals announced they would ban alcohol from the clubhouse as well as on their charter flights. General Manager Walt Jocketty noted that some players were not pleased with the decision, but he saw the incident as a "wake-up call for everybody," pointing out, "The one thing they have to understand is they're not invincible." While not citing any specific previous problems, Club President Mark Lamping supported the decision remarking that the ban "will serve as a reminder. They will know why there is no beer." This policy had already been enacted a few years before by the Florida Marlins, by the Oakland A's the previous season, and following the St. Louis ban, other teams soon set this new policy, including the Baltimore Orioles, New York Yankees, and the Washington Nationals. By the end of May, at least thirteen major league teams prohibited the use of beer and other alcoholic beverages from the clubhouse.[509]

The Cards had a hard time coming back after Hancock's death. That combined with losing pitcher Chris Carpenter for the season and others not coming through as expected, the hope for resurgence in 2007 seemed dim. Nothing helped the team gel. Right before the All-Star break they took six out of ten games, yet they posted a 40-45 record and sat seven and a half games behind the first place Milwaukee Brewers and seven games behind on the wild card side.

Tragedy struck again on August 31st when Juan Encarnacion suffered a serious left eye injury in a freak accident. As he stood in the on-deck circle, the batter's ball hit his face crushing his eye socket on impact. His future playing days were uncertain.

By Labor Day the team reached the .500 mark, but then they fizzled out. The Cardinals drew over three million fans for the eleventh time in their history, but they finished the season in third place with a 78-84 record, seven games behind the first place Chicago Cubs. Emotionally, the fans and players were spent. They needed to pull back and gear up for next season. Management decided that the fresh start would be one with a new general manager. On October 3rd, after 13 years with the Cardinal organization, Walt Jocketty and the team parted ways. John Mozeliak, assistant general manager for the past five years, replaced him. La Russa's contract expired at the end of the season and speculation reigned concerning his return since he and Jocketty appeared to be a team for the past 12 years, but in the end, he agreed to a new two-year contract; that assured him the spot as the manager for the longest time in Cardinal history.[510]

In March, the club sealed a deal with 26-year-old Adam Wainwright, a four-year contact for $15 million. That same month brought changes to the front office when long-time Cards President Mark Lamping left to become the Chief Operating Officer of the New Meadowlands Stadium Company. Bill DeWitt III stepped in to fill the vacancy.[511] The 2008 season did not show much promise, but more of a rebuilding to get back into contention. Trades and signings showed the mainstay of the old team gone, with new players in uniform, including trading Jim Edmonds to the Padres for David Freese. Most pundits did not hold much promise for the Cardinals. In fact, the *Pittsburgh Tribune* overall picked them to finish dead last.[512] As always, loyal fans saw differently.

On April 2, 2008, with an attendance of 39,915, the sellout streak for the St. Louis Cardinals' regular season came to an end at 165 games. The newness had worn off and the season did not appear as promising without the ole stand-by players the fans came to root for. Even with that drop the team continued to draw fans from around the country; some came to see the down numbers in attendance as a positive. Perhaps now they could come to the games spur of the moment and not have to pay the higher prices for scalper tickets or those on Stub Hub. On May 18th, the team found another way to honor longtime St. Louis hero, 87-year-old Stan Musial. They renamed the street in front of Busch Stadium at the main entrance Stan Musial Drive. Musial and his wife Lil were there for the ceremony, to thank the owners and "the greatest fans around."[513]

On November 8th the Bowling Hall of Fame across from Busch Stadium moved to Arlington, Texas, and the St. Louis Cardinals Hall of Fame, located in the same building closed its doors. The Cardinals purchased the building to knock it down and add the space to the purposed Ballpark Village. This $550 million multipurpose project was to sit on the 10-acre site north of the new stadium; but for years the project could not see the light of day. Blame seemed to rest on the city and the citizens for not supporting a bond issue to finance the retail center while others blamed the 2007 economic downturn that caused major developers to back away. The Cardinals were not putting up the money though they continued to market the idea as reality.

Curator of the Hall of Fame Museum, Paula Homan, was a strong proponent of Ballpark Village, especially the reopening of the Hall of Fame Museum. For a while, a few items from the mammoth collection were on display in areas of the new stadium, but until a new space would be opened in Ballpark Village, most of the materials were mothballed. Homan remarked, "We are very excited about what lies ahead for the Cardinals Museum…We have a wonderful collection of artifacts relating to the history of the Cardinals as well as the history of baseball in St. Louis," Homan continued to work for the organization and was eager to show off the over-$1-million-plus collection of pieces representing more than a hundred years of St. Louis baseball history.

Plans for the opening of the Cardinals Museum was originally set for spring 2008, but delays continued. Homan, quite proud of the collection, continued to acquire artifacts and memorabilia. Though many were skeptical that Ballpark Village would ever materialize, Homan trusted DeWitt. She knew his love of the game, the investments he made in the collection, and held high hopes that one day she would be a part of the opening of this majestic museum to honor the franchise and its players.[514] Ballpark Village and the museum opened in April 2014.

Opening day 2009 looked bleak as the team carried over its lackluster results of the previous season. Not many additions had been made to change things up, but quite a few rookies were added to the roster. It resembled a season of investment in youth. La Russa's magical managerial prowess was at its finest as he juggled his team. At the All-Star break the Red Birds posted a 49-41 record in a four-way battle for the National League Central.

St. Louis hosted the 80th All-Star Game on July 14, 2009. It was the first time the city held the event since 1966. Festivities filled the streets that week to include amusement rides, musical concerts, and a homerun derby on the 13th which Prince Fielder of the Milwaukee Brewers won. The Cardinals took the opportunity to show off their new stadium; they had hoped to have Ballpark Village ready too, but that did not materialize. The site of the old stadium, directly across the street from the new home, was simply a vacant lot used for parking and a softball field.

Native St. Louisans from around the nation played in the game, including Phillies Ryan Howard, White Sox Mark Buehrle and Rays

Ben Zobrist.[516] Tony La Russa and Joe Torre were chosen as coaches by All-Star manager Charlie Manuel. Three Cardinals, the leading All-Star vote-getter Albert Pujols, Yadier Molina, and Ryan Franklin were on the roster. Sheryl Crowe sang the National Anthem, while hometown favorite, Stan Musial presented a baseball for President Barack Obama to throw the ceremonial first-pitch to Cardinals Albert Pujols. "God Bless America" was sung by Sara Evans. The American League won the game 4-3, garnering home field advantage for the World Series in the fall.

On July 24th the Cardinals sat in first place with a one and a half game lead, as management secured their shot at the Fall Classic. They acquired 29-year-old Matt Holliday, a .340 hitter in 2007, from the Oakland Athletics. Holliday would be a free agent at the end of the season, and he carried a hefty salary, but Mozeliak believed it was a fair deal. Holliday was excited to join the club, to be back in the National League, and to be in a pennant race. He also knew the Cardinals were a great organization from his off-season work with hitting instructor Mark McGwire. The move added depth to the lineup, a bat to protect Pujols, and strength to left field.[516]

The team took off; they burned up the league in August, taking 20 out of 26 games. Carpenter and Wainwright were solid, posting ERAs of 1.30 and 2.20 respectively. By Labor Day, Wainwright had 17 victories, and on the 5th of September, Carp threw a one-hitter, his first shutout since 2006. Closer Ryan Franklin did not allow a run all of August. The Cardinals clinched the National Central Championship, finishing the season with a 91-71 record. Carpenter was named Comeback Player of the Year, Wainwright and Molina won Gold Gloves, and Pujols picked up his second consecutive Most Valuable Player Award.

The post-season was short-lived. The Cardinals faced the Los Angeles Dodgers and were swept in three. The season was over. Once they recovered from the shock of defeat, the Cardinal Nation mantra became "Wait 'til next year."[517]

The Cards prepared for the 2010 run within weeks after the season ended. La Russa agreed to a one-year contract, marking his 15th year with the Red Birds, and 46-year-old Mark McGwire signed as their new hitting coach. McGwire and some other noted players had been accused or suspected of steroid use which the MLB did not permit. La Russa noted that it was up to McGwire if he wanted to address the steroid incident, what they wanted was for Mark to coach the hitters.

On January 5, 2010, the Cardinals announced the signing of Matt Holliday, the "most sought-after free agent in all of baseball." He signed a seven-year deal worth $120 million with a no-trade clause. This was the largest contract in franchise history. It surpassed the money first baseman Albert Pujols made from a 2004 deal he had worked out, for seven years and $100 million. At the annual three-day fan festival, the Winter Warm-up held January 16-18 at the Hyatt Regency St. Louis, fans were all abuzz. This was exciting news, but there was interesting speculation, if the Cardinals gave that much money to the left fielder, would they have enough to keep Pujols with free agency looming at the end of the 2011 season. At the time, the team showed no signs that they would not sign the mega-superstar, and led fans to believe of course they would, as it was believed Holliday was brought in to bolster Pujols' place in the lineup.[518]

Mark McGwire announced that he had indeed used steroids during his playing years, including 1998, the year he broke the Roger Maris home run record.[519] The long-awaited confession and apology came January 11, 2010. McGwire acknowledged, "It was foolish, and it was a mistake. I truly apologize. Looking back, I wish I had never played during the steroid era." McGwire insisted, "The only reason I took steroids was for health purposes…The steroids could help me recover faster…They would help me heal and prevent injuries, too."[520]

In an interview on ESPN's *Baseball Tonight*, La Russa, McGwire's manager in Oakland and St. Louis, revealed that he did not know McGwire used until the slugger called him before the public announcement to apologize to him. The manager declared "he would put his reputation, his wins, and his Hall of Fame status on the line in support of McGwire," asserting, "he harbors no second thoughts about hiring McGwire as a Cardinals hitting coach or standing behind his character." Commissioner Bud Selig also received an apology phone call from McGwire and was pleased with the confirmation, noting, "This statement of contrition, I believe, will make Mark's re-entry into the game much smoother and easier."[521]

Spring training as always was a fun, relaxed place with a promise of things to come. One bright spot for Cardinals and their fans seemed to be that Pujols seemed relaxed and willing to talk with Bernie Miklasz about his future with the Cardinals. Albert Pujols was the face of the modern St. Louis Cardinals. It was clear in February 2010 that the three-time winner of the MVP loved St. Louis and appreciated the opportunity the Cardinal organization had offered him. He told Miklasz, "People in St. Louis and our fans around the country know where I want to be. And that's St. Louis. There's no city like St. Louis to play baseball…So why would I want to go anywhere else?"

Pujols appreciated the Cardinals, the legacy, the tradition, hanging out with the Hall of Famers, and donning the uniform. He had a profound respect for Cardinal veteran Stan Musial, so much so that he did not want to be known as El Hombre, a nickname fans like to credit him. He noted that there was and would always be only one Stan the Man. Albert stated many times that he wanted to be a Cardinal forever. The only thing he and the franchise had to do was negotiate a contract. He sounded confident that would be worked out.[522]

Many analysts picked the Cards to win the division. Leaving spring training, Chairman Bill DeWitt Jr. was confident fans would turn out to witness a good season.[523] As La Russa shuffled the Cards lineup things looked promising. The first part of the season started well. They took the opener in Cincinnati 11-6.[524] Noted Cardinal dignitaries, including seven Hall of Famers, rode in the ceremonial motorcade and showed their support. Fans loved it. This opening day excitement gets everyone ready for the journey to October ball.

St. Louis fans know the history and tradition of the game. They are privy to the Redbirds' style of playing that had been with the team for its existence. It became known in baseball circuits as "the Cardinal Way." It was a "fighting spirit, dedication to fundamentals" and has been the overall characteristic of each era in Cardinals' history. The tradition of playing hard and giving your all on the field was instilled in all the players, especially those who went through the Cardinals farm system. That formula produced 17 pennants and 10 World Series titles. The Cardinal experience is like no other. When the old-timers get together, they always seem to get around to talking about the good ole days and showing the youngsters what it is really like to be a Cardinal.

The month of May found the team and fans focusing on Cardinal tradition as they sought to bring honor to 89-year-old Cardinal great, Stan Musial. On May 25th, in a program designed in large part by Ron Watermon, a member of the team's media relations staff, the team announced a campaign to acquire for The Man the highest honor of the country. They spearheaded a "Stand for Stan" endeavor. The organization worked privately to get President Obama to award the Cardinal legend the "Presidential Medal of Freedom, the most prestigious award a civilian can receive in the United States."

It became clear that public attention would serve to honor Stan for more than his work on the field. It would be a platform to give "recognition of him as a model citizen." The drive used the latest in social media to spark fans to respond through a special web site, Twitter, and Facebook as well as television and radio announcements and newspaper coverage. Prominent Missouri politicians, and the Cardinal team and owner, all sent letters in support of honoring Musial, a World War II veteran, for helping to safeguard national security and spread world peace. Not only had Musial left baseball at the height of his career to serve the country, but soon after he retired, he served on the President's Council on Physical Fitness and Sports from 1964-1967. DeWitt noted, "Stan has been a true role model—exemplifying the humility, grace, and generosity we so desperately need to see in our American sports heroes."

The team called on fans "to send in their recollections and fond memories and even first-hand stories about the Cardinals' great." They also instituted a "Flat Stanley-like project" where cartoonist Dan Martin designed a "flat" Stan the Man that was distributed to the public with the idea to have fans take their pictures with the likeness and post it to the official site. The idea of drawing attention and positive responses to the campaign was basically to "show some affection for Stan" and appreciation for a lifetime of achievement.

The promotion ignited excitement for Cardinal Nation, and the season ended with a "Stand for Stan" day at the ballpark in October where fans held up "Flat Stan the Man" cutouts and cheered as Musial and his family circled the field.[525] This effort showed commitment of the St. Louis community and the Cardinals organization to work together to bring recognition to a former player they all admired and to the city of St. Louis.

At the All-Star break the Red Birds sat a game behind the first place Cincinnati Reds and held a 47-41 record. All-Star Cardinals Chris Carpenter, Matt Holliday, Yadier Molina, and Adam Wainwright flew to Anaheim, California, with fellow nine-time All-Star pick Albert Pujols, on a charter arranged by the first baseman. The guys went to the west coast ready for a fun experience and to play a little ball. It was an important game to bring in a victory for the National League; since 2003, whichever league won garnered home-field advantage for the World Series. For the first time since 1996, the National League won, 3-1.

DeWitt did not seem ready to work out Pujols' contract. In midseason he had other concerns, to work out ways to get the club to the championship. Historically, since 1965, if the Cardinal team had not been in first place by the time of the All-Star break, they would not capture the division title.[526] The owner did not put stock in that though.[527] On the heels of the Anaheim game, just thirteen days before the trade deadline, DeWitt formalized a contract with General Manager John Mozeliak to extend his deal through 2013 with an option for 2014. To many, this signaled his confidence that Mozeliak would be able to get Pujols to reach an agreement when the time arrived.[528]

Suiting up after the All-Star break, manager La Russa was ready for the challenges ahead. With his philosophy intact, he noted, "You play the first half to put yourself in contention. Now you get to find out if you're good enough."[529] Shuffling the deck they sought ways to bolster pitching, but it simply was not enough.[530] The St. Louis Cardinals missed out on the postseason for the third time in four years. The Cardinals though, once again drew over three million fans that were eager to get through winter and begin anew in the spring.

Once the season ended the Cardinals picked up their final part of Pujols' 2004 $111 million contract. They assumed the $16 million option for Pujols for one more year. That move lined up the negotiations that would follow during the winter in hoping to get Pujols for a long-term deal.[531]

On October 19th, La Russa signed for his 16th season with the Cardinals.[532] The season had been a tough one for everyone involved but, in all probability, more so for the oft impatient La Russa. While La Russa saw the job as challenging,[533] he noted that it "was not as much fun" and blamed that on not just the pressure of the position "but the combination of distractions of players due to money and security…and the proliferation of media." With all of that, La Russa insisted he wanted to come back to help the club get to the postseason.[534]

The winter months turned to getting Pujols to sign and finding ways to beef up the team to get them back to the Fall Classic. DeWitt and his son, team president Bill DeWitt III, had noted throughout the summer that the off-season would be the "optimum" time to discuss terms with the first baseman.[535] Tony La Russa described Pujols as "the perfect player…There is nobody out there better…like Mays, Musial, Aaron. He could hit in their league."[536]

Projected payroll showed the team had committed $80 million to nine players with $50 million of that going to Holliday, Pujols, Carpenter, and Lohse. It was hedging over an annual $100 million, but it takes money to make money. Investments in long-term contracts for substantial players assured long-range plans and let fans know the organization was committed to building and supporting a winning team.[537] Winning teams more than paid for themselves, not only in ticket sales, but the accompanying merchandise and concessions. At the general managers' meeting in Orlando, Mozeliak announced that the "long-anticipated talks regarding a contract extension" with Pujols would begin in December.[538]

At the beginning of December, to deepen the lineup, the franchise brought free agent, switch-hitter Lance Berkman, 34, aboard with an $8 million deal for one year. Berkman had a strong reputation as a former National League Rookie of the Year and five-time All-Star, but, after knee surgery in the previous off-season he had found it hard to fit back into the regular stress of everyday playing. Berkman was excited with this opportunity, noting he wanted "to make 'Mo' a genius."[539] Berkman's acquisition added another powerful bat to the lineup. The middle of the lineup was set with Pujols, Holliday and Berkman.[540] Some speculated, if for any reason the Cardinals lost Pujols, they at least had a backup first baseman in Berkman.

Mid-December came around and still no Pujols' signature on a long-term contract. Ryan Howard had signed for $25 million with the Phillies and others had received enormous deals, including Jayson Werth, Carl Crawford, and Adrian Gonzalez. All those outstanding players were in Albert's age group, but none were as "consistently excellent" as the Cardinals first baseman. Miklasz believed that Pujols, who hit .312 and led the National League in home runs and RBIs in 2010, would stay but he also "wasn't convinced Pujols will bolt after the 2011 season unless a new deal with the Cardinals" could be worked out by spring training.[541]

Bryan Burwell, another St. Louis sports analyst, stated a profound fact that, "Sooner or later, someone is going to pay Albert Pujols an obscene amount of money to keep playing baseball at the Hall of Fame level. Maybe historic money, $28 million to $30 million a season, extended out until the next decade." As early as December 2010, Burwell did not believe that deal would come from the Cardinals.[542] Fans gathered for the holidays talking about the winter deals and wondering what it would take to get Albert signed. Everyone could just breathe a little easier if it was all settled before spring training.[543] The fateful year was at hand.

CHAPTER ELEVEN

THE MIRACLE YEAR!

The 2010 census showed the population for the City of St. Louis fell off 8.3% from that in 2000 and rested at 319,294. Changes to the city occurred over the last 15 years or so with major businesses pulling out of town; but the biggest upset for the city seemed to rest in the sale of Anheuser-Busch to a Belgian firm, InBev, in July 2008. For many, it was uncertain if the brewery would remain in the city; it did, but the company faced layoffs. The name of the stadium remained Busch. The Cardinals had spent five full seasons in their new home and other than 2006 nothing too noteworthy had occurred. It was baseball as usual, fun and exciting. The team had continued to draw the 3 million plus crowds, but the hoped-for wish each spring of competing in the World Series had eluded the Red Birds since their inaugural year. The Cardinal organization showed concern about how to field a competitive team and continue to draw the crowds now that the newness of the stadium had worn off.

In January 2011, the St. Louis Cardinals adopted the new ticket pricing technique, Qcue. The program was used to shift ticket prices based on demand. This setup provided "flexibility to adjust ticket prices to better match the fan experience and to draw more fans to the ballpark to see some of baseball's top teams play each other." Basically, the software works to analyze sales data and to take into consideration "external pricing variables" within minutes. The old way of ticket pricing had the cost of the ticket figured before the season began and was basically unmovable. The new method was figured in real time to allow for adjustments throughout the season as the demand for the venue shifts. Barry Kahn, the economic genius behind Qcue, explained in an interview for *Business Insider*, "Most teams face an internal debate—price for a sell out or price to maximize sales." His system worked to balance those two priorities by offering high-demand seats at an increased price and taking advantage of the lower demand to reduce prices and hopefully fill the stadium. Kahn noted it helped to more accurately price tickets and maintain "price integrity."[544]

Martin Coco, director of ticket sales and marketing with the Cardinals, noted at the end of the 2011 season that the program was "undoubtedly a success for the Cardinals" as it allowed them to more accurately price their tickets according to the overall market demand.

He noted that the system primarily allowed for the fluctuating factors of "opponents they play, time of year, day of the week, team performance, and to a lesser extent, weather, and pitching matchups." Throughout the season the special pricing was used, and Coco remarked that he received positive feedback from the Cardinal fan base. While ticket prices did increase with traditionally popular games such as Opening Day, fans understood that the "increased revenue generated…allows us to have the larger number of low-priced tickets on the lower-demand days." About 20 games in 2011 offered fans a chance to purchase tickets for as low as five dollars each. These were usually games played in mid-week and typically came in the slower months of April, May, and September when kids were in school. The plan has a price protection for season ticket holders. The Cardinals "guarantee all full and half-season ticket plans that the single-game price will not go below the price they paid for a ticket on that given date." The team continues to use this modern ticket approach.

Throughout January, meetings between the organization and Pujols' agent, Dan Lozano were said to have taken place although that was only speculation as it was agreed that all meetings would remain confidential. Albert had made it clear if things could not be worked out in the offseason, before February 15th, he would not discuss the subject until after the season. He did not want a media circus of the issue stating, "Do you want to bring all that into the clubhouse all year…No. I think you need to respect that. And I respect my teammates more than I respect this contract."[545] DeWitt did not seem fazed, "You deal with the situation as it develops. I don't know what else to say."

To the club, Pujols would be considered not on his past record but on his "future performance." Mozeliak also stated that other big signings, such as Howard's with Philadelphia, played no part in Pujols' situation. At the Orlando winter meetings in December, DeWitt conceded that the club had "a limit on how much the franchise could commit to one player and that it would not be hostage to other organizations' excessive deals."[546]

The Cardinals had the support of the fans which showed in the successful drive to bring the Medal of Freedom to St. Louis-great Stan Musial. On Tuesday, February 15, 2011, the beloved St. Louis resident "was among 15 recipients honored during a ceremony at the White House…President Barack Obama called the Hall-of-Famer 'a gentleman you would want your kids to emulate.'"[547]

As spring training began the Cardinals were optimistic about their chances and were a "serious threat to win the NL Central division title."[548] Then a little over a week later the team's chances for making a run for the October playoffs seemed just about over. The team did not look as solid as it had because, on Feb. 23rd, it was announced that the 2010 Cy Young Award runner-up, Adam Wainwright, would be lost for the season with an elbow injury. The right-handed hurler needed Tommy John surgery.[549] Determined to keep the team in strong contention, Mozeliak shopped for ways to strengthen the team. The only two relievers left from April were Mitchell Boggs and Jason Motte.[550]

The dog days of summer hit the Cardinals and blasted them virtually out of any chance of postseason play. They were slipping further and further behind. The Cardinals could not find the right combination to bring the best they could offer onto the field. Fans looked for explanations beyond "oh, we lost Wainwright"; for even without him and other mishaps, to include the failure of Franklin to produce and the slow start by Pujols, the team had been in contention.

They seemed lackluster, and La Russa commented that it was possible they were experiencing a letdown. Rumors floated that perhaps this would be La Russa's last year. Many believed he was being courted by White Sox owner Jerry Reinsdorf to return to Chicago to complete his managerial career, but La Russa insisted if he finished his managerial career it would be with the Cardinals. For him the problem was not so much that the Cardinals were stale in August, but that the team ahead of them was on fire. Tony was not giving up.[551] On Monday, August 22nd, the Cardinals announced that pitching coach Dave Duncan was taking a leave of absence. Bullpen coach Derek Lilliquist took over his duties.[552]

Within a few days a magical turn-around came out of the clubhouse with the leadership of veteran Cardinals. On August 24th, after being swept by the Dodgers, and holding a 67-63 season record, most expected La Russa to hold a clubhouse meeting, but it was the players who came together to discuss the dismal outlook; highly regarded players that included Carp, Pujols, and Berkman led the discussion. They believed they "owed it to their fans and their own self-respect to pick it up." After that, the team caught fire, winning six of their next seven, including a series from the Brewers in Milwaukee.[553]

Late summer 2011, no one truly believed that the Cardinals would win; oh, they hoped, they wished, they kept their fingers crossed, the players played like every game was their last, but truthfully, how could anyone think the impossible would come about. Yet, miracles were known to happen, and things were certainly going the way of the Cardinals. From August 25th until they clinched the World Series on October 28th, nothing stood in their way. Time after time they were the underdog and each time, they overcame defeat. The Cardinals were unstoppable. Play like this binds the fans to the Cardinal organization. Citizens of Cardinal Nation began to believe anything was possible.

La Russa seemed less tense. Remarks were made by sportswriters, analysts, and fans of how low-key La Russa was in some stressful situations. It was almost as if the team knew something others did not. The team solidified as professionals. If you beat them, you had to do it and you better stick around and make sure they were down for the count because in all probability they would find a way to rise again. The team soaked up that never-say-die attitude, not braggadocios, not in an arrogant way, but in a lighthearted, happy-go-lucky way; almost wondering themselves how they did it.

The Cardiac Cardinals came from behind in a consistent basis that would stop one's heart. Those who had lived through the 1964 crazy run, when the Cardinals were 6.5 games out on Labor Day, took the pennant the last day of the season, and beat the Yankees to become World Champions, reminded everyone that "it ain't over 'til it's over." Believe was the mantra that carried the fans on, no matter how outlandish it seemed. Very methodically, the team showed La Russa's secrets to success: they took a series two out of three or three out of four consistently and they made progress toward the play-offs.

The Cards did their job throughout the month, winning 23 of their last 32 games, averaging five runs a game. While the Cards were mowing down their opponents, the Braves lost 17 of their last 25. No amount of miracle-inning would give them the wild card; they needed Atlanta to flail to have any chance of assuring a place at the end, and they did. The wild card went to the Cardinals.

Major League Baseball handled all the ticketing for the postseason play. Season ticket holders received the option to purchase their same seat locations for playoff and World Series games; tickets were made available to Cardinal personnel, and a limited number of single-game tickets were set aside for the general public. Ticket demand was high, so the Cardinals held a website registration and then randomly drew for the opportunity to purchase single-game tickets. Stub Hub and eBay tickets became available as ticket holders weighed their option of attending the game or reaping the financial gain of selling their ticket.[554]

Jubilation filled Cardinal Nation and the Cardinals' locker room in Houston. The team took the happy flight to St. Louis where they rested overnight and then moved onto Philadelphia to begin the battle for the Division Series while the Milwaukee Brewers took on the Tampa Bay Rays. This truly was a "happy flight" celebration.[555]

All that was necessary Thursday, September 29, 2011, was to play each game as they came and see where it ended up. After posting a 90-72 season record, against the greatest odds in baseball, the St. Louis Cardinals were in the play-offs. La Russa lived for this type of pressure and his boys were set. Always the excellent strategist, he was ready to shuffle and play his Cards.

Saturday, October 1st began the show-down in the best-of-five series. Though the Cardinals had the best offense in the National League, the bullpen blew 26 saves that season. The Phillies held the odds with their in-depth pitching. The Cardinal bullpen ranked "as the worst among the playoff contenders," an important element in "tight postseason games."[556]

To some though, the Cards' chances looked good. La Russa had made 13 trips to the postseason and had won the first-round series nine times. La Russa preached short-series games played differently than a full season, and anything could materialize at any time. Over the years, Cardinal fans learned the philosophy of the game by following the maneuvering of the owners and managers. Elated and energized, Cardinal fans packed Busch Stadium, joined by the Rally Squirrel who made an appearance running across the outfield. The little furry critter showed up on the field again the next night before the second-largest crowd in Busch Stadium history (47, 071).[557]

The series went five games. Carp was magic in the last game, pitching a 3-hit shutout to clinch the National League Division Series 1-0. He became the first pitcher to throw a shutout in a Game Five National League Division Championship.

For the past few years, there had been real tension between the Brewers and Cardinals. The Cards represented tradition and sportsmanship, while the Brew Crew flaunted players of showmanship. A few years back the young Brewers had the habit of flipping out their shirt tails after a game in what some perceived as disrespectful and flippant. This season, the teams had been embroiled in some real differences that led to dramatic problems on the field, to include the smart mouth of Nyjer Morgan and the over-the-top personal cheering when they hit a double, triple, or homer. Opposing players and fans thought the Brewers were cocky and disrespectful with their overt body language, trying to push their successful plays in the face of the opponents to show them up. Other irritating issues were the way opposing pitchers set out to put Pujols in his place with the brush-back pitches. Cards fans even took to prayer to help them defeat the Brewers.[558] (See Appendix)

La Russa's genius came through as others sat baffled at his maneuvering. He showed a new way to victory. For the postseason, he lined up the bullpen to pitch its stuff, if only for an out or two, and he moved on to bring the next expert in. It looked odd, seemed strange, but as always, La Russa's magic worked. For the first five playoff games of the NLCS, his bullpen "pitched 21-2/3 of the team's 44 innings in five games, recording a 1.66 ERA." Once again, the virtuoso took center stage and orchestrated another way to avoid the pitfalls of late-inning rallies. La Russa's game plan pitted the batter against the one pitcher he believed could make the out; then he re-evaluated the situation with the next match-up. La Russa used his specialized bullpen committee to make the strategic outs and then go with his closer, Jason Motte, to bring it home. The remarkable line of attack played out beautifully, even La Russa's critics admired his finesse.[559]

Miracle of miracles, for the third time in eight seasons, the Cards found a path to the World Series. The Cards got more innings (28-2/3) from their bullpen than their starters (24-1/3) and posted a 1.88 ERA. Even La Russa was astonished. "The thing that overwhelmed me was that our relievers stood out so much. I figured our starters would at least get us into the last third of the game." The skipper stated, "I've never seen anything like it. It's very weird to be successful when your starters aren't doing what they're supposed to be doing." Except for one win by Carpenter, the bullpen pitchers posted all postseason victories (three with the Phillies and three with the Brewers).[560] Even Freese, the MVP of the series, acknowledged that perhaps the bullpen should have won the award and that he "would have approved cutting up his award and doling it out to the relievers."[561] Wednesday, October 19th, marked Game 1 of the World Series. The 2011 series insignia was painted on the field, and the red, white, and blue celebratory bunting was in place as excitement filled the streets of St. Louis from downtown to the far-reaching suburbs. The fans were decked out in their Cardinal gear from traditional old-timer shirts to the new Rally Squirrel ones, as well as championship and World Series t-shirts; they were bundled up too. Rain throughout the afternoon had cancelled the typical outdoor rallies and for a while threatened the game.

The opening game was a chilly one on a cloudy, windy night where temperatures dipped to the low 40s. The feel was that of a football game. The Cardinals were playing in their 18th World Series and the Rangers were competing in only their second. The Cards franchise had won 52 World Series games, while the Rangers had only won one World Series game.

The Rangers were picked in the beginning of the season to make a return to the Fall Classic after their loss the previous year to the San Francisco Giants. They finished the season posting 96 wins, 10 games ahead of the Los Angeles Angels. They made short order of the wild-card Tampa Bay Rays, beating them in four, and then took care of the Tigers in six. Many considered their offense the best in baseball that season. The Rangers were confident and determined, with desired revenge, to prove they were number one.

Though not eligible to play because of Tommy John surgery, the presence of Wainwright in the dugout inspired the guys and helped the pitcher feel part of the team. They beat the two best teams in the National League. They were hot and confident; they had overcome all the odds to get into the World Series. The team skipper had brought in 12 first place finishes and appeared in six World Series. By many he was considered the finest manager in the game. La Russa instinctively knew the way to maneuver the line-up to get the most out of his team and was supported by his experienced coaching staff.[562]

It appeared to be an evenly matched series, though prognosticators picked the Rangers.[563] MLB used a simulation engine to determine the winner and the results supported the Rangers in seven.[564] Almost all the media billed this series as a high-scoring slug-fest, especially in the hitter's park, Rangers Ball Park in Arlington.

Modernity in technology helped fans stay in touch. The *St. Louis Post-Dispatch* updated its coverage online to include "Cardinals galleries, videos, stats, and scoreboard, along with…award-winning analysis and commentary." They also added "a link to in-game chats with Jeff Gordon." In addition, one could find "Cardinals updates and photos on the *Post-Dispatch* news app for…Android, BlackBerry or iPhone." Each day of the series the newspaper featured a special World Series edition that was available at the newsstands and online.[565]

These Cardinals did not play the speed of "Whitey Ball," in fact, they held the lead in garnering outs in double-plays. They stole just 57 bases and had been caught 39 times. Their Gold Glove catcher Yadier Molina helped to balance that as he was notorious for nailing the opposition in stolen-base attempts. He would be kept busy by the Rangers as they could manufacture runs with the speedy duo of Ian Kinsler and Elvis Andrus who batted first and second in the lineup and were noted for stealing. They had a combined total of 67 steals. The Rangers stole 143 bases and were caught 45 times.[566]

Offense was strong with both teams. St. Louis scored the most runs in the National League, but ranked fifth in the Majors, while the Rangers scored the third most runs in all of baseball. Both sides could get on base and were noted for hitting the long ball when it counted. Hot bats could well rule the day.

The Cardinals had a remarkable fan base, noted for its dedication and overall knowledge, not only about the Cardinals, but about baseball and other teams. They also had a blind faith in their team and a spirit that would not die. Having already won 10 World Series Championships, the chant that took over was 11 in 11.[567]

With the Cards back in the World Series, folks rode on adrenaline.[568] Not only the players had an exhaustive ride for the last few weeks playing to their fullest capacity, traveling around and losing valuable sleep, but so had other Cardinal personnel, media folks, family members, friends, and fans. Some folks were divided which team to root for. For the older generation, Cardinal Nation was in their blood, but some of the younger folks had grown up on baseball in Texas and wanted to see a team that had not won a World Series come out on top. Texas executive, Chief Operating Officer Rick George had roots in the Midwest city. He noted, if the Cards were playing any team other than his Rangers, he would be rooting for St. Louis. His dad Dick was seventy-seven years old and living in Texas. "He watches every Cardinals game, and if he doesn't watch he listens." He followed Rangers baseball, too, but he wanted to see St. Louis, his hometown, win.

Sporting Rangers gear were Jenny and Dean Feaman from Ellis Grove, Illinois. They followed the Cardinals all season, but this time they were cheering for their grandson, Mark Lowe, "a right-handed relief pitcher" for Texas. Jenny noted "Wherever he is, we're going to yell for him."

Michelle Lewis, now living in Oklahoma City, was in St. Louis for the second game. She and her family lived in the Arlington area for a while and she gave high praise to the Rangers organization, especially their reasonable ticket packages that helped families afford games. She and her husband, Rick were lifelong Cardinals fans, but she noted both of her children were born in Texas and the kids were cheering for the Rangers. Her husband had a hard time making up his mind who to cheer for since he so admired what Nolan Ryan had done with the Rangers, having rescued them a few years back. It was clear though, Michelle, all decked out in her Cardinal garb and foam Fredbird head, hoped to bring the World Series championship back to her hometown.[569]

This was the celebration of a lifetime, something everyone had worked hard for whether on or off the field. At least "more than 14 hours before the first pitch was thrown," a host of supporting cast got everything ready, including "cooks and carpenters, broadcasters and baseball executives, security guards, and ticket sellers."[570] The work began at the crack of dawn and lasted into the night. The Cardinals hosted the biggest party of the year and set the stage for not only the additional 100,000 visitors to the city, but also for close to 15 million nationwide TV viewers.

James Fisher, a marketing professor at St. Louis University, reckoned, "if you can show interesting venues and personalities, the things that really make St. Louis what it is, there's a lot of value in that." The city took on tighter security and spruced up. Downtown hotels, bars, and restaurants awaited the mass influx of this new business. The St. Louis Convention and Visitors Commission estimated "that tourists will spend, exactly,

$2,655,140.11 per game here in St. Louis." With homefield advantage, if the games went to seven, the Regional Chamber and Growth Association calculated about between $10.6 and $12.4 million in additional funds for the downtown area alone.[571] The "city officials estimated the team's seven home play-off games have generated almost $2 million in added tax dollars. World Series games six and seven could add an additional $900,000."[572]

The afternoon rain cancelled the pre-game rally, but not the game. Game 1, dedicated to veterans and their families, had tight security as First Lady Michelle Obama and the wife of the Vice President, Jill Biden, attended as part of the pre-game ceremonies.[573] Other celebrity fans that grew up in the area or as fans of the Cardinals were expected too, among those might be Scott Bakula, Jenna Fischer, John Goodman, Jon Hamm, Kevin Kline, rapper Nelly, Phyliss Smith, or Billy Bob Thornton. One might well spot friends of La Russa too, such as Bill Parcells or Bobby Knight. Bob Costas, who grew up in New York rooting for the Cardinals, and Greg Amsinger, who did a stint with KMOX a few years back and was a huge Cardinal fan, would be on hand. With more than 70 former players living in the St. Louis area, one could maybe spot Lou Brock, Jack Clark, Bob Gibson, Joe Magrane, Mike Matheny, Stan Musial, Red Schoendienst, Ozzie Smith, and a host of St. Louis Cardinals "old-timers." Eighty-year-old Whitey Herzog might have made it to the park but he "suffered a nasty fall" about a month before and was on the mend.

Tickets were hard to come by and expensive. Many fans purchased their tickets through eBay, Stub Hub, or on Craigslist; though some still took their chances outside, looking for brokers selling tickets at huge markups.[574] A standing-room-only ticket went for $300 and other tickets ranged in excess of $1000. With a capacity of just under 47,000, that meant a lot of Cardinal Nation, as well as Ranger fans, would have to find alternative ways to view the game. Some liked the privacy of their homes without the distractions of crowds, but others wanted the ambience of watching the game surrounded by other fans. The bars around the stadium were packed, including the newly opened Three Sixty atop Ballpark Hilton. It provided a spectacular view of Busch Stadium across the Ballpark Village parking lot. The office towers bordering the stadium also offered great views and "have enjoyed private baseball watching parties for years."[575]

The 46,406 fans entering the park had to pass through more intense security. Fans received a plastic World Series lanyard to display their ticket and a rally towel. The color scheme for the World Series was controlled by MLB. This year they chose an Army green and beige motif that did not favor the red and white colors of the Cardinals or the red, white, and blue of the Rangers. Many could be spotted sporting World Series jackets for warmth and style including Michelle Obama and Jill Biden, as well the three Cardinal pitchers designated to throw out the first pitches of the game: starter, but on the disabled list all season, Adam Wainwright, and Hall-of-Famers Bob Gibson and Bruce Sutter. It was a memorable trio since all had been "on the mound for the last out in the decisive game of the Cardinals' previous four World Series."[576] The traditional Clydesdales did not make an appearance; instead soldiers from Fort Leonard Wood ceremoniously took the field to unfurl an enormous American flag. The national anthem was sung by Scotty McCreery, an "American Idol" winner. At the seventh inning stretch "God Bless America" was sung by U. S. Air Force Staff Sergeant Brian Owens.[577] After two games, the series split. Now, the only chance for the Cards was to take at least one in Arlington and hope for a chance to return home; for the Rangers, victory at home was the goal.

Fans in Texas presented a mix of die-hard Cardinal enthusiasts and hometown Ranger fanatics. It only made sense that some folks held a strong allegiance to the Midwest city, as for a long time St. Louis was the only major league baseball affiliate close to the southwest region. When growing up in Texas, former President George W. Bush listened to KMOX and the voices of Harry Caray and Jack Buck. He noted, "It made me a baseball fan…To appreciate the value of the St. Louis Cardinals… [with] a fantastic fan base"; but as a former owner and an active part of the Rangers in the 1990s, he claimed his allegiance to them.[578] Cards' top minor-league prospect, Shelby Miller, grew up in Brownwood, Texas, and his Dad, Mitch, a firefighter, would be rooting for the Redbirds.[579] A lot of transplanted Midwesterners, like Jake Evert of Austin and Nick Nolan and his wife Kelly from Houston, had settled in the southwest but remained part of Cardinal Nation. Cards' 1920s star, Rogers Hornsby, grew up in Texas and returned there every off-season as well as after his playing career. In the '50s, he managed minor-league teams in the Lone Star state. A grandson of Hornsby, 64-year-old Rogers Hornsby III, was in Arlington for the series; he lives in Denison, Texas, about 80 miles north of Dallas. He cheered on his grandfather's team as did his cousin, Brad Hornsby, in the games in St. Louis. A lot of fans in Texas continued their love of the Cardinals.

In fact, Tim McLaughlin, who was co-owner of the Smokehouse restaurant, grew up in Town and Country, a St. Louis suburb. During the regular season, he usually kept at least one TV in the establishment fixed on Cardinal games, and he said he got quite a following from local fans who appreciated being able to catch the game. He was tempted to turn the place into a "bar for Cardinals' expatriates," but his co-owner was a Rangers fan, so that probably would not have gone over very well.

There were a lot of St. Louis folks in town for the Saturday and Sunday games. The St. Louis Rams were playing the Dallas Cowboys on Sunday afternoon and the stadiums were within walking distance of each other. Rather than hold a team meeting the night before the big game, Coach Steve Spagnuolo took his entire Rams team to Game Three of the World Series. The football team was off to a bad start with no wins posted, and he thought the Cardinals could provide some inspiration for his team.[580] A huge contingent of Cardinals front office personnel flew down for Game Three.

The game-feel atmosphere in Arlington was quite different from that in St. Louis. The Rangers had been in Texas only since 1972 when the second Washington Senators (1961-1971) moved from the nation's capital. They had a short history compared to the storied tradition of the Cardinals' franchise, especially the ten World Championships, second only to the New York Yankees.

Texans were more supportive of football than baseball. Nick Nolan noticed, on his drive over from Houston, the radio conversation was still about the Cowboys—WHAT?—it is the World Series! Everything in St. Louis, not just the week of the World Series but weeks leading up to it, was about baseball. People sported their Cardinal red, hung signs of support, and talked baseball even to strangers. The Cards ruled the newspapers, radios, blogs, etc. St. Louis showed it is the best baseball town in America. The heart of Cardinal Nation thrives on baseball and it really comes alive during the postseason; that is what the season is all about, fighting to make it to the playoffs and then the World Series. It matters, and one can feel that in the air not only in the stadium but in St. Louis and the surrounding areas.

The Cardinals draw 3 million plus each year, but the Rangers never drew that number. The location of the Rangers' stadium in the suburbs had a similar feel to other newer stadiums that sit away from the heart of the downtown. Complexes where the Cards played in the postseason this year, Philadelphia, Milwaukee, and Arlington, were surrounded by parking lots that lend more to tailgating, while the Cardinals site is a vital part of the city surrounded by hotels, bars, and restaurants.

Kelly Nolan noted she and her husband left Houston "early to soak in the environment, but we can't find any bars around here." Even the opening ceremonies in Arlington were different; the one celebrity brought out was Nolan Ryan and he owned the team; they do not have scores of Hall of Famers to return for the excitement of World Series plays and, of course, no Clydesdales pranced around to electrify the crowd. Bob Hawkins of Wentzville, a suburb of St. Louis, remarked, "There is just a different feel here. The excitement isn't the same."[581]

No ballpark in the majors was more favorable to runs or homers than the Rangers' that season.[582] This was what the Rangers were waiting for, to return home to the American League style of play, gorilla ball, that is a hitter's game with the Designated Hitter rule in effect now that the games had moved to an American League park. The playing conditions proved advantageous to both teams once the games shifted 650 miles southwest. The temperatures were about 30 degrees warmer, predicted to be about 80 degrees, and this being a hitter's park it would seem to benefit both teams, though of course, the edge was given to the Rangers as home team.

That Saturday night in Texas, though, Pujols simply destroyed all pitchers he faced and all logic of how to pitch to him. He bested whoever faced him. He went five for six and drove in six runs, hitting three homers and becoming only the third player in World Series history to accomplish that feat along with Babe Ruth, who did it twice, and Reggie Jackson. Joe Buck remarked that he had "murdered the ball," and his side-kick Tim McCarver marveled, "Staggering…I've got to admit that there are some balls…that are hit that absolutely take your breath away. And that one hit by Pujols did exactly that."[583] Albert came back in the seventh to connect for a two-run homer. The final score was 16-7, as the Cards pulled ahead of the series 2-1. St. Louis "scored their most runs in their World Series history, an expanse of 108 games."[584] Ranger fans were shocked, Cardinal fans elated.

The country was awed by the ability of this St. Louis team, especially the showing of Albert Pujols. La Russa noted, "He's been great for a long time, but this has to be the greatest…Has someone had a better day—ever—in the World Series?" Pujols humbly turned the focus on his teammates. "It shows you the kind of club we have. Everybody was concentrating on the tough loss we had in St. Louis a couple of days ago and how we bounce back." He went on to say, "We flipped the page and came ready to play."[585]

October 23rd, a beautiful, sunny Sunday afternoon, traffic around Rangers Ballpark and Cowboys Stadium was horrendous. It was one of those rare occasions where the Rangers and Cowboys were playing on the same day, so fans arrived early. Over 130,000 fans vied for parking spaces; that small section of real estate was the place to be from early afternoon to late night. It was a football/baseball double-header and involved Texas and Missouri devotees. Just as quickly as the Cards' bats on Saturday sparked red hot, on Sunday they were cold. One could not believe it was the same team. For the first time in postseason play, the Cards failed to score first; in fact, for the first time since August 27th, they were shut out. They lost 4-0.[586] A trip back to St. Louis was assured.

Game 5 on Monday evening at Rangers Ballpark was probably the most bizarrely managed game of Tony La Russa's career. For non-Cardinal fans, and Tony La Russa haters, this was a comedy of errors so enjoyable to watch on a national stage. It could have cost the Cardinals the World Series and sullied the reputation of one of the most winning managers to ever take the field. The strategist had lost his magic touch with the bullpen, not from what he called, but from what was not heard that he called. Supposedly the message was garbled or could not be heard in the loud ballpark, somehow there was miscommunication. Bullpen coach Derek Lilliquist later said he did not understand the message.[587]

The crazy phone mishap filled the air waves until the beginning of Game 6. Tony admitted to embarrassment when he held a press conference to explain his version. He took the blame. But media guys around the country doubted the story and thought surely there was more to it than a phone snafu. When La Russa appeared before the media, he was quite calm which was out of character for the skipper when his tactics were questioned. Media speculated he was covering up for someone else, but no one ever came forward. La Russa said that he thought maybe he had mentioned Motte's name after Lilliquist had already hung up the phone.[588] For the first time, the Cards trailed in the series; Rangers pulled within one game of their first World Series win.

The teams returned to St. Louis. Word came from Commissioner Bud Selig and MLB's executive vice president of baseball operations, Joe Torre, of the postponement of Game 6 until the next evening due to rain.[589] Game 6 moved to Thursday and Game 7, if necessary, would be held Friday evening. Throughout the city visitors busily reshuffled their schedules to assure they would still get to take in the game they had planned.

Game 6 showed the Cards do-or-die efforts. It was simply an unbelievable evening that defied logic. Twice the Cardinals were down to their final out, their final strike, and managed to tie, take it into extra innings, have the Rangers pull ahead, and then, in grand fashion, home towner David Freese hit a walk-off home run to take the series to Game Seven. The Cardinals became "the first team in Series history to score in the 8th, 9th, 10th and 11th innings."[590]

The game was one of the most exciting in the history of baseball, not just for Cardinal Nation, but for anyone who sat through the 11-inning contest; it was a game they would never forget.[591] Cards won 10-9. Busch Stadium rang out with "Don't Stop Believing." The Cardinals did it again! This unbelievable come-from-behind team would not go away. The young hero of the day noted, "It's Cardinal baseball. This is how they teach us. You never give up." Freese continued, "It was all about surviving. It was all about getting to tomorrow, and Game 7."[592]

Ranger's manager, Ron Washington's job was to uplift his team, to get them ready for Game 7.[593] La Russa had a bigger problem. Basically, he advised his players, "Put Game 6 in a box, and put it away." He urged his veterans to reach out to other team members and sell them on the idea that as hard as it was they had to move beyond Game 6.[594] Win the whole thing and it goes down in history as the most spectacular game that allowed the team to move on; lose Game 7 and the Rangers winning their first World Series becomes the story that history writes and fans remember.

Cards won Game 7, 6-2. The 107th World Series was history and the St. Louis Cardinals picked up their 11th title. Bedlam took over Busch Stadium as confetti drifted onto the field, fireworks sparked overhead, and fans and players alike went berserk. Exhilaration hit the field, the town, the state, and Cardinal Nation.

Downtown St. Louis went mad with honking horns, fans climbing on the treasured Cardinal statues, others embracing complete strangers, and some running into the opened stadium gates to become part of the historic post-game celebration. Along with his MVP for the National League Championship Series, Freese picked up the MVP for the World Series with his five extra-base hits, one important home run, and a .348 batting average. He posted more RBIs in a single postseason than any other player. Carpenter, too, had a phenomenal postseason setting a record by winning four postseason games, taking his record to 9-2 overall in his postseasons with St. Louis (7-0 at home with a 2.15 ERA.) La Russa became "only the ninth manager in major-league history to win at least three World Series… [and] gave the St. Louis fans their second World Series title in six years."[595]

On October 30th, Albert Pujols awoke as a free agent. By all accounts, Pujols, a .328 hitter, would remain a Cardinal. As of January, it was reported the team had offered him a $200 million contract for nine years, and Pujols backed away. Now with free agency all would see what the market would bear.[596]

The World Series victory parade was Sunday, October 30th, at 4. The majestic event was done the Cardinal Way with all the tradition, pomp, and ceremony of a team used to the high spirits of World Championship celebrations. Streets were a sea of red as several hundred thousand fans lined the parade route, hung from trees, leaned out of office windows, and planted themselves in the parking garages that overlooked the parade route. Inside the stadium DeWitt noted, "This 11th Cardinals World Championship will always be remembered as one of baseball's greatest achievements." He praised the fans, noting, "I would expect nothing less from these great fans. You are the reason we were able to assemble a team of this caliber." La Russa "paid respect to his team for never surrendering, even when 10.5 games out of wild-card contention on Aug. 25th, or when they faced three postseason opponents with superior records—Philadelphia, Milwaukee, and Texas." Freese stated, "I got the greatest phone call of my life, [December 2007] that I had been traded to the St. Louis Cardinals."

Fans, too, shared their feelings and excitement for the events of October. Chris Ambrose of Chesterfield, Missouri, said "It just seemed improbable. It's one of the greatest World Series of all time." Another Chesterfield resident, Brenda Haalboom, who held season tickets for 30 years, exclaimed, "The thing about St. Louis fans, even when the Cardinals were playing bad, the stadium was filled. The Cardinals are St. Louis." Fireworks ended the rally. It was truly the end of a very eventful and extraordinary season. Little did most people in Cardinal Nation realize it was also the end of an era in the history of the St. Louis Cardinals.[597]

CHAPTER TWELVE

CHANGE IN THE AIR

On October 31, 2011, Tony La Russa announced his retirement in major league baseball managing. La Russa showed little emotion at the press conference except when he referred to "his wife Elaine and two daughters for putting up without him over much of the past 33 years." He stated, "There isn't one (factor) that dominates (my decision). They all just come together telling you your time is over." He emphatically stated that he would not manage again even though he was only 35 wins away from capturing the record for the second-most managerial wins. La Russa hoped to continue in some capacity working for baseball. While with the Cardinals, La Russa took them to three World Series and won two championships. He led the team to the postseason nine times, including his first season in St. Louis. DeWitt Jr. noted, "Tony leaves behind a legacy of success that will always be remembered as one of the most successful eras in Cardinals history."[598]

La Russa, a polarizing figure, gradually came to be embraced by a significant portion of the fan base. Over the years he won over many of the skeptics, but he was constantly facing second-guessing by fans who thought they knew the game, and the way to play it, better than one of the wisest managers in the game. St. Louis fans like to see those of their organizations embrace the city and live there year-round. While Tony was visible during the season and attended many off-season events, it caused ire to some that he did not live there year-round, nor did his family, even during the playing season. Beyond all the personal stuff, though, what really mattered was his ability to lead the team, and for 16 years he brought winning baseball to St. Louis. Over the years, detractors called for La Russa to leave; well now he was gone, but he left "on his terms, not theirs."[599]

Mike Eigenbrod, a fan, remarked, "He brought class to the management with the Cardinals. A true respect for players, management, fans and true love of the game." Another fan, Sara Macke Crook, noted "His achievements speak for themselves…He did St. Louis proud."[600] Cardinal Nation would miss its skipper, the man who racked up 1,408 victories and took the Redbirds to three World Series in eight seasons— more than any other manager, and no one matched his record of winning percentages for divisional races since the three-tiered system began in 1995. His teams "played in nine first-round series, winning seven of them."[601]

On November 14th the Cardinals announced their new manager, 41-year-old Mike Matheny. He signed a two-year contact for an undisclosed amount. Matheny, a .239 hitter, played in the big leagues 13 years and was a member of La Russa's "teams that went to the playoffs four times in five seasons."[602] Many were surprised by the decision. Matheny had no experience managing, but his experience as a leader and respected catcher in major league baseball, who learned to work with diverse personalities as well as strategizing about the game, served him well in knowing how to call the game and work with the team. Mozeliak hoped Matheny would give opportunities to home-grown players from the Cardinals minor league operation and promoted this with Matheny, though he noted, "the approach will always be that the manager writes the lineup."[603]

Matheny invited Whitey Herzog to spring training and extended an invitation to Hall-of-Famer Ozzie Smith, who had virtually been off the scene for most of the La Russa era. Matheny reached out to Musial and Schoendienst and stayed in touch with La Russa. He took time to closely relate with the support staff, "from the video room to the medical staff to the clubhouse managers." He contacted farm director John Vuch to get up-to-date information on the minor league players. Matheny did not want to "reinvent the wheel." He wanted to help the players improve individually and he understood what the organization, the fans, and the players wanted from him, "collectively they all want to repeat what they just did."[604] A new era of Cardinal history began.

December arrived, and the Cardinals were honored as Baseball America's Organization of the Year. Their star, Pujols, had not yet signed. DeWitt and Mozeliak remained confident that Pujols would return to the fold, though everyone knew the decision was nearing and they were eager to get the deal signed. On December 7th, "the Cardinals offered a 10-year contract for $220 million."[605] On December 8th, the Los Angeles Angels ended the suspense. They talked with Pujols' agent, Dan Lozano, and owner Arte Moreno had a 30-minute conversation with Pujols and his wife Deidre. The hometown favorite left with more money, an extensive lengthy contract, the west coast, the American League, and eventually the DH. The Angels signed the 31-year-old to a 10-year, $254 million deal. In addition, there was "a 10-year personal service provision, something the Cardinals were reluctant to discuss, according to sources familiar with the process."[606]

The announcement shocked Cardinal Nation and the baseball world. The complex decision included the money, the length of contract, the post-playing years' commitment, the lack of a personal touch, the perceived lack of respect, and a miscommunication that emerged. All versions were tainted by personal experience and emotion. The bottom line was, Pujols, as other fan-favorite Cardinals of the past, would no longer wear a Cardinal uniform.

It was interesting to see how the fans dealt with the news. Of course, most were upset and showed it in many ways, labeling Pujols, "Lebron James and burning their No. 5 jerseys." Some said, "Good riddance, it was all about money" and "how much money does one need." A few analyzed, what was the "real financial benefit for Albert" between making $21 million a year in St. Louis and $25 million in Los Angeles, and demonstrated that the higher cost of living, higher taxes, and more, meant that Pujols would have benefitted better financially with the St. Louis offer. Others doubted his sincerity about wanting to be a Cardinal for life, and some mocked his Christianity that revealed he received a message from God as to what would be best for him and his family.[607] A group of fans felt insulted that someone would dare turn down the opportunity to be part of the tradition of Cardinal Nation and to have a statue alongside the great Stan the Man.

Others understood the move as an economic decision and did not blame Pujols for accepting a better deal; after all, many folks move around the country for better financial stability. Many faced the reality that the Cardinals should have locked him up a long time ago before he was lured by free agency. Yet, early on it did not appear that fans were upset with either Cardinals' chairman, Bill DeWitt, or General Manager John Mozeliak. They saw that the Cardinals put a good offer forward and that "it would have been foolish for the Cardinals to match the Angels' bid of 10 years and $254 million for a player who turns 32 next month."[608]

Surprisingly, there were mixed views not only in Cardinal Nation but throughout the world of sports. Cardinal fans had a hard time accepting that Pujols did not feel secure with their organization that holds the tradition of the team and closeness with former players. That association with former players is seen as the Cardinal Way—a glorious tradition and respect for those who played throughout the great history of the team. But they also had to know not everyone with a storied career with the team had been openly embraced by the organization. Even the greats of the game, including Bob Gibson and Ozzie Smith, did not fill key roles with the Cardinals organization as did others who had received post-playing employment opportunities. Smith had been invited to many events over the years, but certainly felt miffed by his departure under La Russa. Pujols had seen this, as well as the worship and acceptance of Musial, Schoendienst, Brock, etc. It appeared that Pujols looked for a guarantee more than a playing career to be associated with a team for the rest of his life. Pujols was not the only player since free agency to leave beloved fans and he would not be the last. He gave the fans 11 great years of entertainment and winning records; Cardinal fans are smart and forgiving. They appreciated having seen him play and, likely, would welcome him back; but only time will tell that outcome

Pujols mentioned that the signing "wasn't about the money. I'm going to die saying that, because it wasn't about the money. It was about the commitment." Pujols appeared to be enthusiastic about playing for the Angels and mentioned that his new owner gave him "a greater sense of belonging." He remarked, "It was about the way he made me feel. Arte made me feel like he wanted me to be with the Angels forever. He doesn't want me to be 37 years old and go somewhere else." Perhaps that was the same wish the Cardinals had, but for whatever reason, Albert did not feel the love, the acceptance, as much after 11 years of association with the Cardinal organization as he did in one short phone conversation with Moreno.

Lozano noted the quandary of the public's awareness of the negotiations; "I think a lot of people believe this decision was made on dollars and years. That's not what it was based on. You have to understand there were other outside factors that affected this decision." Perhaps in the end it all came down to "feelings." DeWitt came across much more business-like than the personal approach of a fellow Latino who figuratively "speaks the same language" as Pujols. Albert said that, in just a brief telephone encounter with Moreno, he felt wanted. In Moreno's offer, he saw a swiftness of decision that lacked the cautionary approach of the Cardinals that showed a seriousness of intent. Albert expressed, in his conversation to Moreno, that whatever decision he made, "this was going to be my last contract." Moreno took him at his word and made it happen.

Pujols appeared concerned with how St. Louis fans would react to his departure. "They're calling me 'liar' and all that stuff. That's all good. I went through that when I made the decision. It was tough.[609] Pujols had been part of the St. Louis community since he moved there as a 21-year old rookie. His family was highly invested in the area with a charitable foundation, involvement in the Down Syndrome Center, a home, close relationships, and a restaurant. He acclaimed the community "made me into the man I am right now. Knowing I had to play somewhere else was tough. It was emotional. I still love my fans back in St. Louis. We built a family there." His wife remarked, "We still love St. Louis and that will never change."[610] She also noted that "neither she nor Albert is angry with the Cardinals organization and that they have respect for owner Bill DeWitt and the entire organization." Pujols acknowledged he would carry St. Louis in his heart and "I have been honored to be able to wear the Cardinal uniform the last 11 seasons, and I want to thank the entire Cardinal organization, my teammates, coaches, managers, and staff for everything they have given to me as well."[611] DeWitt and Moreno, both savvy businessmen, looked at the bottom line from their perspectives. At the heart of both offers was the fact that it was a business decision for the Angels and the Cardinals.

John Mozeliak noted his confidence in the Cardinals' wealth of players where the "focus over the last four or five years is really making sure that our minor-league system is going to be able to produce some everyday players or middle to top of the rotation type of starters...we still think we have a lot of positives coming." He continued, "There's no doubt he's been the identity of this organization for the past decade, and trying to push just one button or try to say you're not going to feel that loss would be very difficult to say, especially in this environment."[612] One thing was clear, without Pujols taking down $14 million a year, the Cardinals freed up money to bolster their chances to win in 2012 without their star.

The loss of Pujols highlighted many modern baseball practices. It showed that money matters. Without a salary cap, as other sports have, middle-and small-market teams do not have the financial clout that the larger markets do. The DH, whether wanted or not, is here to stay and the power of the American League to extend a long-ball hitter's career is an advantage over the National League.

Both teams noticed advantages and disadvantages from this one transaction. For the Angels, this was a big gamble, not necessarily in the short-run, but a 10-year playing commitment for a 31-year-old player, even with the caliber of Pujols, was still a chance. Within the first day of signing, the Angels sold 1,000 additional season tickets and 500 online ticket packages.[613] For St. Louis, there was no doubt this would be a great loss in the identity of the team, in a legend of the game, but financially the team was richer and would find ways to use the money. The owners were committed to winning. The team they built around Pujols was strong competitively and that strategy showed he was not the only consistent player. The Cardinals had a good farm system, the same system produced the likes of Pujols; they would continue to bring good players. Disgruntled fans or not, people would come out for good baseball, and the organization would continue to invest in players who performed at high levels. Stars would continue to filter through the Cardinal organization and continue to entertain St. Louis fans.

A New Era in St. Louis

In the meantime, the 2012 season came, and the Cardinals survived without La Russa or Pujols. Matheny's rookie managerial year showed his style. Basically, he worked on a running game to produce smart base-running to block the numerous double-plays the team hit into and worked to move runners along. Fans continued to come out to see the stars of the previous World Series and weigh in on the prowess of Mike Matheny.

St. Louis ended the 2012 season in second place, 88-74, and secured a wild card position. They beat the first place Atlanta Braves in the wild card game, went on to beat the Washington Nationals in five for the NLDS but lost to the San Francisco Giants, 3 games to 1, for the NL Championship.

Baseball changes to embrace the cultural changes of a more modern society while at the same time holding onto some of the nostalgic traditions that continue to make the sport beloved and one that will continue to draw fans no matter what changes. For St. Louis, that love of the game, the loyalty of the Cardinals continued to inspire millions to "meet me in St. Louie" for a delightful heavenly experience at Busch Stadium.

The 2013 season proved an exciting one in the River City with the Cards compiling the best record in the National League with 97-65. St. Louis took the NLDS by besting the Pirates in five and then mowed down the Dodgers 4 games to 2 for their nineteenth National League Pennant. The World Series pitted the Cards against the Boston Red Sox, who went on to win in six. It was an impressive showing for Matheny's second season. Thirty-six of their victories came from rookie pitchers who promised more good years and solidified the Cards' investment in their farm system. Fans continued to show their support for winning baseball. For the 10th consecutive season attendance at Busch soared over the 3 million mark.

Spring 2014 finally ushered in the opening of the long-awaited Ballpark Village adjacent to Busch Stadium. Crowds filled the numerous restaurants and visited the Hall of Fame Museum in record numbers. The whole atmosphere around the ballpark came alive during game time as well as when the team traveled. The television broadcasts picked up the services of longtime FOX network broadcaster and former St. Louis Cardinals player, Tim McCarver, who would handle about 30 games that season.

A highlight of the season was the 50th anniversary reunion of the 1964 World Champion St. Louis Cardinals, a team in which McCarver, Bob Gibson, Lou Brock, and Mike Shannon were a part. Many of the former team participated in the celebration. Tony La Russa was inducted into the Hall of Fame, though chose not to wear a Cardinals uniform feeling that all the teams he had been associated with had influenced the manager he became.

That season witnessed the call of the promising young right fielder, Oscar Taveras, a great prospect and dubbed by many to be the next

Albert Pujols. In his first major league debut, he homered in the fifth against the San Francisco Giants, and the Cards took the game 2-0. For the second straight year, the Cardinals finished the season in first as they racked up a 90-72 season. They beat the Los Angeles Dodgers in the Division Series, but then lost in five games to the San Francisco Giants for a bid at the World Series.

Just ten days later, before the fifth Game of the World Series, it was announced that Taveras, vacationing in his home country of the Dominican Republic, had died, along with his 18-year-old girlfriend, in a car accident. Test results revealed in November that Taveras was intoxicated. It was a sad commentary on the problems of alcohol and its impact on a team that had already suffered from the death of Josh Hancock in 2007. While some of the players benefited from the programs initiated by the team, this young 22-year-old had not heeded the warnings.

The loss would be devastating personally for the team as well as the promise of what his career could have meant. His teammate and fellow Dominican, Carlos Martinez, a pitcher, received permission to change his uniform number to Taveras' 18 as a tribute. In January 2015, DeWitt announced plans to renovate a baseball field in the Dominican Republic to honor Taveras and the team wore black patches throughout the 2015 season to respect the rookie.[614]

Cards got off to a great start in 2015, winning 22 of their first 29 games, and then on September 30th, they took their 100th game and clinched the division title. They went down to defeat at the hands of the Chicago Cubs in the division series. In 2016, they posted a record of 86-76 and did not even make the wild card. It was the first time since 2010 they did not make the playoffs. In 2017 the Cards named Mike Girsch General Manager and promoted John Mozeliak to President of Baseball Operations. That season, their 12th year at Busch Stadium, they posted an 83-79 record, and for the second year in a row, missed appearing in the playoffs. That was uncharacteristic for this franchise since playoff berths have become the common norm in the newer stadium.

Staff changes came pre-season 2018 with the release of pitching coach Derek Lilliquist and bullpen coach Blaise Ilsley. Mike Maddux was named the new pitching coach and Bryan Eversgerd the bullpen coach. They also brought back fan favorite third base coach Jose Oquendo who had spent the last two years as a special assistant to the general manager at the team's Roger Dean Stadium in Jupiter, Florida. Willie McGee joined the coaching staff and Mike Shildt became the bench coach.

Those changes were not enough to help the team find a winning way back to the playoffs. By mid-season they had a 47-46 record and rested in third place, seven games behind the first place Chicago Cubs.

The weekend before the All-Star break, following another loss, the team fired manager, Mike Matheny. It was rumored that there were problems in the clubhouse with Matheny showing favoritism for some players and virtually ignoring others. This was a major change for the Cardinals.

The organization had not fired a manager mid-season since Joe Torre in 1995. De Witt bought the team after the 1995 season and had only two managers. Tony La Russa ruled for 16 years and Matheny was in his 7th year. Overall Matheny had a good run with a 591-473 record. He managed over 1,000 games and his first four years he took the team to the playoffs; but clearly a message was being sent. Lackadaisical play was unacceptable, the team was expected to make the playoffs. That was the Cardinal Way and it appeared this would be the third season in a row where they would be left out.

Mike Shildt was named interim manager. He had experience in that capacity with the Cardinals minor leagues and had led some of the current team in the past. Within six weeks, with a 26-12 record, he agreed to continue in that role until the end of the 2020 season. The Cardinals finished the year in third place with an 88-74 record.

The 2019 season shows promise for Cardinal Nation, promise that the St. Louis Cardinals will once again be hosting playoffs and perhaps capturing their 12th World Series title. A major reason for that confidence rests with the signing of free agent, left-handed relief pitcher Andrew Miller and more importantly a trade the team completed in December 2018. They acquired six-time National League All-Star first baseman and Gold Glover Paul Goldschmidt from the Arizona Diamondbacks. Goldschmidt is seen as a perfect fit for the Cardinals. He loves baseball and is one of the finest players in the game. He will bolster the strong Cardinal lineup and allow Shildt to shift Matt Carpenter to third base and strengthen the bench by delegating Jedd Gyorko to reserve status.

Former Cardinals and current players are happy with the new addition of Goldschmidt. Reggie Jackson sought him out and told *USA TODAY* columnist, Bob Nightengale, "He's a guy I really wanted to meet because I've admired him so long. There were a lot of moves and a lot of money spent this winter, but that was the best acquisition by any team. He's everything you want in a ballplayer." He noted that, "St. Louis is going to love this guy." Adam Wainwright stated, "He comes exactly as advertised, because I don't think you can have higher words of praise going into something. So many of his former teammates texted me and said, 'Dude, this guy is going to be your all-time favorite teammate. Just wait until you see it.'"

Not surprisingly, Goldschmidt reinforces the idea of blest player. He is thrilled to be a Cardinal, stating: "Everything I heard about St. Louis is more than great." He added: "I can't wait to play in front of the St. Louis fans now. I know how much they're really in the game with the reputation of just appreciating good baseball." [615]

Goldschmidt was so eager to prove his loyalty that he agreed to an extended contract while still at spring training in Jupiter, Florida. He signed a $130 million contract that assures his place through 2024. He is open to win and excitingly looks forward to playing on a World Series team.

With Harrison Bader, Paul DeJong, Yadier Molina, Marcell Ozuna, Kolten Wong and other strong teammates the 2019 season will be another fun run for Cardinal Nation, especially if Wacha and Wainwright bring their game. Five *St. Louis Post-Dispatch* sportswriters predict the team will finish either first in the National League Central or capture the wild card.

So Cardinal fans go ahead and once again believe in dreams. Believe you and your team will reach the Fall Classic. Afterall, the beloved St. Louis Blues won their first Stanley Cup in 2019. They went from last to first and proved miracles happen. When they beat the Boston Bruins in Boston, St. Louis fans noted the revenge for the Red Sox stealing the 2004 World Series in a sweep and in St. Louis. Diehard St. Louis sports fans love the Blues and the Cardinals. The best thing they could hope for would be taking the Stanley Cup and the World Series in the same year.

Go Cards! Cardinal Nation believe!

CONCLUSION

St. Louis baseball has certainly changed over the last century. Not just the location of the parks but in the way of economic, political, and social aspects played out within the cultural institution of the sport. The overall culture and society at large have changed too. The changes played out by human actors demonstrate an unbalanced, but coveted relationship that has endured between owners, players, and patrons. Though the game has changed a lot since 1882, customers still support the baseball enterprise in St. Louis. The bond between owner, players, and fans has altered as well, but in the modern era it is probably the strongest it has ever been. In the twenty-first century, baseball purists search to find a way back to the mythical world where the game was played for the love of the sport, if that day ever existed, while newer fans, living a faster-paced lifestyle, want a shorter, faster game.

It is the business of baseball to find intersections through new marketing strategies, inroads of technology, and mass communications that satisfy all markets if the sport is to thrive and survive for future generations. The Cardinal organization, under the DeWitt family, understands its role more than any previous owners in keeping baseball exciting and bringing in the fans as they continually work to bolster their relationship with their fans.

Throughout the years, the owners have shown that for most patrons the connection is with the team, not the individual players. They continue to have favorite players but if a team lets a player go, trades him, or does not offer him the deal he wants, the fans willingly let him move on. They may be quite upset at the loss, but their loyalty remains with the team. Their mantra is "It's what's on the front of the jersey [team name] that matters not on the back [player's name]." Nothing proves this more than the departure of beloved Cardinal Albert Pujols. As well, most folks continue to follow the team of their youth; no matter where they move throughout their lives, their steadfast dedication tends to stay with the team they grew up with.

Old-time photos, newspaper articles, and reminiscences show that while some women followed the game early on, mainly males supported the enterprise; but today, the attendance at baseball events at Busch is 56 percent males compared to 44 percent females. Women over the years have taken some front office positions. Prior to the Winter Meetings, December 2018 MLB hosted the "Take the Field" symposium in Vegas to show support and help for including women in operations of the clubs. This indicates that a strong concern for women in the game exists.

Race and ethnicity show a different story, though. Long after Jackie Robinson broke the color-line, blacks and Latino/Hispanics have taken to the field and changed the face of the game; yet only a few have stepped off the field to seats of power and authority in the sport. The game continues to have a largely white audience with 91 percent being Caucasian, less than 6 percent African American, 2 percent Hispanic, and just 2 percent other.[616] It is difficult to judge who follows the game via social media outlets that garner local, national, and international attention.

Awareness to the issue of class has changed over the years regarding who attends the games. While some teams, including the Cardinals, find ways to give away tickets to "those in need," and to sponsor nights with lower admission rates, the ticket prices, transportation costs, parking fees, and concession expenses have long excluded most of those outside the middle and upper classes from physically attending the events. Though radio broadcasts and newspaper accounts help to keep those on the bottom economic scale abreast of the team's actions, the higher cost of cable, satellite radio, and the internet works to exclude those with discretionary income that spreads only so far.

Today, many continue to attend the games, though that no longer is the only way to be engaged in the sport of baseball. The fast-paced modern society has not taken away from what some see as a slow-paced game compared to other sports; rather, this era draws in more fans via the various media setups that help one stay up on the game. Coverage of the sport has moved far beyond physical attendance or following it through newspapers. Fans have magazines, books, radio, television, as well as films, plays, prayers, and songs devoted to their sport. Players even have individualized music that inspires them when they step up to the plate and die-hard fans easily recognize that signature piece as connected to the player. The message of the world of baseball is delivered 24/7, 365 days a year throughout blogs, chat rooms, message boards, e-mails, Facebook, tweets, MLB, ESPN, and numerous websites that link baseball fanatics through a global connection. The field of baseball's historical research has kept pace with social networking and will continue to do so.

Control and independence of the player has changed drastically from the days where player's professional lives were beholden to owners and organizations. In bygone years, legends were traded, cut, or forced into retirement at the whim of the owners. Control today rests as much with players/agents as with the club. The modern era presents a vast array of sources for fans to examine player deals and shows that clubs have a myriad of decisions to consider as they weigh the strength of the players and the bottom line for the club. Those concerns include the age of the player, the physical conditions, long- or short-term contracts, financial figures, and overall disposition of the athlete; but now the players are backed by the players union and have agents to help negotiate the draft, arbitration, collective bargaining, no-trade clauses, right-of-refusal, and free agency to explore their worth.

Some problems have been with the sport ages on end and continue to surface. Cheating in the game is difficult to nail down, and some see no problem with certain antics that others consider not playing by the rules. Substance on the ball or bat and stealing signs to some are considered a real taboo but others say it is all part of the game. Betting on contests was a part of the culture in the early years but the 1919 Black Sox Scandal exposed the damage cheating would bring to the game and in modern times gambling on the outcome is so frowned upon it continues to block baseball great Pete Rose from the Hall.

Drugs caused problems in society during the '70s and '80s that drifted into professional sports and ruined many a player's life. The steroid controversy has been taken on by Major League Baseball to the extent that testing has become routine, though it continues to be a problem as shown with the accusation against the National League MVP Ryan Braun and Yankee Alex Rodriguez. The sport will have to deal with what to do with the steroid-enhanced players when it comes time for the greats of that era to be considered for the Hall.

Alcohol, for society at large, was a problem in the nineteenth, twentieth, and twenty-first centuries—that endures. Repercussions of bad behavior from alcohol abuse plagued the game early on with rowdiness on and off the field, and the storied Cardinals were no exception. Modern day tales of the problems of drink still surface; but it seems the team, the patrons, and the players are learning to respectively address this issue. The higher price for alcoholic drinks, the limit of the number of drinks sold to an individual, and the no-sales after the seventh inning have shown a genuine concern for how to address the drinking, as has the support of a designated driver. For players and associates of the team, assisted programs of intervention and rehabilitation come on the heels of the tragedy of the consequences of a habitual problem. It demonstrates a commitment to recognize what might block one from achieving his full potential. That attention and recognition of possible setbacks has helped steer the team on a more compassionate path that benefits all, brings celebration in its own way, and saves lives. Tragically, the message did not resonate with their young prospect Oscar Taveras.

Within the context of baseball as an entertainment source, positions of power and powerlessness played out over the years to influence gender relations, racial hierarchy, and social control. Progressively throughout the twentieth century, government and big business united to increase control over a public space of entertainment, but unions and agents helped to level the playing field. Fans became more clearly under the financial and physical control of the owners, and social divisions distinctly separated the social classes that tended to mirror the societal structure outside the walls of the stadium.

Baseball has gone from an all-American fun pastime to a multi-billion-dollar industry that is competing more than ever with other sports such as football, basketball, hockey, and car racing. To recapture the feeling of the early twentieth century, new stadiums have been built throughout the last fifteen years. These post-modern structures, referred to as new-old traditional, have attempted to capture the spirit of days gone by. Owners believe that restoring the physical structure of the look of old parks and adding modern amenities to the newer stadiums will revive fan interest in the game.

Other changes to the game occurred throughout its history, and somehow the game survived, and fans adjusted. It is interesting that some things, like the DH, was only adopted by the American League, but with players hoping to extend their playing days it might well be that the National League will need to adopt that part of the game if they hope to hold onto players the quality of Pujols and Fielder. The changes to the traditional sport seemed to have paid off with increased revenues, but will the "newness" of the game pass that love of the game on to future generations? Only time will tell if baseball stays an integral part of the American identity, but it has endured a lot over the past century and continues to thrive.

American sports-venue architecture provides a notion of a throwaway society where it becomes cheaper to tear down and start afresh rather than restore. Except for Wrigley Field in Chicago and Fenway Park in Boston, no baseball stadium has lasted more than about a sixty-year time span. The building created helps to structure and create a revived community response. The life history of the structure enshrines the ideas, thoughts, values, and spirit of that interconnection of the neighborhood, owners, players, and patrons. For as long as it lasts, and some would say long after it is gone, the baseball park/stadium creates memories of the embodied values of a time and place. It memorializes the past and the memories connected to what went on many years before.

The structure of the playing arena as an object of design is important, but more paramount to saving baseball as a respected enterprise is the ability to capture the essence of the sport and sell that to the fan. To discover the innocence of the sport prior to the overzealous involvement of capitalism is a tall order and is probably impossible in today's consumer-oriented world. With the current player's salaries, lavish sporting venues, and expected profits, has baseball out priced itself for the common working-class fan? Does it matter? Will the scandals of the game, especially the steroid controversy, ruin the image of baseball? After the public announcement by Mark McGwire about his steroid use, St. Louis fans did not seem to have problems with his past. Most acknowledge that seeing him put the uniform back on as the team's hitting coach was Cardinal tradition at its best. Along with Tim McCarver and Pepper Martin, Mark McGwire was inducted into the 2017 St. Louis Hall of Fame. As this study concludes, the real controversy for loyal St. Louis fans is the money in the game and the lack of what is perceived as loyalty to a team, though not necessarily misdeeds by their former players.

The Albert Pujols departure may well serve as more damaging to the image of star power than the steroid era. The Pujols decision proved what ole Chris Von der Ahe, Sam Breadon, and Gussie Busch knew all along—that it does not matter who puts on the uniform. The allegiance rests with those who follow the front of the uniform, the birds on the bat. The tradition of Cardinal baseball lives on even without Albert, and the new era will show a continued devotion to the spirit of St. Louis, the Cardinals.

The combination of economic greed, alcohol, drugs, steroid use, and attempts of social control has ended baseball as it was a hundred years ago; but overall, American society's cultural phenomena has changed over that century too. The great American pastime continues, and die-hard fans are determined to stick with it. Cardinal Nation endures.

People have come to recognize that the buildings may be destroyed, but it is hard to believe that anything will ever kill the enthusiasm for the Cardinals. The team, a traditional institution, has survived numerous owners, managers, players, scandals, stadiums, and setbacks. While some fans have given up, others swear faithfulness to Cardinal Nation that is hard to extricate.

The buildings are paramount to the physical experience of the game, yet at the same time demolition of the brick and mortar help fans realize the game is not just about place. Place changes; but the sport, the spirit, the generational connection, and the team are a state of mind. The shrine can be destroyed but the bond, the relationship lives through the association with the designated place in the hearts and minds of those who follow the sport. Amid their memories of place, a desire to remember the sacred space of the game, fans pass the torch to a new generation that will continue to remember the way "baseball ought to be played."

Capitalism built America, and baseball is and has always been about business. It is the bottom line. The current baseball owners tend to believe the association between fans, owners, and the city favors no one because with higher player salaries and other expenses, the revenues seem to be dwindling each year; yet if that were true these capitalist owners would have long ago closed the doors and moved on.

Fans still flock to the games and revenues are up. It might not be the same folks filling the seats or the party rooms, but in cities like St. Louis, where baseball matters, the seats are full. Many, including former Cardinal star Bill White and sports historian Dr. Chuck Korr have espoused that the game "has always been about the money." That is true for players, owners, and fans. Love of the game plays an important part of the attraction of the sport; but if the game was free who would play, who would sponsor it, and who would watch? The more romantic times of yesteryear saw baseball as all-American as mom and apple pie, but in more recent time, folks clearly see the money, too, and realize its overall importance to how the game operates. Baseball, especially the St. Louis Cardinals, continues to be a rich tapestry that weaves together the influences of owners, players, and fans with the field.

Nothing is stagnant in relationships among individuals, organizations, or institutions. The historic continuum of the heritage of the Cardinals will be an interesting cultural study to follow through the twenty-first century and to note the changes that are sure to occur. A new era of Cardinal history will unfold that will unite a group of followers who come alive with spring training and live to capture the championship. It is a way of life that leaves a legacy many simply do not want to miss, for it is the spirit that stays alive no matter where the physical play happens. Cardinal Nation is a congregation of believers looking for that stimulating environment of the field of play that will keep the game alive and continue to prove that place matters in the realm of historical events, and all play their part.

APPENDIX

(1)

For America (9/11 Tribute)
A Poem by Jack Buck

Since this nation was founded, under God
More than 200 years ago
We have been the bastion of freedom
The light which keeps the free world aglow.

We do not covet the possessions of others,
We have rushed to help other nations,
Anything, Anytime, Anywhere,
To protect what we know is right.

We have been challenged by a cowardly foe,
Who strikes and then hides from our view!
With one voice, we say,
"There is no choice today,
There is only one thing to do."

Everyone is saying the same thing,
And praying that we end those senseless moments we are living.
As our fathers did before, we shall win this unwanted war.
And our children will enjoy the future we'll be giving.

(2)

NOT TODAY

Busch Stadium is not our house.
I will not waste your time this morning talking about the importance
of the Cardinals protecting our house in Game 6 of the NLCS.
I will not broach the obscenity of seeing Houston players
spilling champagne on our living-room carpet.

Busch Stadium is not our house.
It's much more important than that.

It's where many of us watched our first game,
caught our first foul ball, begged for our first autograph.
It's where Gibby ruled the mound, where Brock ran like the wind,
and where Ozzie made all the folks go crazy.

It's where the El Birdos dominated, where Sutter
struck out the last batter of 1982, where Mike Shannon
has worked since the joint opened in 1966.

The Ol' Redhead managed there.
Stan the Man played his harmonica there.
The White Rat led us back to glory there.

This is where Gussie drove the Clydesdales,
where Willie McGee tracked down fly balls,
where Joaquin Andujar summed up his philosophy
of life in one simple word. Youneverknow.

This is where Big Mac smacked No. 70,
where Tommy Lawless flipped his bat, where
GOOD GOD ALMIGHTY...
BRUMMER'S STEALING HOME!!!!!!!!

This is where the greatest St. Louis team
in Busch Stadium's history performed.
That's right, the 2004 Cardinals.

They had the best home-record in baseball. Right on that field.
Ted Simmons played there. Kenny Boyer managed there.
And a beloved old man in a bright red jacket told a mournful
nation why it was good and right to play baseball after Sept. 11.

My friends, Jack Buck's coffin rested on that field.
Darryl Kile pitched his last game there.
And many of us cannot walk into that stadium
without thinking of loved ones who are no longer with us.

Not today.
We don't lose today.

Not against the Houston Astros. Not against a wild-card team.
Not in Busch Stadium. No, it's not our house.

It's simply the place where our memories congregate,
where our baseball dreams are stored,
where the voices of millions of fans and
the ghosts of seasons past await their call to arms.

Folks, it's time to wake 'em up.

This is the year.

(3)

Our Father

Our Father who art in Saint Louis, Baseball be thy game.
Thy will be done, NL division will be won,
on the field, as well as in the bull pen.
Give us this day our bat and glove,
and forgive us our errors, as we forgive those who home run against us.
Lead us not into defeat, but…help us BEAT THE BREWERS.
In the name of the fans, Albert Pujols, and the Cardinals.

Amen

ABOUT THE AUTHOR
Connie F. Sexauer

Dr. Sexauer has taught at the University of Wisconsin–Marathon County for the past 16 years. She teaches U.S. History and Gender Studies. She attended St. Louis Community College, University of Missouri–St. Louis, and received her Ph.D. in history from the University of Cincinnati with a specialty in urban history. Connie was born and raised in St. Louis, MO and the subject of the St. Louis Cardinals has been a passion of hers for over fifty years. This book brings together her love of history, cultural studies, social change, and sports. She has had several articles published and has delivered national papers on this subject of America's favorite pastime.

You may contact Connie at connie.sexauer@yahoo.com

ENDNOTES

Introduction

1   Bruce Kuklick, *To Every Thing a Season: Shibe Park and Urban Philadelphia 1909-1976* (Princeton: Princeton University Press) 193.

2   Dolores Hayden, *The Power of Place: Urban Landscapes as Public History* (Cambridge, MA: The MIT Press, 1997) 15.

3   Joan M. Thomas, *St. Louis' Big League Ballparks* (Charleston: Arcadia, 2004) 9.

4   This book does not propose to offer a comprehensive study of the St. Louis Cardinals or certainly not of the stadiums as mere material culture. There are numerous books of that genre.

Chapter One

5   Rich Wolfe, *For Cardinal Fans Only!* (Phoenix: Lone Wolfe Press, 2003) 6. Another benefit of the game is its educational value as "the best math and geography teacher" that one could hope for.

6   Curt Smith, *Storied Stadiums: Baseball's History Through Its Ballparks* (New York: Carroll & Graf Publishers, 2001) 317; Rich Wolfe, *Remembering Jack Buck* (Phoenix: Lone Wolfe Press, 2002) 31.

7   Alan Ross, *Cardinals Glory* (Nashville: Cumberland House, 2005) 21. *St. Louis Post-Dispatch*, Jan. 19, 2015;

8   Jason McKee, "Bud Selig calls St. Louis best baseball town in America," *Kansas City Star*, Jan. 20, 2015.

9   Pre-game comments made by Joe Buck on FOXSPORTS, July 14, 2009.

10   Rich Wolfe, *For Cardinal Fans Only!* (Phoenix: Lone Wolfe Press, 2003) 94; Bob Costas, *Fair Ball: A Fan's Case for Baseball* (New York: Broadway Books, 2001) 76.

11   David Claerbaut, *Cardinals Essential: Everything You Need to Know to be a Real Fan!* (Chicago: Triumph Books, 2006) 2-4.

12   Tim McCarver, et al, *Diamond Gems: Favorite Baseball Stories from the Legends of the Game* (New York: McGraw Hill, 2008) 1-2.

13   Alan Ross, *Cardinals Glory* (Nashville: Cumberland House, 2005) 68-69.

14   Ron Green, Jr., *101 Reasons to Love the Cardinals* (New York: Stewart, Tabori & Chang, 2006) 57.

15   Tim McCarver, et al, *Diamond Gems: Favorite Baseball Stories from the Legends of the Game* (New York: McGraw Hill, 2008)140; Alan Ross, *Cardinals Glory* (Nashville: Cumberland House, 2005) 218.

16   Tim McCarver, et al, *Diamond Gems: Favorite Baseball Stories from the Legends of the Game* (New York: McGraw Hill, 2008) 45.

17   Rob Rains, *The Cardinals Fan's Little Book of Wisdom* (South Bend: Diamond Communications, Inc., 1994) 19.

18   Rob Rains, *Mark McGwire Home Run Hero* (New York: St. Martin's Press, 1998) 217.

19   Ibid., 211-212.

20   As in "We won the World Series," etc.

21   Rich Wolfe, *Remembering Jack Buck* (Phoenix: Lone Wolfe Press, 2002) 8-9.

22   Pre-game comments made by President Barack Obama on FOX-TV, July 14, 2009.

23   *Baseball as America: Seeing Ourselves Through Our National Game* (Washington, D. C.: National Baseball Hall of Fame and Museum, National Geographic) 28.

24   Rich Wolfe, *For Cardinal Fans Only!* (Phoenix: Lone Wolfe Press, 2003) 96.
25   Edward J. Rielly, *Baseball: An Encyclopedia of Popular Culture* (Lincoln: University of Nebraska Press, 2000) 253-254
26   Ron Green, Jr., *101 Reasons to Love the Cardinals* (New York: Stewart, Tabori & Chang, 2006) 97.
27   Roger Angell, *The Summer Game* (New York, Viking Press, 1972) 103. Mickey Mantle, Bob Feller, Bill Clinton, George W. Bush, John Goodman, George McGovern, Billy Bob Thornton, Warren Buffet, the list of noted celebrities who have acknowledged their faithful following of St. Louis teams throughout the years goes on and on. Bob Costas grew up on Commack, Long Island with fond memories of listening "to KMOX on my father's car radio through the crackle and static." He reflects, "I heard Harry and Jack Buck and I knew there was a certain romance about the team." Rich Wolfe, *For Cardinal Fans Only!* (Phoenix: Lone Wolf Publishing, 2003) 73, 96; Knowledge picked up by C. F. Sexauer from public interviews with some of these people.
28   Ron Green, Jr., *101 Reasons to Love the Cardinals* (New York: Stewart, Tabori & Chang, 2006) 98.
29   John Snyder, *Cardinals Journal* (Cincinnati: Emmis Books, 2006) 7.
30   Curt Smith, *Storied Stadiums: Baseball's History Through its Ballparks* (New York: Carroll & Graf Publishers, 2001) 57.
31   "Tampa Bay's Joe Maddon tips his cap, grew up St. Louis Cardinals Fan," Derrick Goold, *St. Louis Post-Dispatch*, Oct. 22, 2008; Rob Rains. *The Cardinals Fan's Little Book of Wisdom* (South Bend: Diamond Communications, Inc., 1994) 86.
32   September 11, 1969 Roger turned nine. For his birthday he received an AM transistor radio and tickets to a Cards-Mets game.
33   Interviews and email correspondence by C. F. Sexauer with Roger Drake and Glen Drake, January and March 2009. For other interesting and unusual stories of Cardinals fans see Rick Wolfe, *For Cardinal Fans Only!* (Phoenix: Lone Wolfe Press, 2003). This strange fascination for the Cardinals runs in the Drake family. His nephew, TJ lives in Atlanta where his mom, Bernie is a lifetime Braves fan and his dad, Glen avidly follows the Yankees, but TJ is a huge Cards fan. TJ, like his uncle Roger, believes that the St. Louis Cardinals are the best team in baseball. In the modern age T. J. is luckier than his uncle was growing up as he follows the box scores on the internet and TiVo's the games, as well as programs on the Cardinals that he might not be able to watch in real time. His room is decorated with Cardinal memorabilia, and his wardrobe consists of Cardinal shirts, sweatshirts and jackets. There are thousands of fans throughout the world who did not grow up in St. Louis, but they bleed red and have a fierce passion for the Cardinals.
34   Inscription credited to Baseball Commissioner Ford Frick at a ceremony honoring The Man at Stan's last game. Bob Broeg, *Memories of a Hall of Fame Sportswriter* (Champaign: Sagamore Publishing, 1995) 292.
35   Bob Broeg, *Memories of a Hall of Fame Sportswriter* (Champaign: Sagamore Publishing, 1995) 293.

Chapter Two
36   Joan M. Thomas, *St. Louis' Big League Ballparks* (Charleston: Arcadia, 2004) 9.
37   Robert Burnes, "From Nine Inches to Nine Acres to Ninety Years," *St. Louis Globe-Democrat*, May 1966. Some referred to the park as Grand Avenue Grounds and others came to call it Solari Park.

38 Joan M. Thomas, *St. Louis' Big League Ballparks* (Charleston: Arcadia, 2004) 9.
39 Benjamin G. Rader, *Baseball: A History of America's Game* (Urbana: University of Illinois Press, 2002) 38. Or to some it was known as Solari Park, as Solari lived in a two-story home on the property.
40 Peter Golenbock, *The Spirit of St. Louis: A History of the St. Louis Cardinals and Browns* (New York: Harper Entertainment, 2000) 7, 9, 13. The name of this park changed several times throughout the years including Grand Avenue Park. In 1881 it was renamed Sportsman's Park.
41 Ibid., 13
42 Mike Eisenbath, *The Cardinals Encyclopedia* (Philadelphia: Temple University Press, 1999) 8; Frederick G. Lieb, T*he St. Louis Cardinals: The Story of a Great Baseball Club* (New York: G. P. Putnam's Sons, 1950) 5; Peter Golenbock, *The Spirit of St. Louis: A History of the St. Louis Cardinals and Browns* (New York: Harper Entertainment, 2000) 9; Benjamin G. Rader, B*aseball: A History of America's Game* (Urbana: University of Illinois Press, 2002) 52. Players included W. H. Craver, James A. Devlin, A. H. Nichols, and G. W. Hall.
43 Peter Golenbock, *The Spirit of St. Louis: A History of the St. Louis Cardinals and Browns* (New York: Harper Entertainment, 2000) 13.
44 Joan M. Thomas, *St. Louis' Big League Ballparks* (Charleston: Arcadia, 2004) 33; Frederick G. Lieb, *The St. Louis Cardinals: The Story of a Great Baseball Club* (New York: G. P. Putnam's Sons, 1950) 6.
45 Ibid.
46 Peter Golenbock, *The Spirit of St. Louis: A History of the St. Louis Cardinals and Browns* (New York: Harper Entertainment, 2000) 13.
47 Ibid., 12.
48 Benjamin G. Rader, *Baseball: A History of America's Game* (Urbana: University of Illinois Press, 2002) 55.
49 Steven A. Riess, *Sport in Industrial America 1850-1920* (Wheeling, IL: Harlan Davidson, Inc., 1995) 158.
50 John Snyder, *Cardinals Journal* (Cincinnati: Emmis Books, 2006) 41.
51 Frederick G. Lieb, *The St. Louis Cardinals: The Story of a Great Baseball Club* (New York: G. P. Putnam's Sons, 1944) 6;
52 Peter Golenbock, *The Spirit of St. Louis: A History of the St. Louis Cardinals and Browns* (New York: Harper Entertainment, 2000) 16.
53 Ibid., 18.
54 Von der Ahe spoke his broken English with a German accent. John Snyder, *Cardinals Journal* (Cincinnati: Emmis Books, 2006) 17.
55 Frederick G. Lieb, T*he St. Louis Cardinals: The Story of a Great Baseball Club* (New York: G. P. Putnam's Sons, 1944) 7; Lawrence S. Ritter, *The Glory of Their Times: The Story of the Early Days of Baseball Told by the Men Who Played It* (New York: Macmillan Company, 1966) 79.
56 Steven A. Riess, *Sport in Industrial America 1850-1920* (Wheeling, IL: Harlan Davidson, Inc, 1995) 15. Other changes took place too, batters no longer were allowed to request the area they wanted the ball to be pitched, overhanded pitches were required, the regulation count became four balls and three strikes, the walk did not count as a hit, and the pitcher had to throw from sixty feet six inches. Mainly those changes became the gist of the baseball regulations of the modern era.
57 Peter Golenbock, *The Spirit of St. Louis: A History of the St. Louis Cardinals and Browns* (New York: Harper Entertainment, 2000) 19. He eventually became owner of the American League Chicago White Sox.

58   Ibid., 19; George F. Will, *Men at Work: The Craft of Baseball* (New York: Macmillan Publishing Co., 1990) 306. Baseball statistician Bill James sees this type of play leading to the coach's box.

59   Peter Golenbock, *The Spirit of St. Louis: A History of the St. Louis Cardinals and Browns* (New York: Harper Entertainment, 2000) 19.

60   Benjamin G. Rader, *Baseball: A History of America's Game* (Urbana: University of Illinois Press, 2002) 47.

61   John Snyder, *Cardinals Journal* (Cincinnati: Emmis Books, 2006) 14; Peter Golenbock, *The Spirit of St. Louis: A History of the St. Louis Cardinals and Browns* (New York: Harper Entertainment, 2000) 16.

62   Benjamin G. Rader, *Baseball: A History of America's Game* (Urbana, University of Illinois Press, 2002) 40-41; Steven A. Riess, *Sport in Industrial America 1850-1920* (Wheeling, IL: Harlan Davidson, Inc., 1995) 60, 70. White collar jobs consisted of such positions as "telegraph operators, printers… travelling [sic] men [salesmen]…men of leisure…barkeepers…hotel clerks, actors and employees of theater, policemen and firemen on their day off…clerks and salesmen temporarily out of work…butchers [and] bakers" Manual workers "were employed about eight hours a day with a half-holiday on Saturday that left considerable discretionary time for sports or other uplifting recreations."

63   Peter Golenbock, *The Spirit of St. Louis: A History of the St. Louis Cardinals and Browns* (New York: Harper Entertainment, 2000) 13.

64   Ibid.

65   John Snyder, *Cardinals Journal* (Cincinnati: Emmis Books, 2006) 14-15.

66   Ibid., 18-21.

67   Frederick G. Lieb, *The St. Louis Cardinals: The Story of a Great Baseball Club* (New York: G. P. Putnam's Sons, 1944) 7.

68   Frederick G. Lieb, *The St. Louis Cardinals: The Story of a Great Baseball Club* (New York: G. P. Putnam's Sons, 1944) 7; "Origins - The Spirit of St. Louis in the History of Professional Baseball May 4-8, 1875" J. D. Cash, *Gateway Heritage*, Quarterly Magazine of the Missouri Historical Society, Spring 1995, 16.

69   John Snyder, *Cardinals Journal* (Cincinnati: Emmis Books, 2006) 23-27; Joan M. Thomas, *St. Louis' Big League Ballparks* (Charleston, SC: Arcadia, 2004) 23; Frederick G. Lieb, *The St. Louis Cardinals: The Story of a Great Baseball Club* (New York: G. P. Putnam's Sons, 1944) 8.

70   John Snyder, *Cardinals Journal* (Cincinnati: Emmis Books, 2006) 12, 30. This Chicago team eventually became the Chicago Cubs in 1902 so one can see that the rivalry between these two mid-western cities goes back a long way.

71   Mike Eisenbath, *The Cardinals Encyclopedia* (Philadelphia: Temple University Press, 1999) 423.

72   John Snyder, *Cardinals Journal* (Cincinnati: Emmis Books, 2006) 15.

73   Eric Enders, *Ballparks: Then and Now* (San Diego: Thunder Bay Press, 2002) 134.

74   John Snyder, *Cardinals Journal* (Cincinnati: Emmis Books, 2006) 15.

75   Frederick G. Lieb, *The St. Louis Cardinals: The Story of a Great Baseball Club* (New York: G. P. Putnam's Sons, 1944) 9-13; Benjamin G. Rader, *Baseball: A History of America's Game* (Urbana: University of Illinois Press, 2002) 59.

76   Peter Golenbock, *The Spirit of St. Louis: A History of the St. Louis Cardinals and Browns* (New York: Harper Entertainment, 2000) 17.

77   Ibid., 20

78   Benjamin G. Rader, *Baseball: A History of America's Game* (Urbana: University

of Illinois Press, 2002) 64. Nineteenth century "father of baseball" Henry Chadwick "estimated that at least a fifth of all big-leaguers worked in saloons in the off-season"

79   Ibid., 65.

80   Benjamin G. Rader, *Baseball: A History of America's Game* (Urbana: University of Illinois Press, 2002) 58.

81   Ibid.

82   John Snyder, *Cardinals Journal* (Cincinnati: Emmis Books, 2006) 42-43.

83   Benjamin G. Rader, *Baseball: A History of America's Game* (Urbana: University of Illinois Press, 2002) 60; Steven A Riess, *Sport in Industrial America 1850-1920* (Wheeling, IL: Harlan Davidson, Inc, 1995) 113.

84   Ibid., 74.

85   Frederick G. Lieb, *The St. Louis Cardinals: The Story of a Great Baseball Club* (New York: G. P. Putnam's Sons, 1944) 18.

86   Peter Golenbock, *The Spirit of St. Louis: A History of the St. Louis Cardinals and Browns* (New York: Harper Entertainment, 2000) 49.

87   Ibid., 51; John Snyder, *Cardinals Journal* (Cincinnati: Emmis Books, 2006) 48.

88   Steven A. Riess, *Sport in Industrial America 1850-1920* (Wheeling, IL: Harlan Davidson, Inc, 1995) 155.

89   John Snyder, *Cardinals Journal* (Cincinnati: Emmis Books, 2006) 17, 2122, 48-49, 76; Peter Golenbock, *The Spirit of St. Louis: A History of the St. Louis Cardinals and Browns* (New York: Harper Entertainment, 2000) 30.

90   John Snyder, *Cardinals Journal* (Cincinnati: Emmis Books, 2006) 54, 87; Steven A Riess, *Sport in Industrial America 1850-1920* (Wheeling, IL: Harlan Davidson, Inc, 1995) 65. Reiss reports that "virtually all (over 90 percent) … American-born, and predominantly of native-born white American ancestry… [and] four-fifths (83 percent) came from cities at a time when only one-fourth of the population was urban."

91   Frederick G. Lieb, *The St. Louis Cardinals: The Story of a Great Baseball Club* (New York: G. P. Putnam's Sons, 1944) 11-13. On his power to buy and sell players and the reaction of the fans Von der Ahe, in his broken English, remarked, "They talked of poycotting my team. I made more money than with my old wonder poys. I guess I am a pretty smart fellar."

92   Benjamin G. Rader, *Baseball: A History of America's Game, 3rd ed.* (Urbana: University of Illinois Press, 2008) 25.

93   Ibid.

94   Ibid., 82; Edward J. Rielly, *Baseball: An Encyclopedia of Popular Culture* (Lincoln: University of Nebraska Press, 2000) 109-111; Steven A. Riess, *Sport in Industrial America 1850-1920* (Wheeling, IL: Harlan Davidson, Inc, 1995) 176.

95   Michael Benson, *Ballparks of North America: A Comprehensive Historical Reference to Baseball Grounds, Yards and Stadiums, 1845 to Present* (Jefferson, N.C.: McFarland and Co., 1989) 345-351. The silk handkerchief collection C. F. Sexauer saw in February 1998 on display at the St. Louis Cardinal Hall of Fame Museum.

96   John Snyder, *Cardinals Journal* (Cincinnati: Emmis Books, 2006) 64; Steven A. Riess, *Sport in Industrial America 1850-1920* (Wheeling, IL: Harlan Davidson, Inc, 1995) 157. Benjamin G. Rader, *Baseball: A History of America's Game* (Urbana: University of Illinois Press, 2002) 48-49.

97   *Baseball as America: Seeing Ourselves Through Our National Game* (Washington, D.C.: National Baseball Hall of Fame and Museum) 25.

98   Mike Eisenbath, *The Cardinals Encyclopedia* (Philadelphia: Temple University Press, 1999) 396.

99   Ibid., 17.

100   John Snyder, *Cardinals Journal* (Cincinnati: Emmis Books, 2006) 65.

101   Joan M. Thomas, *St. Louis' Big League Ballparks* (Charleston: Arcadia, 2004) 24.

102   John Snyder, *Cardinals Journal* (Cincinnati: Emmis Books, 2006) 55.

103   Ibid., 69; Eric Enders, *Ballparks: Then and Now* (San Diego: Thunder Bay Press, 2002) 134.

104   John Snyder, *Cardinals Journal* (Cincinnati: Emmis Books, 2006) 69. Note: "The Star-Spangled Banner" did not officially become the National Anthem until 1933 and wasn't played regularly at sporting events until the 1940s.

105   Ibid., 18; Frederick G. Lieb, *The St. Louis Cardinals: The Story of a Great Baseball Club* (New York: G. P. Putnam's Sons, 1950) 18.

106   Peter Golenbock, *The Spirit of St. Louis: A History of the St. Louis Cardinals and Browns* (New York: Harper Entertainment, 2000) 54.

107   Mike Eisenbath, *The Cardinals Encyclopedia* (Philadelphia: Temple University Press, 1999) 386.

108   John Snyder, *Cardinals Journal* (Cincinnati: Emmis Books, 2006) 6588.

109   Benjamin G. Rader, *Baseball: A History of America's Game* (Urbana: University of Illinois Press, 2002) 39.

110   John Snyder, *Cardinals Journal* (Cincinnati: Emmis Books, 2006) 55, 89; Frederick G. Lieb, *The St. Louis Cardinals: The Story of a Great Baseball Club* (New York: G. P. Putnam's Sons, 1944) 20.

111   John Snyder, *Cardinals Journal* (Cincinnati: Emmis Books, 2006) 86; Frederick G. Lieb, *The St. Louis Cardinals: The Story of a Great Baseball Club* (New York: G. P. Putnam's Sons, 1944) 20.

112   Mike Eisenbath, *The Cardinals Encyclopedia* (Philadelphia: Temple University Press, 1999) 387.

113   John Snyder, *Cardinals Journal* (Cincinnati: Emmis Books, 2006) 18, 55, 81, 90. Note: Von der Ahe finished his years mainly out of the spotlight in poverty and died in 1913; Frederick G. Lieb, T*he St. Louis Cardinals: The Story of a Great Baseball Club* (New York: G. P. Putnam's Sons, 1944) 21.

114   Mike Eisenbath, *The Cardinals Encyclopedia* (Philadelphia: Temple University Press, 1999) 387; Peter Golenbock, *The Spirit of St. Louis: A History of the St. Louis Cardinals and Browns* (New York: Harper Entertainment, 2000) 56.

Chapter Three

115   Film Series: *Decades: A Century Turns*, (St. Louis: KETC/Channel 9) 1997; Lincoln Steffens, *Shame of the Cities* (New York: McClure, Philips & Co., 1904) 56.

116   Ibid., 31-32.

117   Ernest Kirschten, *Catfish and Crystal* (Garden City, NY: Doubleday & Company, Inc., 1960) 317.

118   At the time, there was no rule barring the owners from owning more than one major league ball club. In fact, the owners of the Baltimore Orioles also owned the Brooklyn team.

119   Mike Eisenbath, *The Cardinals Encyclopedia* (Philadelphia: Temple University Press, 1999) 387.

120   Frederick G. Lieb, *The St. Louis Cardinals: The Story of a Great Baseball Club* (New York: G. P. Putnam's Sons, 1944) 24.

121 Ibid., 23; Steven A. Riess, *Sport in Industrial America 1850-1920* (Wheeling, IL: Harlan Davidson, Inc, 1995) 163.

122 Mike Eisenbath, *The Cardinals Encyclopedia* (Philadelphia: Temple University Press, 1999) 388.

123 Frederick G. Lieb, T*he St. Louis Cardinals: The Story of a Great Baseball Club* (New York: G. P. Putnam's Sons, 1944) 23.

124 Ibid., 26.

125 *St. Louis Post-Dispatch*, April 15, 1899, 1-2.

126 John Snyder, *Cardinals Journal* (Cincinnati: Emmis Books, 2006) 11.

127 Frederick G. Lieb, *The St. Louis Cardinals: The Story of a Great Baseball Club* (New York: G. P. Putnam's Sons, 1944) 24.

128 *St. Louis Post-Dispatch*, April 16, 1899, 16.

129 John Snyder, *Cardinals Journal* (Cincinnati: Emmis Books, 2006) 85-93; *Frederick G. Lieb, The St. Louis Cardinals: The Story of a Great Baseball Club* (New York: G. P. Putnam's Sons, 1944) 22; 25-26.

130 Mike Eisenbath, *The Cardinals Encyclopedia* (Philadelphia: Temple University Press, 1999) 387.

131 Joan M. Thomas, *St. Louis' Big League Ballparks* (Charleston: Arcadia, 2004) 27.

132 John Snyder, *Cardinals Journal* (Cincinnati: Emmis Books, 2006) 54, 90, 97. For continuity the first few years both names applied to the organization.

133 John Snyder, *Cardinals Journal* (Cincinnati: Emmis Books, 2006) 98.

134 John Snyder, *Cardinals Journal* (Cincinnati: Emmis Books, 2006) 95.

135 Ibid., 103; Steve Steinberg, *Baseball in St. Louis 1900-1925* (Charleston: Arcadia, 2004) 10.

136 Ibid., 9-12.

137 Note: Those four players were John McGraw, Wilbert Robinson, Patsy Donovan and Cy Young. He lost McGraw and Young to the new league anyway. Mike Eisenbath, *The Cardinals Encyclopedia* (Philadelphia: Temple University Press, 1999) 388.

138 Mike Eisenbath, *The Cardinals Encyclopedia* (Philadelphia: Temple University Press, 1999) 388.

139 Steve Steinberg, *Baseball in St. Louis 1900-1925* (Charleston: Arcadia, 2004) 10.

140 Benjamin G. Rader, *Baseball: A History of America's Game* (Urbana: University of Illinois Press, 2002) 97.

141 Ibid., 96.

142 "Robison Plans Improvements: Big Fireproof Grand Stand and Pavilion Will be Erected at League Park," *St. Louis Globe-Democrat*, Oct. 18, 1905.

143 John Snyder, *Cardinals Journal* (Cincinnati: Emmis Books, 2006) 128.

144 Steven A. Riess, *Sport in Industrial America 1859-1920* (Wheeling, IL: Harlan Davidson, Inc., 1995) 26.

145 Lawrence S. Ritter, *The Glory of Their Times: The Story of the Early Days of Baseball Told by the Men Who Played It* (New York: Macmillan Company, 1966) 34; Davy Jones, of the Detroit Tigers (1906-1910), recalled that during the turn of the century they "had stupid guys, smart guys, tough guys, mild guys, crazy guys, college men, slickers from the city, and hicks from the country."

146 Ibid. 34; Frank Deford, *The Old Ball Game* (New York: Grove Press, 2005) 15; Edward J. Rielly, *Baseball: An Encyclopedia of Popular Culture* (Lincoln: University of Nebraska Press, 2000) 148. The *Sporting News* in 1923, boasted "The Mick, the Sheeny, the Wop, the Dutch and the Chink, the Indian, the Jap or the so-called

Anglo-Saxon—his nationality is never a matter of moment if he can pitch, hit, or field," but that was not necessarily the case.

147 Benjamin G. Rader, *Baseball: A History of America's Game* (Urbana: University of Illinois Press, 2002) 103; Lawrence S. Ritter, *The Glory of Their Times: The Story of the Early Days of Baseball Told by the Men Who Played It* (New York: Macmillan Company, 1966) 52. Entertainer Eddie Cantor recalled that when his grandmother wanted to insult him, she would call him a baseball player. Players might bring fun and excitement to the game, but they were not well-regarded. They had a reputation of being "pretty crude."

148 Edward J. Rielly, *Baseball: An Encyclopedia of Popular Culture* (Lincoln: University of Nebraska Press, 2000) 48, 123, 129, 131; Benjamin G. Rader, *Baseball: A History of America's Game* (Urbana: University of Illinois Press, 2002) 93; Frank Deford, *The Old Ball Game* (New York: Grove Press, 2005) 9, 13, 4950, 91, 102; Steven A. Riess, *Sport in Industrial America 1850-1920* (Wheeling, IL: Harlan Davidson, Inc, 1995) 62, 164-165. In 1908 the whole National League scored only about 6.7 runs per game, down from the 1894 average of 14.7 runs; the same year the American League posted six no-hitters.

149 Lawrence S. Ritter, *The Glory of Their Times: The Story of the Early Days of Baseball Told by the Men Who Played It* (New York: Macmillan Company, 1966) The pitching distance extended to sixty feet and six inches, in 1900 the size of home plate went from twelve to seventeen inches and the shape went from "a square to a five-sided figure." By 1903 both leagues decided to speed the game up by counting the first two foul balls as strikes; before foul balls did not count and hitters could foul off numerous pitches without penalty of striking out. This latter change saw a fifty per-cent increase in strikeouts and a decline in hits and runs per game. These changes alone were not the only reasons for a decline in hitting in the "dead ball era." The dirty ball was common practice. Players hardly ever saw a new, clean ball. Balls cost money so owners tried to use the ball if it was playable. The only time umpires brought in a new ball was if the ball went into the stands and they could not retrieve it. Consequently, the balls would get dirty, but they could also deliberately be soiled "with tobacco juice and dirt" or licorice. Saliva was used to produce the "spitball." Some guys threw an emery ball that had been roughed and caused the ball to break. A dark ball is difficult to see, a scuffed ball difficult to hit. Those conditions gave the edge to the pitcher. In 1911 "baseball juiced up the balls some...putting cork in the center...this helped the batters enough so that there were more hits."

150 Ibid., 33, 54, 91, 183, 242, 246. The spitball was outlawed in December 1920; Frank Deford, *The Old Ball Game* (New York: Grove Press, 2005) 104; Steven A. Riess, *Sport in Industrial America 1850-1920* (Wheeling, IL: Harlan Davidson, Inc, 1995) 173.

151 Lawrence S. Ritter, *The Glory of Their Times: The Story of the Early Days of Baseball Told by the Men Who Played It* (New York: Macmillan Company, 1966) 35, 52.

152 Benjamin G. Rader, *Baseball: A History of America's Game* (Urbana: University of Illinois Press, 2002) 98-100.

153 John Snyder, *Cardinals Journal* (Cincinnati: Emmis Books, 2006) 108.

154 "Frank Robison Dies Suddenly: Former President of Cardinals Victim of Apoplexy at Cleveland," *St. Louis Globe-Democrat*, Sept. 26, 1908; Lawrence S. Ritter, *The Glory of Their Times: The Story of the Early Days of Baseball Told by the Men Who Played It* (New York: Macmillan Company, 1966) 241.

155 John Snyder, *Cardinals Journal* (Cincinnati: Emmis Books, 2006) 126; Steve Steinberg, *Baseball in St. Louis 1900-1925* (Charleston: Arcadia Publishing, 2004) 36.

156 Bill Borst, "The Matron Magnate," *Baseball Research Journal*, 1977, 2530; "Bresnahan Goes After Knockers," *St. Louis Globe-Democrat*, Apr. 13, 1910.

157 "Sporting Comment," *St. Louis Globe-Democrat*, Mar. 25, 1911.

158 Mike Eisenbath, *The Cardinals Encyclopedia* (Philadelphia: Temple University Press, 1999) 388; As noted in Benjamin G. Rader, *Baseball: A History of America's Game* (Urbana: University of Illinois Press, 2002) 112 -Baseball historian Harold Seymour's careful estimates, by 1910 "established regulars" earned "in the neighborhood of $3,000 per season...steelworkers average annual pay of about $700 or a skilled craftsman's $1200."

159 "Sporting Comment," *St. Louis Globe-Democrat*, Mar. 25, 1911.

160 Marguerite Martyn, "Mrs. Schuyler Britton: New Owner of the Cardinals," *St. Louis Post-Dispatch*, April 9, 1911, 1; John Snyder, *Cardinals Journal* (Cincinnati: Emmis Books, 2006) 133, 136-137; Steven A. Riess, *Sport in Industrial America 1850-1920* (Wheeling, IL: Harlan Davidson, Inc, 1995) 65.

161 *Sporting News*, March 3, 1911, 2.

162 "Steininger New Cardinal Head," *St. Louis Globe-Democrat*, April 7, 1911. Steininger was a friend of the late Stanley Robison and administrator of his estate. Steininger also headed his own construction firm.

163 "Helene Britton: My Experience as a Big League Owner," *Baseball Magazine*, Feb. 1917, 13-14.

164 Marguerite Martyn, "Mrs. Schuyler Britton: New Owner of the Cardinals," *St. Louis Post-Dispatch*, April 9, 1911, 1.

165 Alan Ross, *Cardinals Glory* (Nashville: Cumberland House, 2005) 16.

166 Marguerite Martyn, "Mrs. Schuyler Britton: New Owner of the Cardinals," *St. Louis Post-Dispatch*, April 9, 1911, 1.

167 Frederick G. Lieb, *The St. Louis Cardinals: The Story of a Great Baseball Club*, (New York: G. P. Putnam's Sons, 1944) 46.

168 Ibid., 46.

169 Note: During this era in baseball it was very common for a player to serve as managers too.

170 John Snyder, *Cardinals Journal* (Cincinnati: Emmis Books, 2006) 138; Frederick G. Lieb, *The St. Louis Cardinals: The Story of a Great Baseball Club* (New York: G. P. Putnam's Sons, 1944) 44; Steve Steinberg, *Baseball in St. Louis 1900-1925* (Charleston: Arcadia, 2004) 34.

171 John Snyder, *Cardinals Journal* (Cincinnati: Emmis Books, 2006) 137.

172 Frederick G. Lieb, *The St. Louis Cardinals: The Story of a Great Baseball Club* (New York: G. P. Putnam's Sons, 1944) 47.

173 Bob Broeg, *The Greatest Moments in St. Louis Sports* (St. Louis: Missouri Historical Society Press, 2000) 12.

174 Mike Eisenbath, *The Cardinals Encyclopedia* (Philadelphia: Temple University Press, 1999) 399.

175 John Snyder, *Cardinals Journal* (Cincinnati: Emmis Books, 2006) 137.

176 Mike Eisenbath, *The Cardinals Encyclopedia* (Philadelphia: Temple University Press, 1999) 399.

177 Frederick G. Lieb, *The St. Louis Cardinals: The Story of a Great Baseball Club* (New York: G. P. Putnam's Sons, 1944) 48

178 Bob Broeg, *The Greatest Moments in St. Louis Sports* (St. Louis: Missouri Historical Society Press, 2000) 12.
179 Frederick G. Lieb, *The St. Louis Cardinals: The Story of a Great Baseball Club* (New York: G. P. Putnam's Sons, 1944) 48.
180 Steve Steinberg, *Baseball in St. Louis 1900-1925* (Charleston: Arcadia, 2004) 11, 55.
181 Benjamin G. Rader, *Baseball: A History of America's Game* (Urbana: University of Illinois Press, 2002) 113; Three starting outfielders from the Cardinals went to the Terriers while additional players fled with lucrative contracts to other Federal League teams. Major league owners "blacklisted players who had deserted organized baseball, obtained court injunctions, and raise player salaries…Salary averages more than doubled, climbing from $3,187 in 1913 to $7,327 in 1915." Lawrence S. Ritter, *The Glory of Their Times: The Story of the Early Days of Baseball Told by the Men Who Played It* (New York: Macmillan Company, 1966) 79; Steven A. Riess, *Sport in Industrial America 1850-1920* (Wheeling, IL: Harlan Davidson, Inc, 1995) 175.
182 Miss Anna Gene Witzig, "Woman Artist Describes First Experience at Baseball Game," *St. Louis Globe-Democrat*, April 6, 1914.
183 "Topics in the Sport World," *St. Louis Globe-Democrat*, April 3, 1914.
184 John Snyder, *Cardinals Journal* (Cincinnati: Emmis Books, 2006) 154,155; Steve Steinberg, *Baseball in St. Louis 1900-1925* (Charleston: Arcadia, 2004) 12; Ibid., 58.
185 John Snyder, *Cardinals Journal* (Cincinnati: Emmis Books, 2006) 149; Steven A Riess, *Sport in Industrial America 1850-1920* (Wheeling, IL: Harlan Davidson, Inc, 1995) 175.
186 Ibid., 137, 143; "Mrs. Britton Sues to Divorce Cardinal Head," *St. Louis Globe-Democrat*, Nov. 18, 1916.
187 John Snyder, *Cardinals Journal* (Cincinnati: Emmis Books, 2006) 164; Frederick G. Lieb, *The St. Louis Cardinals: The Story of a Great Baseball Club* (New York: G. P. Putnam's Sons, 1944) 59.
188 http://bioproj.sabr.org Helene Britton by Joan M. Thomas
189 http://www.findagrave.com Helene Hathaway Robison Britton.
190 Mike Eisenbath, *The Cardinals Encyclopedia* (Philadelphia: Temple University Press, 1999) 9. Underprivileged kids could not afford to attend a game, they would peer through knotholes in the park fence to catch a glimpse of the game.
191 Dan O'Neill, *Sportsman's Park: The Players, the Fans & the Game* (Chesterfield, Mathis Jones Communications, 2007) 24.
192 Peter Golenbock, *The Spirit of St. Louis: A History of the St. Louis Cardinals and Browns* (New York: Harper Entertainment, 2000) 83; Steve Steinberg, *Baseball in St. Louis 1900-1925* (Charleston: Arcadia, 2004) 85.
193 Peter Golenbock, *The Spirit of St. Louis: A History of the St. Louis Cardinals and Browns* (New York: Harper Entertainment, 2000) 82; John Snyder, *Cardinals Journal* (Cincinnati: Emmis Books, 2006) 164-165; Frederick G. Lieb, *The St. Louis Cardinals: The Story of a Great Baseball Club* (New York: G. P. Putnam's Sons, 1944) 67.
194 John Snyder, *Cardinals Journal* (Cincinnati: Emmis Books, 2006) 166.
195 Ibid., 168.
196 Ibid., 170.
197 Mike Eisenbath, *The Cardinals Encyclopedia* (Philadelphia: Temple University Press, 1999) 9.
198 John Snyder, *Cardinals Journal* (Cincinnati: Emmis Books, 2006) 171.

199 Ibid., 169.

200 Ernest Kirschten, *Catfish and Crystal* (New York: Doubleday & Co., Inc., 1960) 182.

201 Steve Steinberg, *Baseball in St. Louis 1900-1925* (Charleston: Arcadia, 2004) 91.

202 Geoffrey C. Ward and Ken Burns, *Baseball: An Illustrated History* (New York: Alfred A. Knopf, 1994) 179.

203 Frederick G. Lieb, *The St. Louis Cardinals: The Story of a Great Baseball Club* (New York: G. P. Putnam's Sons, 1944) 63.

Chapter Four

204 Film Series: *Decades: A Century Turns* (St. Louis: KETC/Channel 9) 1997.

205 James N. Giglio, *Musial: From Stash to Stan the Man* (Columbia: University of Missouri Press, 2001) 69-70; Lawrence S. Ritter, *The Glory of Their Times: The Story of the Early Days of Baseball Told by the Men Who Played It* (New York: The Macmillan Company, 1966) 245; Jules Tygiel, *Past Time: Baseball as History* (New York: Oxford University Press, 2000) 11; Steven A. Riess, *Sport in Industrial America 1850-1920* (Wheeling, IL: Harlan Davidson, Inc., 1995) 33-34; Edward J. Rielly, *Baseball: An Encyclopedia of Popular Culture* (Lincoln: University of Nebraska Press, 2000) 153.

206 Frederick G. Lieb, *The St. Louis Cardinals: The Story of a Great Baseball Club* (New York: G. P. Putnam's Sons, 1944) 77. Bing Devine, *The Memoirs of Bing Devine: Stealing Lou Brock and Other Winning Moves by a Master GM* (Sports Publishing, LLC, 2004) 58. Sportsman's Park sat at Grand, Dodier, Sullivan and Spring.

207 Tim McCarver, *Oh, Baby, I Love it!* (New York: Villard Books, 1987) 8. In 1958 the New York Giants and the Brooklyn Dodgers moved to California.

208 John Snyder, *Cardinals Journal* (Cincinnati: Emmis Books, 2006) 178, 184.

209 Mike Eisenbath, *The Cardinals Encyclopedia* (Philadelphia: Temple University Press, 1999) 402; Frederick G. Lieb, *The St. Louis Cardinals: The Story of a Great Baseball Club* (New York: G. P. Putnam's Sons, 1944) 74.

210 Mike Eisenbath, *The Cardinals Encyclopedia* (Philadelphia: Temple University Press, 1999) 387, 402.

211 Frederick G. Lieb, *The St. Louis Cardinals: The Story of a Great Baseball Club* (New York: G. P. Putnam's Sons, 1944) 75-77.

212 John Snyder, *Cardinals Journal* (Cincinnati: Emmis Books, 2006) 178-179; Frederick G. Lieb, *The St. Louis Cardinals: The Story of a Great Baseball Club* (New York: G. P. Putnam's Sons, 1944) 79.

213 John Snyder, *Cardinals Journal* (Cincinnati: Emmis Books, 2006) 188.

214 Ibid., 195. The practice did not take off around the league though until 1932 when all the major league clubs adopted it.

215 James N. Giglio, *Musial: From Stash to Stan the Man* (Columbia: University of Missouri Press, 2001) 63.

216 First-hand personal recollections of C. F. Sexauer and photos of the time period.

217 Philip Lowry, *Green Cathedrals: The Ultimate Celebration of 271 Major League and Negro League Ballparks Past and Present* (Reading, Mass: Addison Wesley, 1992) 229.

218 Ron Smith, *The Ballpark Book: A Journey Through the Fields of Baseball Magic* (St. Louis: Sporting News, 2000) 289.

219 Curt Smith, *Storied Stadiums: Baseball's History Through its Ballparks* (New York: Carroll & Graf Publishers, 2001) 132.

220 Bob Broeg, *Memories of a Hall of Fame Sportswriter* (Champaign: Sagamore Publishing, 1995) 23.

221 John Snyder, *Cardinals Journal* (Cincinnati: Emmis Books, 2006) 244.

222 Richard Sandonair, "Rising Above the Field," *Design* (8-5-91). Osborn built a reputation on rebuilding and designing ballparks that caught the spirit of baseball. The company designed and built seven new major league stadiums and rebuilt seven, including Wrigley in 1988. John Snyder, *Cardinals Journal* (Cincinnati: Emmis Books, 2006) 200, 207.

223 Frederick G. Lieb, *The St. Louis Cardinals: The Story of a Great Baseball Club* (New York: G. P. Putnam's Sons, 1944) 79.

224 John Snyder, *Cardinals Journal* (Cincinnati: Emmis Books, 2006) 210.

225 Ibid., 208, 214 Note: These numbers would be surpassed on July 12, 1931 when the Cardinals hosted a doubleheader against the Cubs and 45,714 were in attendance "about 13,000 more than the stands could hold. The remainder encircled the outfield." John Snyder, *Cardinals Journal* (Cincinnati: Emmis Books, 2006) 245.

226 Jules Tygiel, *Past Time: Baseball as History* (New York: Oxford University Press, 2000) 70, 72.

227 http://www.stlradio.com/articles-stlcards.htm; Jules Tygiel, *Past Time: Baseball as History* (New York: Oxford University Press, 2000) 66. The Cardinals and Browns had two common broadcasters, Garnett Mark and Thomas Patrick Convey announced the home games. They did not finish the season out as this "was costing too much money." The following season a couple of stations picked up the games to include KMOX, KFVE, and WIL. By the end of the 1920s "St. Louis, Cleveland, Detroit, Cincinnati, Boston, and Chicago all featured regular broadcasts of home games, but none of the New York, Washington, D.C., or Pennsylvania teams followed suit." In 1929 France Laux served as the radio voice of both teams on KMOX but WIL also broadcasted the games. The exclusive rights for KMOX did not come about until 1955 and lasted until 2006 when they switched to KTRS, a station 50-percent-owned by the ball club. Cardinal broadcasts returned to KMOX the beginning of the 2011 season.

228 Roger Angell, *Five Seasons: A Baseball Companion* (New York: Simon & Schuster, 1977) 114.

229 John Snyder, *Cardinals Journal* (Cincinnati: Emmis Books, 2006) 213.

230 Lawrence S. Ritter, *The Glory of Their Times: The Story of the Early Days of Baseball Told by the Men Who Played It* (New York: Macmillan Company, 1966) 236.

231 John Snyder, *Cardinals Journal* (Cincinnati: Emmis Books, 2006) 212-213. 2

232 Rob Rains, *The Cardinals Fan's Little Book of Wisdom* (Lanham, MD: Diamond Communications, 1994) 1.

233 Frederick G. Lieb, *The St. Louis Cardinals: The Story of a Great Baseball Club* (New York: G. P. Putnam's Sons, 1944) 126-127.

234 John Snyder, *Cardinals Journal* (Cincinnati: Emmis Books, 2006) 215.

235 Frederick G. Lieb, *The St. Louis Cardinals: The Story of a Great Baseball Club* (New York: G. P. Putnam's Sons, 1944) 128-131.

236 Jules Tygiel, *Past Time: Baseball as History* (New York: Oxford University Press, 2000) 92; John Snyder, *Cardinals Journal* (Cincinnati: Emmis Books, 2006) 217-218. Note: Some notable Cardinal favorites traded by Breadon over the years included: Burleigh Grimes (1931), Chick Hafey (1932), Jim Bottomley (1932), Dizzy Dean (1938), Joe Medwick (1940), Johnny Mize (1941), and Walker Cooper (1946).

237 Alan Ross, *Cardinals Glory* (Nashville: Cumberland House, 2005) 58.

238 John Snyder, *Cardinals Journal* (Cincinnati: Emmis Books, 2006) 215-216. Note: Hornsby had to sell his stock in the Cardinals in order to move to his new team. He garnered $110,000 for the stock that he purchased in 1925 for less than half that amount. Alan Ross, *Cardinals Glory* (Nashville: Cumberland House, 2005) 234.

239 KTEC film series, *Decades*, Vol. IV; James Neal Primm, *Lion of the Valley: St. Louis, Missouri*, 2nd ed. (Boulder: Pruett Publishing Co., 1990) 469, 484.

240 Robert Burnes, "Down Memory Lane," *St. Louis Globe-Democrat*, May 7, 1966.

241 Frederick G. Lieb, T*he St. Louis Cardinals: The Story of a Great Baseball Club* (New York: G. P. Putnam's Sons, 1944) 45.

242 Bob Broeg, *Memories of a Hall of Fame Sportswriter* (Champaign: Sagamore Publishing, 1995) 22-23.

243 Frederick G. Lieb, *The St. Louis Cardinals: The Story of a Great Baseball Club* (New York: G. P. Putnam's Sons, 1944) 79-80.

244 Rob Rains. *The Cardinals Fan's Little Book of Wisdom* (South Bend: Diamond Communications, Inc., 1994) 17.

245 Curt Smith, *Storied Stadiums: Baseball's History Through its Ballparks* (New York: Carroll & Graf Publishers, 2001) 156.

246 Bob Broeg, *Memories of a Hall of Fame Sportswriter* (Champaign: Sagamore Publishing, 1995) 67.

247 Frederick G. Lieb, *The St. Louis Cardinals: The Story of a Great Baseball Club* (New York: G. P. Putnam's Sons, 1944) 154-156.

248 Ibid., 184.

249 Edward J. Rielly, *Baseball: An Encyclopedia of Popular Culture* (Lincoln: University of Nebraska Press, 2000) 48; Geoffrey C. Ward and Ken Burns, *Baseball: An Illustrated History* (New York: Alfred A. Knopf, 1994) 263.

250 Jules Tygiel, *Past Time: Baseball as History* (New York: Oxford University Press, 2000) 98. Alan Ross, *Cardinals Glory* (Nashville: Cumberland House, 2005) 215.

251 Alan Ross, *Cardinals Glory* (Nashville: Cumberland House, 2005) 59.

252 Ibid., 29.

253 Rob Rains. *The Cardinals Fan's Little Book of Wisdom* (South Bend: Diamond Communications, Inc., 1994) 27.

254 John Snyder, *Cardinals Journal* (Cincinnati: Emmis Books, 2006) 234, p. Note: John Snyder, *Cardinals Journal* (Cincinnati: Emmis Books, 2006) 264-65 reports that the name "Gas House Gang" did not begin until late in the 1935 season. It is believed "the origins of the name are somewhat murky. The most probable explanation derived from a doubleheader the Cards played in Boston in June 1935. It rained during the second game, leaving their uniforms caked with dirt. The team had to grab a late train to New York for a game against the Giants and there was no time to dry-clean the jerseys. They were still mud-stained when they took the field at the Polo Grounds. A reporter in the press box commented that the Cardinals looked as though they were from the Gas House District, an area on the Lower East Side of Manhattan that housed several large gas tanks. It was a rough neighborhood...writers and cartoonists began calling the Cardinals the Gas House Gang because of the club's unkempt appearance and its willingness to do anything possible to win, including fisticuffs, and the nickname stuck."

255 Bob Broeg, *Memories of a Hall of Fame Sportswriter* (Champaign: Sagamore Publishing, 1995) 48; Ron Green, Jr. *101 Reasons to Love the Cardinals* (New York: Stewart, Tabori & Chang, 2006) In addition to Martin, the band consisted of Lon Warneke on guitar, Bob Weiland on the jug; Frenchy Bordagaray on the washboard, whistle, and car horn; and Bill McGee on the fiddle.
256 Frederick G. Lieb, *The St. Louis Cardinals: The Story of a Great Baseball Club* (New York: G. P. Putnam's Sons, 1944) 175.
257 Mike Eisenbath, *The Cardinals Encyclopedia* (Philadelphia: Temple University Press, 1999) 402.
258 KTEC film series, *Decades, Vol. V*; James Neal Primm, *Lion of the Valley: St. Louis, Missouri,* 2nd ed. (Boulder: Pruett Publishing Co., 1990) 473.
259 Frederick G. Lieb, *The St. Louis Cardinals: The Story of a Great Baseball Club,* (New York: G. P. Putnam's Sons, 1944) 189, 193, 204.
260 James N. Giglio, *Musial: From Stash to Stan the Man* (Columbia: University of Missouri Press, 2001) 67; Bill Gilbert, *They Also Served: Baseball and the Home Front, 1941-1945* (New York: Crown Publishers, Inc., 1992) 3, 42, 75, 83.
261 Michael D'Antonio, *Forever Blue: The True Story of Walter O'Malley, Baseball's Most Controversial Owner, and the Dodgers of Brooklyn and Los Angeles* (New York: Riverside Books, 2009) 57; Jules Tygiel, *Past Time: Baseball as History* (New York: Oxford University Press, 2000) 93; Bill Gilbert, *They Also Served: Baseball and the Home Front, 1941-1945* (New York: Crown Publishers, Inc., 1992) 57.
262 James N. Giglio, *Musial: From Stash to Stan the Man* (Columbia: University of Missouri Press, 2001) 80; Mike Eisenbath, *The Cardinals Encyclopedia* (Philadelphia: Temple University Press, 1999) 58.
263 Alan Ross, *Cardinals Glory* (Nashville: Cumberland House, 2005) 59; Jules Tygiel, *Past Time: Baseball as History* (New York: Oxford University Press, 2000) 93. James N. Giglio, *Musial: From Stash to Stan the Man* (Columbia: University of Missouri Press, 2001) 80.
264 Alan Ross, *Cardinals Glory* (Nashville: Cumberland House, 2005) 231.
265 Bill Gilbert, *They Also Served: Baseball and the Home Front, 1941-1945* (New York: Crown Publishers, Inc., 1992) 73; John Snyder, *Cardinals Journal* (Cincinnati: Emmis Books, 2006) 304.
266 Ibid., 337; Bill Gilbert, *They Also Served: Baseball and the Home Front, 1941-1945* (New York: Crown Publishers, Inc., 1992) 113.
267 James N. Giglio, *Musial: From Stash to Stan the Man* (Columbia: University of Missouri Press, 2001) 92-93.
268 Michael D'Antonio, *Forever Blue: The True Story of Walter O'Malley, Baseball's Most Controversial Owner, and the Dodgers of Brooklyn and Los Angeles* (New York: Riverside Books, 2009) 69; James N. Giglio, *Musial: From Stash to Stan the Man* (Columbia: University of Missouri Press, 2001) 94; John Snyder, *Cardinals Journal* (Cincinnati: Emmis Books, 2006) 336-343. Two interesting things from Snyder's work: One, the managers were never in town on the same days during the season, they shared the rent on one apartment; since they had to be in town for the series it posed a problem but Southworth moved to another apartment in the building for the duration of the Fall Classic. Also, the first game of the 1944 World Series happened on October 4th, the day that Tony La Russa, future Cards manager was born in Tampa, Florida.
269 Frederick G. Lieb, *The St. Louis Cardinals: The Story of a Great Baseball Club* (New York: G. P. Putnam's Sons, 1944) 220; Bill Gilbert, *They Also Served: Baseball and the Home Front, 1941-1945* (New York: Crown Publishers, Inc., 1992) 209, 228.

270 John Snyder, *Cardinals Journal* (Cincinnati: Emmis Books, 2006) 348.

271 James N. Giglio, *Musial: From Stash to Stan the Man* (Columbia: University of Missouri Press, 2001) 83; Alan Ross, *Cardinals Glory: For the Love of Dizzy, Ozzie, and the Man* (Nashville: Cumberland House, 2005) 21. Breadon also reminded current players that other big leaguers serving the war effort only pulled down twenty-one dollars a month so they should be grateful for their full salaries.

272 Frederick G. Lieb, *The St. Louis Cardinals: The Story of a Great Baseball Club* (New York: G. P. Putnam's Sons, 1944) 220-232.

273 Ibid., 234-237.

274 Eric Enders, *Ballparks: Then and Now* (San Diego: Thunder Bay Press, 2002) 136.

275 Edward J. Rielly, *Baseball: An Encyclopedia of Popular Culture* (Lincoln: University of Nebraska Press, 2000) 53-54, 77, 168.

276 Richard S. Kirkendall, *A History of Missouri Vol. V 1919 to 1953* (Columbia: University of Missouri Press, 1986) 332.

277 John Snyder, *Cardinals Journal* (Cincinnati: Emmis Books, 2006) 359.

278 Richard S. Kirkendall, *A History of Missouri Vol. V 1919 to 1953* (Columbia: University of Missouri Press, 1986) 332; James N. Giglio, *Musial: From Stash to Stan the Man* (Columbia: University of Missouri Press, 2001) 149-158; Edward J. Rielly, *Baseball: An Encyclopedia of Popular Culture* (Lincoln: University of Nebraska Press, 2000) 258. There was no clear understanding if a strike discussion officially occurred as Slaughter, Schoendienst and Marion have gone on record saying they knew nothing of it. Dick Sisler has reported that "very definitely there was something going on...whereby they said they weren't going to play" though he does not clarify who they were. Musial has said that the talk around the clubhouse "was rough and racial...I thought the racial talk was just hot air."

279 Bob Broeg, *Memories of a Hall of Fame Sportswriter* (Champaign: Sagamore Publishing, 1995) 167.

280 John Snyder, *Cardinals Journal* (Cincinnati: Emmis Books, 2006) 359-360; James N. Giglio, *Musial: From Stash to Stan the Man* (Columbia: University of Missouri Press, 2001) 149-158; Richard S. Kirkendall, *A History of Missouri Vol. V 1919 to 1953* (Columbia: University of Missouri Press, 1986) 332, 334; David Halberstam, *October 1964* (New York: Fawcett Books, 1994) 57.

281 James N. Giglio, *Musial: From Stash to Stan the Man* (Columbia: University of Missouri Press, 2001) 60; Eric Enders, *Ballparks: Then and Now* (San Diego: Thunder Bay Press, 2002)136. An Associated Press release on May 4th noted that "The St. Louis major league baseball teams, the Cardinals and Browns, have discontinued their old policy of restricting Negroes to the bleachers and pavilion at Sportsman's Park."

282 Mike Eisenbath, *The Cardinals Encyclopedia* (Philadelphia: Temple University Press, 1999) 423; Bill Gilbert, *They Also Served: Baseball and the Home Front, 1941-1945* (New York: Crown Publishers, Inc., 1992) 124. In 1964 when the Cardinals played their last World Series in Sportsman's Park most of the people with seats in the pavilion section were white fans who could afford the tickets and the time to take the day off work to attend the game.

283 Edward J. Rielly, *Baseball: An Encyclopedia of Popular Culture* (Lincoln: University of Nebraska Press, 2000) 174-177; Mike Eisenbath, *The Cardinals Encyclopedia* (Philadelphia: Temple University Press, 1999) 325, 351; John Snyder, *Cardinals Journal* (Cincinnati: Emmis Books, 2006) 51; Bill Gilbert, *They Also Served: Baseball and the Home Front, 1941-1945* (New York: Crown Publishers, Inc., 1992) 117-119. Gilbert notes that during the 1940s most of the Latin players

were hired by Clark Griffin and the Washington Senators. The story of the player who decided to hang around and take a chance on not being drafted is that of pitcher Alex Carrasquel.

284 John Snyder, *Cardinals Journal* (Cincinnati: Emmis Books, 2006) 359.

285 Frederick G. Lieb, *The St. Louis Cardinals: The Story of a Great Baseball Club* (New York: G. P. Putnam's Sons, 1944) 238; James N. Giglio, *Musial: From Stash to Stan the Man* (Columbia: University of Missouri Press, 2001) 160; Bob Broeg, *Memories of a Hall of Fame Sportswriter* (Champaign: Sagamore Publishing, 1995) 171.

286 Ibid., 171; Mike Eisenbath, *The Cardinals Encyclopedia* (Philadelphia: Temple University Press, 1999) 403; John Snyder, *Cardinals Journal* (Cincinnati: Emmis Books, 2006) 364.

287 Mike Eisenbath, *The Cardinals Encyclopedia* (Philadelphia: Temple University Press, 1999) 403; John Snyder, *Cardinals Journal* (Cincinnati: Emmis Books, 2006) 364.

288 Frederick G. Lieb, *The St. Louis Cardinals: The Story of a Great Baseball Club* (New York: G. P. Putnam's Sons, 1944) 239.

289 Mike Eisenbath, *The Cardinals Encyclopedia* (Philadelphia: Temple University Press, 1999) 403.

290 Ibid., 403.

291 Ibid., 404; Harold Rosenthal, *The 10 Best Years of Baseball: An Informal History of the 'Fifties* (Chicago: Contemporary Books Inc., 1979) 8.

292 Mike Eisenbath, *The Cardinals Encyclopedia* (Philadelphia: Temple University Press, 1999) 404.

293 Ibid., 404.

294 Ibid., James N. Giglio, *Musial: From Stash to Stan the Man* (Columbia: University of Missouri Press, 2001) 161, 168; Michael D'Antonio, *Forever Blue: The True Story of Walter O'Malley, Baseball's Most Controversial Owner, and the Dodger of Brooklyn and Los Angeles* Note: during this time Dodgers Campanella, Hodges and Snider were pulling down $18,000-22,000 and Robinson received $36,000.

295 Michael D'Antonio, *Forever Blue: The True Story of Walter O'Malley, Baseball's Most Controversial Owner, and the Dodgers of Brooklyn and Los Angeles* (New York: Riverside Books, 2009) 128, 93.

296 John Snyder, *Cardinals Journal* (Cincinnati: Emmis Books, 2006) 377-378.

297 Mike Eisenbath, *The Cardinals Encyclopedia* (Philadelphia: Temple University Press, 1999) 405; John Snyder, *Cardinals Journal* (Cincinnati: Emmis Books, 2006) 397. Several prominent figures had been discovered holding ill-gotten financial wealth that amounted to considerably more than his offense. He believed because of those circumstances and other "political factors" he not only incurred the financial payment with a fine but also received a prison sentence

298 Mike Eisenbath, *The Cardinals Encyclopedia* (Philadelphia: Temple University Press, 1999) 405.

299 Mike Eisenbath, *The Cardinals Encyclopedia* (Philadelphia: Temple University Press, 1999) 405; Peter Hernon and Terry Ganey, *Under the Influence: The Unauthorized Story of the Anheuser-Busch Dynasty* (New York: Simon & Schuster, 1991) 212.

300 Mike Eisenbath, *The Cardinals Encyclopedia* (Philadelphia: Temple University Press, 1999) 405.

301 Ibid., 405.

302 Ibid., 422.

303 Dan O'Neill, *Sportsman's Park: The Players, the Fans & the Game* Chesterfield, MO: Mathis Jones Communications, LLC, 2007) 108.

Chapter Five

304 Ibid.

305 Mike Eisenbath, *The Cardinals Encyclopedia* (Philadelphia: Temple University Press, 1999) 405; Bob Broeg, *Memories of a Hall of Fame Sportswriter* (Champaign: Sagamore Publishing, 1995) 219.

306 Mike Eisenbath, *The Cardinals Encyclopedia* (Philadelphia: Temple University Press, 1999) 405.

307 Peter Hernon and Terry Ganey, *Under the Influence: The Unauthorized Story of the Anheuser-Busch Dynasty* (New York: Simon & Schuster, 1991) 215.

308 Curt Smith, *Storied Stadiums: Baseball's History Through its Ballparks* (Carroll & Graf Publishers: New York, 2001) 161.

309 Michael D'Antonio, *Forever Blue: The True Story of Walter O'Malley, Baseball's Most Controversial Owner, and the Dodgers of Brooklyn and Los Angeles* (New York: Riverside Books, 2009) 178. Howard Hughes too supported this move and was said to have "sent a $1 million check to back up" that bid. Veeck figured that with the modern air transportation he could work out a schedule that would get opposing teams to the west coast. He wanted to pioneer the move to Los Angeles.

310 Curt Smith, *Storied Stadiums: Baseball's History Through its Ballparks* (Carroll & Graf Publishers: New York, 2001) 161; John Snyder, *Cardinals Journal* (Cincinnati: Emmis Books, 2006) 399, 405. Veeck was a showman without polish. He was noted as a gimmick guy with his publicity stunts and over the top promotions. He once used a midget as a pinch-hitter and signed a one-arm pitcher. Other owners wanted his garishness out of the game.

311 John Snyder, *Cardinals Journal* (Cincinnati: Emmis Books, 2006) 405.

312 "Owners OK Cards Sale Without One Balk," Tim O'Neil, *St. Louis Post-Dispatch*, Mar. 22, 1996, 1A; Mike Eisenbath, *The Cardinals Encyclopedia* (Philadelphia: Temple University Press, 1999) 422-423; John Snyder, *Cardinals Journal* (Cincinnati: Emmis Books, 2006) 399.

313 Mike Eisenbath, *The Cardinals Encyclopedia* (Philadelphia: Temple University Press, 1999) 423; Dan O'Neill, *Sportsman's Park: The Players, the Fans & the Game* (Chesterfield, MO: Mathis Jones Communications, LLC, 2007) 121.

314 Mike Eisenbath, *The Cardinals Encyclopedia* (Philadelphia: Temple University Press, 1999) 422.

315 Ibid.

316 Dan O'Neill, *Sportsman's Park: The Players, the Fans & the Game* (Chesterfield, MO: Mathis Jones Communications, LLC, 2007) 115. 317

317 Mike Eisenbath, *The Cardinals Encyclopedia* (Philadelphia: Temple University Press, 1999) 423.

318 E-mail message between Tom P. Schneider and C. F. Sexauer, Oct. 24, 2006.

319 Oral interview with Judy Clark Dwyer and Fran Dwyer by C. F. Sexauer.

320 Oral interview with Isabelle Lenhardt by C. F. Sexauer. Before long they also opened the club up to front office personnel and the wives of those workers, and to the wives of the sportswriters who covered the team.

321 Bruce Kuklick, *To Every Thing a Season: Shibe Park and Urban Philadelphia 1909-1976* (Princeton: Princeton University Press, 1991) 12-13.

322 Dan O'Neill, *Sportsman's Park: The Players, The Fans & The Game* (Chesterfield, MO: Mathis Jones Communications, LLC, 2007) 22.

323 Personal memories of C. F. Sexauer; Rich Wolfe, *For Cardinal Fans Only!* (Phoenix: Lone Wolfe Press, 2003) 193.

324 Oral interview with George H. Fields II by C. F. Sexauer. Fields, a fan who knows the history of the game, noted that in 1950s ticket prices per game were "$2.25 for a box seat, $1.75 for a reserved seat, $1.35 for a general admission seat, $.75 for a pavilion seat and $.50 for a bleacher seat. His 1964 World Series ticket in the pavilion was $4.00 and one in the bleachers only $2.00. Concessions were not too expensive with prices ranging from .10 to .50 for hot dogs throughout the 40 years the Cardinals played at Sportsman's Park," but you could also bring you own refreshments. Quite a few fans could be seen bringing jugs of Kool Aid, sandwiches, and snacks from home.

325 Oral interview with George H. Fields II by C. F. Sexauer.

326 Oral interview with Judith Campana by C. F. Sexauer, fall 1985.

327 Oral interview with Mary Anne Hagedorn by C. F. Sexauer. Also, personal reflections of C. F. Sexauer.

328 Conversation between C. F. Sexauer and Jane Devine Pilkington at the Fall Classic in St. Louis, 2006.

329 David Claerbaut, *Cardinals Essential: Everything You Need to Know to be a Real Fan!* (Chicago: Triumph Books, 2006) 75.

330 David Halberstam, *October 1964* (New York: Fawcett Books, 1994) 57.

331 Peter Golenbock, *The Spirit of St. Louis: A History of the St. Louis Cardinals and Browns* (New York: Harper Entertainment, 2000) 412.

332 Richard S. Kirkendall, *A History of Missouri Vol. V 1919 to 1953* (Columbia: University of Missouri Press, 1986) 333; David Halberstam, *October 1964* (New York: Fawcett Books, 1994) 56-58; Peter Golenbock, *The Spirit of St. Louis: A History of the St. Louis Cardinals and Browns* (New York: Harper Entertainment, 2000) 411-414.

333 John Snyder, *Cardinals Journal* (Cincinnati: Emmis Books, 2006) 407.

334 Ibid., 449; Bob Gibson, *Stranger to the Game* (New York: Penguin Books, 1994) 49-50, 57. The Brooklyn Dodgers were the only team that managed to work around the laws; they trained in Vero Beach, Florida at their complex, Dodgertown. All other major league teams had to split their players up to white hotels and black hotels or private establishments.

335 John Snyder, *Cardinals Journal* (Cincinnati: Emmis Books, 2006) 449; Bing Devine, *The Memories of Bing Devine* (Sports Publishing, LLC, 2004) 86; Bob Gibson, *Stranger to the Game* (New York: Penguin Books, 1994) 57-59; James N. Giglio, *Musial: From Stash to Stan the Man* (Columbia: University of Missouri Press, 2001) 253; David Halberstam, *October 1964* (New York: Fawcett Books, 1994) 58-60; David Claerbaut, *Cardinals Essential: Everything You Need to Know to be a Real Fan!* (Chicago: Triumph Books, 2006) 80.

336 KTEC film series *Decades, vol. VII.*

337 John Snyder, *Cardinals Journal* (Cincinnati: Emmis Books, 2006) 470. Busch fired Devine August 17, 1964 but the St. Louis team went on to win the NL pennant and the World Series that fall.

338 Bob Broeg, *Memories of a Hall of Fame Sportswriter* (Champaign: Sagamore Publishing, 1995) 271.

339 James N. Giglio, *Musial: From Stash to Stan the Man* (Columbia: University of Missouri Press, 2001) 243-248. Stan only hit .255 in 1959. He felt he could perform and add to the team; he still had a love of the game and he was close to records he wanted to break. Stan was having some hitting problems in 1960. Hemus benched him and called on him as a pinch-hitter, a role Musial was not accustomed to playing and consequently he did not produce consistent hitting. Broeg "felt that

Hemus had prematurely given up on Musial, and his mismanagement of him had been detrimental to the club." Musial was in both All-Star games that year as a pinch hitter and delivered a single and home run. The National League took both games.

340 Bob Gibson, *Stranger to the Game* (New York: Penguin Books, 1994) 5254, 43, 62; McCarver, et al, *Diamond Gems: Favorite Baseball Stories from the Legends of the Game* (New York: McGraw Hill, 2008) 168-169. As a player/ manager Hemus played in one of the games and was hit by a pitch. The opposing pitcher, Bennie Daniels, happened to be black. His retort at a postgame clubhouse meeting was to call Daniels a "nigger." Hemus did not seem to care that White, Flood, George Crowe, and Gibson were there nor did he stop to think such language would insult the white players too. It was difficult to play for a manager "who unapologetically regarded black players as niggers." Gibson, a right-handed pitcher, noted Hemus did not even know his players by name as "he kept calling me Bridges, confusing me with Marshall Bridges, who was several years older than me, skinnier, and pitched left-handed. But he was black. Solly got that much right." Years later Hemus defended the comment and others that certainly appeared to be racist by telling Gibson "it wasn't a matter of racism; rather, he was a master motivator doing what he could to fire up the ballclub. Hemus suggested that Flood quit and Gibby give up baseball to pursue basketball. Gibson had a talent for that sport too and had played for the Globetrotters, but he was invested in making it in baseball.

341 James N. Giglio, *Musial: From Stash to Stan the Man* (Columbia: University of Missouri Press, 2001) 258; Roger Angell, *The Summer Game* (New York: Viking Press, 1972) 104.

342 The extended season ended a fifty-seven-year tradition of 154 games.

343 James N. Giglio, *Musial: From Stash to Stan the Man* (Columbia: University of Missouri Press, 2001) 258; John Snyder, *Cardinals Journal* (Cincinnati: Emmis Books, 2006) 455-462. Musial wanted to break Wagner's hits record and Cobb's total bases record).

344 Ernest Kirschten, *Catfish and Crystal* (New York: Doubleday & Company, Inc., 1960) 358; John Snyder, *Cardinals Journal* (Cincinnati: Emmis Books, 2006) 460-462.

345 Rob Rains, *The Cardinals Fan's Little Book of Wisdom* (South Bend: Diamond Communications, Inc., 1994) 42; Bob Gibson, *Stranger to the Game* (New York: Penguin Books, 1994) 85.

346 Rob Rains, *The Cardinals Fan's Little Book of Wisdom* (South Bend: Diamond Communications, Inc., 1994) 43; Bob Uecker and Mickey Herskowitz, *Catcher in the Wry* (New York: Jove Book, 1982) 45; Dan O'Neill, *Sportsman's Park: The Players, The Fans & The Game* (Chesterfield, MO: Mathis Jones Communications, LLC, 2007) 47.

347 Roger Angell, *The Summer Game* (New York: The Viking Press, 1972) 104; Bob Gibson, *Stranger to the Game* (New York: Penguin Books, 1994) 85.

348 Bob Gibson, *Stranger to the Game* (New York: Penguin Books, 1994) 86-87. Keane thought that Groat was undermining the team so right after the All-Star game the manager called a team meeting. He let it be known that he was not about to take the "second guessing...and grumbling behind his back." In a matter of fact way, Keane told the players, "You guys might get me fired, goddamnit, but if you do you can bet your asses that I'm taking some of you bastards with me."

349 Rob Rains, *The Cardinals Fan's Little Book of Wisdom: 101 Truths...Learned the Hard Way* (Lanham, MD: Diamond Communications, 2002) 33. Devine defended his position by stating that "this kind of thing went on with all clubs occasionally. You settled it in the clubhouse, and that was it."

350 Roger Angell, *The Summer Game* (New York: Viking Press, 1972) 104-108. Pavilion tickets sold for $4 each.

351 Bob Gibson, *Stranger to the Game* (New York: Penguin Books, 1994) 101.

352 Bob Uecker and Mickey Herskowitz, *Catcher in the Wry* (New York: Jove Book, 1982) 48; Bob Gibson, *Stranger to the Game* (New York: Penguin Books, 1994) 106; Roger Angell, *The Summer Game* (New York: Viking Press, 1972) 108. Keane knew that Durocher had been in St. Louis that summer for a meeting with Busch at Grant's Farm. For all he knew he was on his way out. He had admired Devine and they worked "closely to build a championship team." The firing of his colleague helped him realize that at no time was his position secure. On the Monday of the final week of the season, long before the clinching of the pennant and the superior victory of the world championship, Keane had been approached by Busch to sign a one-year contract but Keane explained that he wanted to wait until the season had officially ended. Then, with his decision already made, he secretly and promptly wrote out his letter of resignation dated September 26, 1964.

353 Costas Spirou and Larry Bennett, *It's Hardly Sportin': Stadiums, Neighborhoods, and the New Chicago* (DeKalb: Northern Illinois University Press, 2003) 37-38.

354 Dan O'Neill, *Sportsman's Park: The Players, The Fans and The Game* (Chesterfield, MO: Mathis Jones Communications, LLC, 2007) ix.

355 Joan M. Thomas, *St. Louis' Big League Ballparks* (Charleston: Arcadia, 2004) 75.

356 Dan O'Neill, *Sportsman's Park: The Players, the Fans, and the Game 1940-1950*(Chesterfield, MO: Mathis Jones Communications, LLC, 2007) 17, 27.

Chapter Six

357 George Lipsitz, "Sports Stadia and Urban Development: A Tale of Three Cities," *Journal of Sport and Social Issues,* v. 8 n. 2 (1984) 1-18.

358 Ibid.

359 *Busch Stadium Moments*, ed. Mike Smith (Marceline, MO: Walsworth Publishing, 2005) 41.

360 Riverfront Stadium in Cincinnati, Three Rivers in Pittsburgh, and Veterans Stadium in Philadelphia.

361 Michael Benson, *Ballparks of North America: A Comprehensive Historical Reference to Baseball Grounds, Yards and Stadiums, 1845 to Present* (Jefferson, N.C.: McFarland and Co., 1989) 351.

362 Oral interview with Judy Clark Dwyer and Fran Dwyer by C. F. Sexauer.

363 E-mail message between Tom P. Schneider and C. F. Sexauer, Oct. 24, 2006.

364 Rob Rains, T*he Cardinals Fan's Little Book of Wisdom: 101 Truths... Learned the Hard Way* (Lanham, MD: Diamond Communications, 2002) 20.

365 Bing Devine, *The Memoirs of Bing Devine: Stealing Lou Brock and Other Winning Moves by a Master GM* (Sports Publishing, LLC, 2004) 18-21.

366 Bob Broeg, *Memories of a Hall of Fame Sportswriter* (Champaign: Sagamore Publishing, 1995) 315.

367 Roger Angell, *The Summer Game* (New York: Viking Press, 1972) 17475.

368 John Snyder, *Cardinals Journal* (Cincinnati: Emmis Books, 2006) 498; Alan Ross, *Cardinals Glory* (Nashville: Cumberland House, 2005) 233.

369 Roger Angell, *The Summer Game* (New York: The Viking Press, 1972) 176-180. World Series bleacher tickets went for $2.

370 Bing Devine, *The Memoirs of Bing Devine: Stealing Lou Brock and Other Winning Moves by a Master GM* (Sports Publishing, LLC, 2004) 1-4; Devine answered quizzical reporters who questioned his return, "They can take me away from the Cardinals, but they can never take the Cardinals away from me." James N. Giglio, *Musial: From Stash to Stan the Man* (Columbia: University of Missouri Press, 2001) 286.

371 Tim McCarver, et al, *Diamond Gems: Favorite Baseball Stories from the Legends of the Game* (New York: McGraw Hill, 2008)173; Rob Rains, *The Cardinals Fan's Little Book of Wisdom: 101 Truths…Learned the Hard Way* (Lanham, MD: Diamond Communications, 2002) 80.

372 John Snyder, *Cardinals Journal* (Cincinnati: Emmis Books, 2006) 500.

373 Roger Angell, *The Summer Game* (New York: Viking Press, 1972) 188; *Busch Stadium Moments*, ed. Mike Smith (Marceline, MO: Walsworth Publishing, 2005)54-57; "A hitter's game: rule changes promoting offense have favored batters over pitchers," Mark Herrmann, *Baseball Digest*, July 2003. World Series standing room only ticket went for $4.

374 Roger Angell, *The Summer Game* (New York: Viking Press, 1972) 182, 203. The season was an excellent show of pitching control with three hundred and forty shutout games, one perfect game by Catfish Hunter, two no-hitters on consecutive days in the same ballpark by Gaylord Perry of the San Francisco Giants and Ray Washburn of the Cardinals. Gibby led all with his 1.12 earned run-average, though five in the American League finished with an ERA below 2.00 and Detroit Tigers, Denny McLain racked up thirty-one wins. Los Angeles Dodger Don Drysdale kept the opposition scoreless for fifty-eight and two-third innings and New York Mets rookie Jerry Koosman threw seven shutouts.

375 Roger Angell, *The Summer Game* (New York: Viking Press, 1972) 183-184.

376 Ibid., 200-02.

377 In 1961, the American League added the Los Angeles Angels (changed to the California Angels in 1965, to the Anaheim Angels in 1997 and to the Los Angeles Angels of Anaheim in 2005), and the Washington Senators moved to Minneapolis and became the Twins. The Washington D. C. area got a new Senators team (in 1972 they moved to the Dallas area to become the Texas Rangers). In 1962, the National League added two teams, the New York Metropolitans (Mets) and the Houston Colt 45s (they changed their name to the Astros in 1965). In 1966 the Braves moved from Milwaukee to Atlanta. In 1968, the Kansas City Athletics moved to become the Oakland A's. Then in 1969, new American League teams popped up with the Kansas City Royals and the Seattle Pilots (they moved to Milwaukee the following year to become the Brewers and after the 1997 season they switched to the National League). The National League added the San Diego Padres and the Montreal Expos in 1969. In 1993, the National League added the Florida Marlins and the Colorado Rockies. The National League added the Arizona Diamondbacks in 1998, and the American League added the Tampa Bay Devil Rays (changed to the Rays in 2008).

378 KETC series *Decades, Vol. VIII.*

379 *Busch Stadium Moments*, ed. Mike Smith (Marceline, MO: Walsworth Publishing, 2005) 74.

380 "Ernie Hays: Cardinals' Organist Retiring After 40 Years," Chad Garrison, *Riverfront Times*, Aug. 27, 2010. Memorable tunes from those days, including "Take Me Out to the Ball Game," certainly got fans into the spirit of the game as did the chant of "Charge" and the rhythmic clapping of hands. The song most associated with the Cardinals was the theme song of Budweiser beer, the "King of Beers," played at each game and when the Clydesdales marched onto the field.

381 John Snyder, *Cardinals Journal* (Cincinnati: Emmis Books, 2006) 526-527; George F. Will, *Men at Work: The Craft of Baseball* (New York: Macmillan Publishing Co., 1990) 301; Alan Ross, *Cardinals Glory: For the Love of Dizzy, Ozzie, and the Man* (Nashville: Cumberland House, 2005) 221.

382 Shannon has now been behind the microphone for over forty-five years and is still the main Cards announcer.

383 *Busch Stadium Moments*, ed. Mike Smith (Marceline, MO: Walsworth Publishing, 2005) 70; 90. Certainly 1979 was not uneventful for Brock as he received his 3,000th hit on August 13, 1979.

384 Ibid., 86.

385 Ibid., 72.

386 Ibid., 90. One day Busch made an appearance in the clubhouse that astonished the players. He asked his team, "Whatever you do, finish in front of the Mets." Forsch noted it was bad when the owner "has to ask you not to finish last."

387 John Snyder, *Cardinals Journal* (Cincinnati: Emmis Books, 2006) 576-577.

388 Rob Rains. *The Cardinals Fan's Little Book of Wisdom* (South Bend: Diamond Communications, Inc., 1994) 48.

389 John Snyder, *Cardinals Journal* (Cincinnati: Emmis Books, 2006) 593; Whitey Herzog and Kevin Horrigan, *White Rat: A Life in Baseball* (New York: Harper & Row Publishers, 1987) 114-117. Gussie wanted Herzog to take on the general manager spot with the team after he had fired John Claiborne in early August. Herzog admitted he did not want that position because one had to work year-round in the office and he wanted to spend the off-season "fishing, hunting and skiing." Besides, "a general manager's job is nothing but putting up with bullshit and bullshitters, day in and day out." He did not want to spend his time "sitting across a desk from some clown who'd never worn a jockstrap in his life, who was trying to tell me what a great player his client was when he'd probably never seen him play."

390 Whitey Herzog and Kevin Horrigan, *White Rat: A Life in Baseball* (New York: Harper & Row Publishers, 1987) 133. He traded for 13 players and acquired 8 more while he built his dream team.

391 Ibid.

392 Ibid., 134.

393 Ibid., 133.

394 Ibid.

395 Ibid., 119-122. Herzog wanted to move Simmons from catcher to first base and Keith Hernandez to the outfield. Simmons did not want to take the chance of being compared to Hernandez who had been playing at first. "He didn't want to embarrass himself in the field."

396 Ibid., 129-132. The trade also included pitchers Rollie Fingers and Pete Vuckovich, to the then American League Brewers helped to set up a winning team for the 1982 season where Milwaukee played the Cardinals in the World Series.

397 Ibid., 133.

398 Ibid.

399 Ibid.,134. Early in the day, one that was a Ladies' Day game, the shortstop informed Herzog he did not feel like playing but Whitey put him in any way. Templeton retorted with obvious lackadaisical play. When Templeton entered the dugout after his ejection for grabbing his crotch and giving the finger to the fans, Whitey "grabbed him by the shirt and backed him against a wall... fined him $5,000 and suspended him indefinitely for making obscene gestures at fans." Templeton agreed to professional help for his depression and chemical imbalance. He returned to the lineup on September 15th. It was possible that his absence, the benefit he could have brought to the team, cost the Cardinals a postseason slot.

400 Tim McCarver ed., *Tim Carver's Diamond Gems: Favorite Baseball Stories from the Legends of the Game* (New York: McGraw Hill, 2008) 9899. Whitey Herzog and Kevin Horrigan, *White Rat: A Life in Baseball* (New York: Harper & Row Publishers, 1987) 140.

401 Phone interview May 9, 2012, between Roger Drake and C. F. Sexauer.; "It's the bottom of the 9th for longtime Cards organist," Stephen Deere, *St. Louis Post-Dispatch*, Sept. 30, 2010.

402 *Busch Stadium Moments*, ed. Mike Smith (Marceline, MO: Walsworth Publishing, 2005) 110. Players of the 1980s' teams included Darrell Porter, Ozzie Smith, Vince Coleman, Tommy Herr, Lonnie Smith, Willie McGee, and pitchers Bob Forsch, Joaquin Andujar, Danny Cox, Jeff Lahti, Joe Magrane, Rick Horton, Greg Mathews, Todd Worrell, John Tudor, Bruce Sutter.

403 Ibid., 134.

404 John Snyder, *Cardinals Journal* (Cincinnati: Emmis Books, 2006) 604-608.

405 Ibid., 612, 614.

406 *Busch Stadium Moments*, ed. Mike Smith (Marceline, MO: Walsworth Publishing, 2005) 104; 114.

407 John Snyder, *Cardinals Journal* (Cincinnati: Emmis Books, 2006) 616.

408 Ibid., 624-626.

409 George F. Will, *Men at Work: The Craft of Baseball* (New York: Macmillan Publishing Co., 1990) 43, 170.

410 John Snyder, *Cardinals Journal* (Cincinnati: Emmis Books, 2006) 633.

411 Ibid., 634-636.

412 The traditional seats for the most part were priced: field box - infield $19.00; field box - outfield $16.00; loge box - infield $18.00; loge box - outfield $16.00; terrace box - infield $14.00; terrace box - outfield $12.00; loge reserved - infield $13.00; loge reserved - outfield $12.00; terrace reserved - infield $11.00; terrace reserved - outfield $10.00; terrace reserved - outfield: children 15 and under $6.00; upper terrace reserved - outfield $6.00; upper terrace: children $2.00; bleachers $6.00. Scorecards cost a $1.00 and no longer offered the line-up and stats that those of a bygone era did.

413 Whitey Herzog, *You're Missin' a Great Game* (New York: Simon & Schuster 1999) 71.

414 Peter Hernon and Terry Ganey, *Under the Influence: The Unauthorized Story of the Anheuser-Busch Dynasty* (New York: Simon & Schuster, 1991) 402.

415 Rob Rains, *Cardinal Nation* (St. Louis: Sporting News, 2003), p. 250. Peter Golenbock, *The Spirit of St. Louis* (New York: Harper Entertainment, 2000) 626, footnote. John Snyder, *Cardinals Journal* (Cincinnati: Emmis Books, 2006) 647.

Chapter Seven

416 Peter Golenbock, *The Spirit of St. Louis* (New York: Harper Entertainment, 2000) 580

417 Rob Rains, *Cardinal Nation*, 2nd ed. (St. Louis: Sporting News, 2003) 251.

418 John Snyder, *Cardinals Journal* (Cincinnati: Emmis Books, 2006) 650.

419 Ibid., 655-682.

420 *Busch Stadium: Commemorative Yearbook Cardinals* (St. Louis: St. Louis Cardinals, LLC, 2005) 147.

421 "Ozzie, Cards Show Loyalty is Gone," *St. Louis Post-Dispatch*, Dec. 6, 1991, 1C. Local sportscaster Mike Bush aired a hard-hitting commentary about the handling of Smith. Things were so hostile that the sportscaster from KMOV-TV, Zip Rzeppa, "called on Anheuser-Busch to sell the Cardinals." By the end of

1991 though, Miklasz expanded his thinking on this issue, acknowledging that "modern baseball" had taken over and the days of sticking by players for their past performances and their loyalty to a team was on the way out. He saw a different picture in the financial arena of the sport, not that he supported the treatment of Smith, but that he saw the bottom line had become a paramount interest of the team owners.

422 "Ozzie, Cards Show Loyalty is Gone," *St. Louis Post-Dispatch*, Dec. 6, 1991, 1C.

423 *Busch Stadium: Commemorative Yearbook Cardinals* (St. Louis: St. Louis Cardinals, LLC, 2005) 147 and 154. In 1992 the power alleys went from 383 feet to 375 feet and center field came in from 414 feet to 402 feet.

424 Ibid., 158.

425 Charles P. Korr, T*he End of Baseball as We Knew It: The Players Union, 1960-1981* (Urbana: University of Illinois Press, 2002) 256.

426 Former Cardinals showed up as well as Manager Joe Torre and his coaching staff. The Sunday afternoon crowd toured the stadium, including the clubhouses, and romped around the field playing carnival type games, and picked up certificates for admission to a 1995 Cardinals' game. In October 1994, former Cardinal Dal Maxvill was fired as Cards general manager and replaced with Walt Jocketty.

427 "The NFL's Return Meant St. Louis Found the Road to Pay Dirt in '95," Bernie Miklasz, *St. Louis Post-Dispatch*, Dec. 24, 1995.

428 George F. Will, *Men at Work: The Craft of Baseball* (New York: Harper Perennial, 1991) 61.

429 Ibid., 39, 48-49, 74; Buzz Bissinger, *3 Nights in August: Strategy, Heartbreak, and Joy Inside the Mind of a Manager* (Boston: Houghton Mifflin Co., 2005) xv, xvii. He was noted for not putting the pitcher as the ninth batter and notorious for using his relief pitchers based on individual batters they would face. It was not unusual for him to switch from right-hander to lefty after only one batter.

430 Ibid., xi, xxi. There were men in baseball he did respect and listen to, particularly Dave Duncan, but once La Russa made the decision that was the way it was, no discussion. Tony learned along the way from some of the best men in the game and he stressed all the experience in the world would not do one any good without good fortune.

431 George F. Will, *Men at Work: The Craft of Baseball* (New York: Harper Perennial, 1991) 49, 52.

432 "Anheuser-Busch to sell Cardinals," *Pittsburgh Post-Gazette*, Oct. 26, 1995, B7; *George F. Will, Men at Work: The Craft of Baseball* (New York: Harper Perennial, 1991) 22-23; Buzz Bissinger, *3 Nights in August: Strategy, Heartbreak, and Joy Inside the Mind of a Manager* (Boston: Houghton Mifflin Co., 2005) xxi, 4-5.

433 "La Russa's Cardinal Decision A's lose manager, Duncan to St. Louis," *San Francisco Chronicle*, Oct. 24, 1995, B1. "Cardinals are Staying put, Herzog says," *St. Louis Post-Dispatch*, Oct. 26, 1995, 2D.

434 Ibid.

435 Mike Smith, ed., *Busch Stadium Moments* (Marceline, MO: Walsworth Publishing Co., 2005) 138.

436 "Busch to sell Cardinals, snack unit Company, decides to stick to beer," *Globe and Mail*, Canada, Oct. 26, 1995.

437 "Anheuser-Busch to Sell Cardinals," *Dayton Daily News*, Oct. 26, 1995, 2D.

438 Bernie Miklasz, *St. Louis Post-Dispatch*, December 24, 1995, 3F. It got so bad that the owner rarely attended a game. Even on opening night, Busch would be out of the park by the third inning.

Chapter Eight

439 "Anheuser-Busch to sell Cardinals," *Pittsburgh Post-Gazette*, Oct. 26, 1995, B7. The core of the beer industry included Budweiser, Busch, Michelob, and about 35 other beer brands. The sale would include Eagle Snacks, Inc., and they would consolidate brewing operations.

440 "Letters from the People: Selling of Cardinals Is No Surprise," *St. Louis Post-Dispatch*, Oct. 26, 1995, 6B. Note: Both General Dynamics and Southwestern Bell left St. Louis in the 1990s. At this time A-B employed close to 1,600 people in the St. Louis area.

441 "Cardinals are Staying put, Herzog says," *St. Louis Post-Dispatch*, Oct. 26, 1995, 2D. Some folks wondered if the national landmark A-B brewery on Pestalozzi Street, too dated, and too expensive, would continue operations or be gone next. Once the team was sold, would the company follow other major industries and flee the city?

442 "Busch to Sell Cardinals," *New York Times*, Dec. 23, 1995, 3B. The group included some local and some out-of-town backers. Attorney Fred Hanser, a partner in the law firm of Armstrong, Teasdale, Schlafly & Davis of downtown St. Louis led the team of investors. His great-grandfather, Adolph M. Diez, held a minor investment in the Cardinals from 1917-1947. Others involved in the deal were Andrew Baur, chairman of Southwest Bank in St. Louis, Donna DeWitt Lambert, a board member and director of Southwest Bank, Stephen F. Brauer, president of Hunter Engineering Co., John K. Wallace, Jr., a local businessman, and William DeWitt Jr. of Cincinnati who grew up in St. Louis as a son of the former owner of the American League's St. Louis Browns and former executive of the Cardinals, William DeWitt Sr. In addition, business partners of DeWitt, to include his past baseball club investments. G. Watts Humphrey of Pittsburgh, Robert H. Castellini, and Mercer Reynolds of Cincinnati invested in the venture. One last investor appeared, Pulitzer Sports II, a subsidiary of Pulitzer Publishing and owner of the *St. Louis Post-Dispatch*.

443 Ibid. "Anheuser-Busch to Sell Cardinals for $150 million;" Richard Gibson, *Wall Street Journal*, Dec. 26, 1995, 3B. "Other Members of Group That Bought Cards," *St. Louis Post-Dispatch*, Dec. 24, 1995, 6A.

444 "New Cards Owners: 'We Want to Win'; Group Purchases Team from Brewery for $150 million," Rick Hummel, *St. Louis Post-Dispatch*, Dec. 23, 1995, 1A.

445 "Musial is Thumbs up for Hands-on Owners," Mike Eisenbath, *St. Louis Post-Dispatch*, Dec. 24, 1995, 1F. In fact, Musial had been approached by Baur, Hanser and DeWitt Jr. about joining their investment adventure but he declined stating, "At 75, I felt I should be retiring from a lot of activities. I might consider it if they want to talk to me again. Really, I'll do anything I can to help baseball in St. Louis."

446 Ibid. Henke played in Texas and Toronto and said it was different there, especially in Toronto where the owner always inquired what they could do to improve things.

447 "Cards' New Owners Get a Hearty Salute," Bob Broeg, *St Louis Post-Dispatch*, Dec. 27, 1995, 6B; Frederick G. Lieb, *The St. Louis Cardinals: The Story of a Great Baseball Club*, (New York: G. P. Putnam's Sons, 1944) 91.

448 Dan O'Neill, *Sportsman's Park: The Players, the Fans, and the Game 1940-1965* (Chesterfield: Mathis Jones Communications, LLC, 2007) 9, 116.

449 "You Can't Beat Fun at Cards' Ballpark," Dave Van Dyck, *Chicago Sun Times*, Feb. 11, 1996, 20.

450 "Owners OK Cards Sale Without One Balk," Tim O'Neil, *St. Louis Post-Dispatch*, Mar. 22, 1996, 1A. Pulitzer Publishing Co. removed its name from ownership since it had a limited partnership in the Arizona Diamondbacks that would begin play in 1998. Unlike the days of the Robison brothers, Major League Baseball prohibits ownership in more than one team. Pulitzer lent "$5 million to the new group's subsidiary that bought the stadium parking garages as part of the deal."

451 Ibid. Note: As stated in this article, the sale price of $150 million was the second highest amount paid for a baseball team, trailing only the $175 million paid by Peter Angelos' group for the Baltimore Orioles in 1993.

452 "The Eagle Flies," *St. Louis Post-Dispatch*, Mar. 10, 1996, 2B.

453 "Fans Saying 'Thank You' to Cardinals at Ticket Office," *St. Louis Post-Dispatch*, Mar. 16, 1996, 3C.

454 Ibid.; "New Owners Loosen the Grip on Wallets, Rejuvenate Cards on Wallets," George Schroeder, *Arkansas Democrat-Gazette*, Mar. 29, 1996, 4C.

455 "New Owners Loosen the Grip on Wallets, Rejuvenate Cards on Wallets," George Schroeder, *Arkansas Democrat-Gazette*, Mar. 29, 1996, 4C.

456 "Phone Lines Busy as Fans Seek Cards Playoff Tickets," Carolyn Bower, *St. Louis Post-Dispatch*, Sept. 16, 1996, 3B.

457 "These Birds Put a New Face on Old Legacy," Bernie Miklasz, *St. Louis Post-Dispatch*, Sept. 25, 1996, 1D.

458 "Where are the Fans? Spontaneity is Missing from the Turnstile Mix," Bernie Miklasz, *St. Louis Post-Dispatch*, Sept. 6, 1996, 1D.

459 "Woe is Baseball; The Game's Problems are Many, and Little is Done to Solve them," Mike Eisenbath, *St. Louis Post-Dispatch*, June 25, 1995, 1F.

460 "These Birds Put a New Face on Old Legacy," Bernie Miklasz, *St. Louis Post-Dispatch*, Sept. 25, 1996, 1D.

Chapter Nine

461 "The NFL's Return Meant St. Louis Found the Road to Pay Dirt in '95," Bernie Miklasz, *St. Louis Post-Dispatch*, Dec. 24, 1995.

462 The new team players that first year included: Ray Lankford, Brian Jordan, Andy Benes, Ron Gant, Gary Gaetti, Todd Stottlemyre, Dennis Eckersley and Royce Clayton.

463 "C.O.D.: Cards Delivered; Now it's Time for Fans to Pay," Bernie Miklasz, *St. Louis Post-Dispatch*, Nov. 29, 1996, 1B.

464 Rob Rains, *Cardinal Nation* (Chesterfield: Sporting News, 2006) 252; Rob Rains, *Mark McGwire: Home Run Hero* (New York: St. Martin's Press, 1998) 211; Eric Enders, *Ballparks: Then and Now* (San Diego: Thunder Bay Press, 2002) 137. McGwire promptly took the field and hit a 517-foot home run at home.

465 Bing Devine, *The Memoirs of Bing Devine: Stealing Lou Brock and Other Winning Moves by a Master GM* (Sports Publishing, LLC, 2004) 18-21.

466 Tim McCarver, *The Perfect Season: Why 1998 was Baseball's Greatest Year* (New York: Villard Books, 1999) xii.

467 Rob Rains, *Cardinal Nation* (Chesterfield: Sporting News, 2006) 252

468 *Cardinals Busch Stadium Commemorative Yearbook* (St. Louis: St. Louis Cardinals, LLC, 2006)

469 Letters to the Editor: A New Ballpark: Ugly or Visionary? *St. Louis Post-Dispatch*, April 13, 2000, B8.

470 "Harmon says voters should decide on any stadium tax plan; Cardinals urge officials to consider proposal," *St. Louis Post-Dispatch*, April 14, 2000, A1.

471 "Harmon says voters should decide on any stadium tax plan; Cardinals urge officials to consider proposal," *St. Louis Post-Dispatch*, April 14, 2000, A1.

472 "Regional Officials agree any new baseball stadium should be downtown," *St. Louis Post-Dispatch*, May 25, 2000, C1.

473 "Harmon says voters should decide on any stadium tax plan; Cardinals urge officials to consider proposal," *St. Louis Post-Dispatch*, April 14, 2000, A1.

474 "Officials discuss new Cards home," *St. Louis Post-Dispatch*, May 29, 2000, 5.

475 John Snyder, *Cardinals Journal* (Cincinnati: Emmis Books, 2006) 730-731; Rich Wolfe, *Remembering Jack Buck* (Phoenix: Lone Wolfe Press, 2002) See Appendix.

476 Ibid., 736.

477 Ibid., 737. His father had died in his 40s from a heart attack, yet the son had no history of heart disease.

478 Ibid.

479 Ibid., 734, 740-741.

480 "New Home base: A 32-page guide to Busch Stadium," *St. Louis Post- Dispatch*, April 9, 2006.

481 http://stlouis.cardinals.mlb.com/NASApp/mlb.stl/news/stl_news

482 "Ballpark Village: Earth will move today, Cards say," *St. Louis Post-Dispatch*, August 5, 2008, 1D.

483 "Cards look forward to new Busch," stlcardinals.com

484 "Broadcasters ready for new Busch," stlcardinals.com

485 This poem was delivered to me via email from Jennifer Borcherding with a message that a Cardinal fan wrote it before Game 6 and posted it on the *Post-Dispatch* website. Bernie Miklasz wrote that Tim McKernan, a local sports guy, gave it to La Russa before the game. He passed it around to several players, and it was well received in the clubhouse. Oct. 21, 2004. See Appendix.

486 John Snyder, *Cardinals Journal* (Cincinnati: Emmis Books, 2006) 755-758.

487 "Cards honor fans in Busch ceremony," Stephen A. Norris/Mlb.com, stlcardinals.com

488 "Busch Stadium Countdown," stlcardinals.com Those participating in the ceremonial display included current and former Cardinal baseball players, broadcasters, organist, band leader, front office personnel, team physician, and mascot Fredbird; current St. Louis Rams football players and former Cardinal football players; other local sports celebrities; Mrs. Frank Robinson; St. Louis sports columnists, and artist Amadee; military personnel, and a police officer.

489 "Busch Stadium Countdown," stlcardinals.com

490 "Busch gears for final weekend," stlcardinals.com

491 Personal recollections of C. F. Sexauer: These included McGwire's 70th home run 1998, Brock's 1979 3,000 hit, the NLCS game 7 clinch in 2004, Brock's 105 stolen-base record, Edmonds' walk-off homer in game 6 of the NCLS 2004, Jack Buck's reading of his original poem "For America" following the 9/11 disaster, Gibson's 17-K game 1 of the 1968 World Series, Bruce Sutter closes out Game 7 of the 1982 Cards' World Series win, McGwire's 62nd homer in 1968, and the number one moment in Busch history: Ozzie Smith's homer in the ninth inning of game 5 of the 1985 NLCS that led to the famous Jack Buck announcement "Go crazy, folks! Go crazy!"

492 The team included current Redbirds who had participated in five postseason events over the last six seasons: Albert Pujols, Scott Rolen and Jim Edmonds. The team consisted of three members of the Hall of Fame: Lou Brock, Bob Gibson and

Ozzie Smith. Others included those that made the 1980s so special in St. Louis: manager Whitey Herzog, Tommy Herr, Bruce Sutter, and current third base coach Jose Oquendo. Named to the team as well were: Ted Simmons from the 1970s teams and the late Roger Maris from the 1967 and 1968 pennant winning seasons.
493 Oral interview memories of Michelle and Rick Lewis shared with the C. F. Sexauer.
494 "Fans share memories of Busch," stlcardinals.com
495 "Cards honor fans in Busch ceremony," Stephen A. Norris/MLB.com, stlcardinals.com
496 John Snyder, *Cardinals Journal* (Cincinnati: Emmis Books, 2006) 765.

Chapter Ten
497 "St. Louis Cardinals," *Sports Network*, December 3, 2007, 1:42 PM, EST.
498 *St. Louis Cardinals GameDay: Take a Stairway to Heaven*, 2006, no. 1.
499 Oral interview with Judy Clark Dwyer and Fran Dwyer by C. F. Sexauer. They note that in these more "modern times" game times are subject to change on short notice to accommodate television revenue.
500 E-mail correspondence between Tom P. Schneider and C. F. Sexauer, Oct. 24, 2006.
501 In the final days of the season some questioned whether the Cards should be in the playoff season; La Russa believes "if a team make[s] it to October, it's good enough to win a Series, I told my players that baseball pays the team that plays the best." La Russa proved right in his evaluation.
502 Tim McCarver, et al, *Diamond Gems: Favorite Baseball Stories from the Legends of the Game* (New York: McGraw Hill, 2008) 24-25.
503 "St. Louis Cardinals 2007 Preview," Mike Castiglione, *The Sports Network*, March 26, 2007. 12:40 PM EST.
504 http://sports.espn.go.com/mlb/news/story?id=2807935. In December 2007 when La Russa went to court, he was placed on probation, assigned community service and issued a fine.
505 "Death report leads Cards to ban booze in clubhouse," Bob Nightengale, *USA TODAY*, May 7, 2007, 2C.
506 "Cardinals fans pay respects to the pitcher's memory", Betsy Taylor, *Associated Press*, April 30, 2007.
507 "Signs of Mourning Follow the Cardinals," Jack Curry, *New York Times*, May 1, 2007, 4D.
508 "Cardinals take part in service for Hancock," *Globe and Mail* (Canada *New York Times*), May 1, 2007, 4D.
509 "Police: Hancock was drunk," *San Jose Mercury News*, May 5, 2007; "Death Report leads Cards to ban booze in clubhouse," Bob Nightengale, *USA TODAY*, May 7, 2007, 2C; "Nats ban alcohol in locker rooms; Hancock death prompts policy," Bob Cohn and Mark Zuckerman, *Washington Times*, May 9, 2007, A1;
510 The Official Site of the St. Louis Cardinals: News: Cardinals name Mozeliak new GM; The Official Site of the St. Louis Cardinals: News: La Russa remains Cardinal manager
511 "Izturis deal edges out Eckstein" Joe Strauss, *St Louis Post-Dispatch*, Dec. 1, 2007; Rolen Enjoying New Address: With Toronto, and Far Away From La Russa, Jack Curry, *New York Times*, March 4, 2008; Mr. Cards lock up Wainwright, *Socratic Gadfly* March 20, 2008, 5:11 PM EST; Baseball: Spiezio gets probation, *Ottawa Citizen*, April 8, 2008, C5.

512 Predictions: "How Trib writers see the NL Central", *Pittsburgh Tribune* March 31, 2008

513 "St. Louis Cardinals' sellout streak ends at 165 games", R. B. Fallstrom, *Associated Press*, April 3, 2008.

514 Interview by C. F. Sexauer with Paula Homan, summer 2011.

515 "St. Louis: Home is where the arch is," Bob Nightengale, *USA TODAY*, Jul. 14, 2009.

516 "Cardinals net Holliday from A's for playoff run Janie McCauley, *Virginia Pilot*, Jul. 25, 2009, C4.

517 "To Live and Thrive in LA," Tom Verducci, *Sports Illustrated*, Oct. 19, 2009, 46-50.

518 "Holliday is happy with the outcome: New $120 million deal with Cardinals puts slugger where he wants to be, he says" Joe Strauss, *St. Louis Post-Dispatch*, Jan. 7, 2010, C1; ""Mozeliak should get the credit Cards GM took right approach, got it done," Bryan Burwell, *St. Louis Post-Dispatch*, Jan. 6, 2010, C1; "Cards now are clear-cut Central pick," Joe Strauss, *St. Louis Post-Dispatch*, Jan. 10, 2010, C1

519 "McGwire Offers No Denials at Steroid Hearings," Duff Wilson, *New York Times*, Mar. 18, 2005. In a choked-up voice, McGwire "My lawyers have advised me that I cannot answer these questions without jeopardizing my friends, my family or myself."

520 "'I used steroids' Why he used," Joe Strauss, *St. Louis Post-Dispatch*, Jan. 12, 2010, A1

521 "McGwire apologizes to La Russa, Selig," http://sports.espn.go.com/ mlb/ news/story?id=4816607; "Mark McGwire: The day after," *St. Louis Post-Dispatch*, Jan. 13, 2010, A1.

522 "Camp puts smile on Pujols' face Cardinals' star talks about elbow, contract status, La Russa and more," Feb. 27, 2010, http://business.highbeam.com/435553/ article-1G1-220028141 Miklasz appreciated the "human wrecking ball that destroys pitchers and breaks open games with one swing of his bat." Back in June he had cautioned the team to start working with the slugger to keep him on the Cardinals' payroll.

523 "Playoff Deep? Cardinals are picked to win the division, but questions remain about their depth," Joe Strauss, *St. Louis Post-Dispatch*, Apr. 5, 2010, B1; "Cardinals are deep enough, DeWitt says," Joe Strauss, *St. Louis Post-Dispatch*, Mar. 17, 2010, C1.

524 "Herzog looks back at '85 team he led to the Series," Rick Hummel, *St. Louis Post-Dispatch*, Apr. 18, 2010, B4.

525 "Cards start 'Stand for Stan' campaign," Derrick Goold, *St. Louis Post-Dispatch*, May 25, 2010; "5,000 and counting 'Stand for Stan,'" Christopher Tritto, *St. Louis Business Journal*, May 28, 2010; "Musial takes lap as fans 'Stand for Stan,'" Matthew Leach, MLB.com, Oct. 2, 2010, http://mlb.mlb.com/news/article. jsp?ymd=20101002&content_id=1532943&vkey=news

526 "Cards rarely rally after the break," Rick Hummel, *St. Louis Post-Dispatch*, Jul. 11, 2010, C9. Hummel noted: The exception to that rule, as all Cardinal Nation knows, was in 2001 split-season, when the Cardinals rallied from eight games out at the All-Star break to tie Houston for the best records in the division, but Houston officially was declared the winner.

527 "'Reason for excitement' Cardinals chairman Bill DeWitt Jr. remains optimistic about the team despite the frustrations of the first half," Joe Strauss, *St. Louis Post-Dispatch*, Jul. 11, 2010, C1.

528 "Cardinals' GM gets new deal," Joe Strauss, *St. Louis Post-Dispatch*, Jul. 16, 2010, C; "Uncertainty of Penny makes Cards needier," Joe Strauss, *St. Louis Post-Dispatch*, Jul 18, 2010, C7.

529 "Spring Dreams – Summer Reality," Joe Strauss, *St. Louis Post-Dispatch*, Jul. 15, 2010, C1.

530 "La Russa, Mozeliak defend trade," Joe Strauss, *St. Louis Post-Dispatch*, Sep. 10, 2010

531 "Cardinals pick up option on Pujols," Derrick Goold, *St. Louis Post-Dispatch*, Oct. 7, 2010, C6.

532 "Mozeliak flexes by firing Mason," Bernie Miklasz, *St. Louis Post-Dispatch*, Oct. 19, 2010, B1; "Pujols' contract talks to heat up," Joe Strauss, *St. Louis Post-Dispatch*, Nov. 16, 2010, B1.

533 "La Russa says job is getting tougher," Joe Strauss, *St. Louis Post-Dispatch*, Sept. 13, 2010.

534 "Skipper to return," Joe Strauss, *St. Louis Post-Dispatch*, Oct. 19, 2010, B1.

535 "Plenty for Cards to review after bagging season," Joe Strauss, *St. Louis Post-Dispatch*, Sept. 6, 2010.

536 "The brightest star," Derrick Goold, *St. Louis Post-Dispatch*, Oct. 31, 2010, L7.

537 "Payroll pushes Cards," Joe Strauss, *St. Louis Post-Dispatch*, Oct. 5, 2010, B1.

538 "Pujols' contract talks to heat up," Joe Strauss, *St. Louis Post-Dispatch*, Nov. 16, 2010, B1.

539 "A make-or-break opportunity for Berkman," Joe Strauss, *St. Louis Post-Dispatch*, Jan. 14, 2011; "A hard nine questions for Cardinals," Joe Strauss, *St. Louis Post-Dispatch*, Feb. 11, 2011.

540 "Berkman's arrival may affect Holliday in Cardinals' outfield," Joe Strauss, *St. Louis Post-Dispatch*, Dec. 6, 2010, 2.

541 "Cardinals will pay for delay on Pujols: Team would have been better off getting a deal done last winter," Bernie Miklasz, *St. Louis Post-Dispatch*, Dec. 11, 2010, B1.

542 "Early Skirmishes: Cards appear ready to test greed angle," Bryan Burwell, *St. Louis Post-Dispatch*, Dec. 8, 2010, C1.

543 "Pujols talks meet reality," Joe Strauss, *St. Louis Post-Dispatch*, Jan. 26, 2011.

Chapter Eleven

544 "How Qcue Prices Tickets to Pack the Stands," Russell Scibetti, *Business Insider*, May 19, 2011.

545 "Contract? Don't ask Pujols," Joe Strauss, *St. Louis Post-Dispatch*, Jan. 16, 2011.

546 "Deadline nears for deal with Pujols," Joe Strauss, *St. Louis Post-Dispatch*, Feb. 4, 2011.

547 "Stan Musial Awarded Medal of Freedom," Feb. 15, 2011, http://www. aolnews. com/2011/02/15/stan-musial-awarded-medal-of-freedom

548 "2011 MLB Preseason preview: NL Central – St. Louis Cardinals," Jeffrey Brown, MLB Preseason Preview, *Bleacher Report*, Mar. 16, 2011.

549 "Adam Wainwright Elbow Injury: Cardinals Ace Might Miss Season," R. B. Fallstrom, *Associated Press*, Feb. 23, 2011. Wainwright had a 20-11 record and over the last four years with the team he posted 64-34.

550 Mozeliak made a major trade on July 27 with the Toronto Blue Jays when he gave up dissatisfied Colby Rasmus as well as three pitchers Trever Miller, Brian Tallet, and P. J. Walters, to improve the pitching situation. In return he picked up young outfielder Corey Patterson, right-handed starter Edwin Jackson, and

two relievers, lefty Marc Rzepczynski and righty Octavio Dotel. He also traded Alex Castellanos to the Dodgers for shortstop Rafael Furcal. On August 11, the Cardinals signed free agent lefty Arthur Rhodes who had been released from the Texas Rangers. These deals drastically changed the makeup of the bullpen overnight.

551 "La Russa positive about the future," Joe Strauss, *St. Louis Post-Dispatch*, Aug. 28, 2011.

552 "Cards Pitching Coach Takes Leave of Absence," Aug. 22, 2011, http:// stlouis. cbs.local.com/2011/08/22/cards-pitching-coach-takes-leve-ofabsence; Duncan was to help care of his wife, Jeanine who had major brain surgery and would need additional tests and rehabilitation. "A Month to Remember," Derrick Goold, *St. Louis Post-Dispatch*, World Series Edition, Oct. 30, 2011, 13.

553 "Leader on and off field, Carp starts in Game 1," Alden Gonzalez/MLB.com, Oct. 18, 2011; "The St. Louis Cardinals rallied from a 3-2 game deficit to claim the 2011 World Championship. David Freese was named Series MVP," Brian Walton, TheCardinalNation.com, http://stlcrdinals.scout. com/2/1122594.html

554 Interview by C. F. Sexauer with Martin Coco, Feb. 14, 2012.

555 The origin of the term happy flight, which the team adopted after a win, is unclear, but it seems to have originated with Rafael Furcal to bring the team luck and became the chant, first among the players and then adopted by fans.

556 "NLDS Preview: Cardinals vs. Phillies," Craig Calcaterra, HardballTalk, Sept. 29, 2011, http://hardballtalk.nbcsports.com/2011/09/29/nlds-previewcardinalsvs-phillies

557 "Wild Cards force Game 5 in Philly Mr. Freese beats playoff nemesis, driving in four runs off Roy Oswalt as series gets squirrelly for Phillies," *The Hamilton Spectator*, Oct. 6, 2011. The Rally Squirrel became an instant favorite with thousands sporting his presence the following night; other items appeared too, fur squirrel tails, and a popular chocolate Rally Squirrel at landmark Crown Candy in St. Louis.

558 See Appendix for prayer.

559 "Bullpen leads Cardinals past Brewers for 3-2 NLCS lead," Mike Dodd, *USA TODAY*, Oct. 15, 2011.

560 "'Improbable postseason' continues for Cards with World Series berth," Joe Lemire, Oct. 17, 2011, http://sportsillustrated.cnn.com/2011/writers/ joe_lemire/10/17/cardinals.brewers.nlcs.game

561 "Hit Parade," Joe Strauss, *St. Louis Post-Dispatch*, Oct. 19, 2011, 4.

562 "Duncan redefines his 'big day,'" Greg Hansen, *Arizona Daily Star*, Dec. 7, 2011. Tigers' manager, Jim Leyland, who had coached for Tony, said, "It's like he was born to manage." Hitting coach McGwire, Oquendo at third, and McKay at first; and Dave Duncan was back at his side for this all-important series.

563 "Prognosticators: Rangers will win first world Series title," Scott Boeck, *USA TODAY*, Oct. 19, 2011; "Rangers' 25-Man Roster," *St. Louis Post-Dispatch*, Oct. 19, 2011, 10; "Scouting the Rangers," Derrick Goold, *St. Louis Post-Dispatch*, Oct. 19, 2011, 10; "2011 CBSSports.com World Series predictions, Oct. 19. 2011, http:// www.cbssports.com/mcc/blogs/ entry/22297882/32820517

564 "Rangers Best Cards to Capture First Title," Joel Beall, WhatifSports.com, Oct. 18, 2011.

565 "We've updated the *Post-Dispatch* on the iPad just in time for the World Series," *St. Louis Post-Dispatch*, Oct. 20, 2011, 1.

566 Stats from Buck and McCarver, FOX network TV coverage.

567 Poetry has been a strong favorite too, see Appendix

568 "Living a Dream," Dan O'Neill, *St. Louis Post-Dispatch*, World Series Edition, Oct. 20, 2011, 5.

569 "Red Ranger," Dan O'Neill, *St. Louis Post-Dispatch*, World Series Edition, Oct. 21, 2011, W11; "We're All Fans," Phillip O'Connor, *St. Louis Post-Dispatch*, World Series Edition, Oct. 21, 2011, W13; personal interview by C. F. Sexauer with Michelle Lewis, Oct. 20, 2011.

570 "Role players," Phillip O'Connor, *St. Louis Post-Dispatch*, World Series Edition, Oct. 20, 2011, 10.

571 "The art of selling St. Louis," Tim Logan, *St. Louis Post-Dispatch*, World Series Edition, Oct. 19, 2011, 14.

572 "Furloughs trumped by Cards' success," David Hunn, *St. Louis Post-Dispatch*, Oct. 21, 2011, A8.

573 "Vets get top billing in visit by Michelle Obama," Tim O'Neil, *St. Louis Post-Dispatch*, Oct. 20, 2011, A10. Both women had been involved in an effort called "Joining Forces" that aided military families; they were only too happy to lend their name and support to Major League Baseball's charitable effort, Welcome Back Veterans, "that has distributed $110 million to help veterans' families."

574 "Brotherhood of the Scalper," Steve Giegerich, *St. Louis Post-Dispatch*, World Series Edition, Oct. 26, 2011, 8.

575 "What a View," Steve Giegerich, *St. Louis Post-Dispatch*, World Series Edition, Oct. 26, 2011, 8.

576 "Trio of Cardinals greats to throw first pitches in Game 1,"Stan McNeal, *Sporting News*, http://aol.sportingnews.com/mlb/story/2011-10-19/trio-ofcrdinals-greatsto-throw-first-pitches-in-game-1

577 "2011 World Series," Baseball Almanac, http://www.baseball-almanac. com/ws/yr2011ws.shtml; Since the terrorist attacks of 9-11, "God Bless America" has been sung during the 7th-inning stretch of all MLB postseason games.

578 "2 cities, 2 very different takes on the revered game," Nicholas J. C. Pistor, *St. Louis Post-Dispatch*, World Series Edition, Oct. 23, 2011, 14.

579 "Small-town Agony," Dan O'Neill, *St. Louis Post-Dispatch*, World Series Edition, Oct. 23, 2011, 12.

580 "Rams coach, players attend Game 3," Tom Timmermann, *St. Louis Post-Dispatch*, World Series Edition, Oct. 23, 2011, 11.

581 "2 cities, 2 very different takes on revered game," Nicholas J. C. Pistor, *St. Louis Post-Dispatch*, World Series Edition, 14.

582 "Looking strong 'top to bottom,'" Derrick Goold, *St. Louis Post-Dispatch*, World Series Edition, Oct. 19, 2011, 10.

583 "Buck's call sounds just like the old days," Dan Caesar, *St. Louis Post-Dispatch*, World Series Edition, Oct. 23, 2011, 15.

584 "Greatest Game," Joe Strauss, *St. Louis Post-Dispatch*, World Series Edition, Oct. 23, 2011, 3.

585 Ibid,

586 "Freese's streak is over," Derrick Goold, *St. Louis Post-Dispatch*, World Series Edition, Oct. 24, 2011, 7.

587 "Tony call bullpen, gets wrong numbers," Jenifer Langosch, MLB.com, Oct. 25, 2011,

588 "Tony La Russa, Cardinals try to explain Game 5 mix-ups," David Lennon, Newsday.com,http://www.newsday.com/sports/baseball/tony-larussa-cardinalstry-to-explain-game-5-mix-ups

589 "Weather forecast postpones Game 6 of Series," Barry M. Bloom, MLB. com, Oct. 26, 2011,

590 "Comeback Special," Joe Strauss, *St. Louis Post-Dispatch*, World Series Edition, Oct. 28, 2011, W3.

591 "Spellbind Game 6 leaves pundits stunned," A. J. Cassavell and Scott Merkin, MLB.com, Oct. 28, 2011.

592 "Comeback Special," Joe Strauss, *St. Louis Post-Dispatch*, World Series Edition, Oct. 28, 2011, W3.

593 "Rangers Regroup," Tom Timmermann, *St. Louis Post-Dispatch*, World Series Edition, Oct. 28, 2011, 8.

594 "'Great Guts,'" Bernie Miklasz, *St. Louis Post-Dispatch*, World Series Edition, Oct. 30, 2011, 2.

595 "Cardinals Rule," Joe Strauss, *St. Louis Post-Dispatch*, World Series Edition, Oct. 29, 2011, 3.

596 "Pujols hits free agent market for first time," Derrick Goold, *St. Louis Post-Dispatch*, Oct. 31, 2011.

597 St. Louis Cardinals World Series Victory Parade," Jim Salter, *Huffington Post*, http://www.huffingtonpost.com/2011/10/30/st-louiscardinalsworld-series-parade-photos.

Chapter Twelve

598 "La Russa retires as Cardinals manager," Derrick Goold, *St. Louis PostDispatch*, Oct. 31, 2011; "I Have no Regrets," Joe Strauss, *St. Louis Post-Dispatch, Special Section on Tony La Russa* "'It's Time to End It,'" Nov. 1, 2011, 2; "Cool Way to Finish,'" Derrick Goold, *St. Louis Post-Dispatch, Special Section on Tony La Russa* "'It's Time to End It,'" Nov. 1, 2011, 6; "La Russa goes out on top St. Louis players shocked as veteran manager retires after emotional run to the World Series victory," Jim Salter, *Waterloo Region Record*, Nov. 2, 2011. The skipper had made his decision in August and shared that at the time with John Mozeliak, Mark McGwire, Dave McKay and Dave Duncan; but it was Sunday evening after all the festivities had ended that he addressed Bill DeWitt and the players with his decision.

599 "Leaving on His Terms," Bryan Burwell, *St. Louis Post-Dispatch, Special Section on Tony La Russa* "'It's Time to End It,'" Nov. 1, 2011, 3.

600 "What They're Saying," *St. Louis Post-Dispatch, Special Section on Tony La Russa* "'It's Time to End It,'" Nov. 1, 2011, 8.

601 "Lasting Legacy," Rick Hummel, *St. Louis Post-Dispatch, Special Section on Tony La Russa* "'It's Time to End It,'" Nov. 1, 2011, 9. La Russa's teams won 23 out of 33 games in the best-of-five competition. He also is just one of two managers to win the World Series in both the American and National Leagues. La Russa, named manager of the year four times, led his teams to six World Series. La Russa is respected throughout baseball.

602 "Mike Matheny to become new Cardinals manager," Stephen Borelli, *USA TODAY*, Nov. 14, 2011; "Matheny's guiding principles are faith and hard work," Derrick Goold, *St. Louis Post-Dispatch*, Feb. 13, 2012. The team leader played from 2000-2004 with the Cardinals and won three Gold Gloves.

603 "Matheny's hiring shows the Cardinals' priorities," Joe Strauss, *St. Louis Post-Dispatch*, Nov. 15, 2011.

604 "Cards retain Duncan, McGwire, Oquendo," Matthew Leach, Nov.16, 2011, http://stlouis.cardinals.mlb.com/news/article.jsp?ymd=20111116&co; "Matheny reaching out to Whitey, Ozzie and others," Derrick Goold, *St. Louis Post-Dispatch*, Dec. 7, 2011.

605 "Bernie to Cards, Albert: Just bend a little," Bernie Miklasz, *St. Louis Post-Dispatch*, Dec. 4, 2011; "Cardinals make a new offer to Pujols that is believed to be more than $220 million for 10 years," Joe Strauss, *St. Louis Post-Dispatch*, Dec. 7, 2011.

606 "Pujols: 'It was about the commitment,'" Joe Strauss, *St. Louis Post-Dispatch*, Dec. 12, 2011. The Cardinals offered nine years at $200 million. Pujols was wooed by the Miami Marlins, certainly not a winning team with having lost 90 games in 2011, but the money seemed good at $200 million plus for ten years. It was alleged that the Cubs presented a five-year contract and two unidentified teams were part of the bidding as well.

607 There will always be numerous interpretations of what took place from DeWitt, Mozeliak, Lozano and Pujols. The truth probably lies somewhere in between.

608 "Bernie: Cardinals have a debt to fans," Bernie Miklasz, *St. Louis Post-Dispatch*, Dec. 10, 2011.

609 "Cardinals' word questioned," Joe Strauss, *St. Louis Post-Dispatch*, Dec. 13, 2011." His wife noted that the couple had mixed feelings, "brokenhearted and delighted, all at the same time." She noted that she and her husband were experiencing much of the same hurt feelings about leaving St. Louis as the fans were about seeing them go. She remarked, "I don't want Albert to be a possession. He's a human being. I can't tell you deeper than that. He's a man."

610 "Deidre Pujols speaks up about split with Cardinals," Roger Hensley, *St. Louis Post-Dispatch*, Dec. 12, 2011.

611 "Pujols: St. Louis will always remain in my heart," Dec. 9, 2011, *St. Louis Post-Dispatch*. That came through clearly in an ad where Albert and Deidre expressed their "thanks and gratitude to the City of St. Louis and Cardinal Nation" in a letter appearing on the back page of the Sports section in Friday's [Dec. 9] *St. Louis Post-Dispatch*.

612 "Cards ponder life without Pujols," Joe Strauss, *St. Louis Post-Dispatch*, World Series Edition, Oct.25, 2011, 8.

613 "Halos' Saturday news conference to air live," Alden Gonzalez, MLB.com, Dec. 10,2011, http://losangeles.angels.mlb.com/news/article.jsp?ymd=20111209&61

614 Derrick Goold, "Cards plan to honor Taveras in several ways," *St. Louis Post-Dispatch*, Jan. 20, 2015.

615 Bob Nightengale, "Goldschmidt happy to be with Cardinals," *USA TODAY*, Mar. 6, 2019, 6C.

Chapter Thirteen

616 Figures derived from an online interview with Ron Watermon by C. F. Sexauer, spring 2017. In 2012 Magic Johnson became one of the owners of the Los Angeles Dodgers.

INDEX

B

Dickson, Murray 82
Dodier Avenue 66
Dominican Republic 86, 205
Don't Stop Believing 195
Double-Header 38, 60, 71, 81, 83, 99, 109, 194
Down Syndrome Center 202
Drake, Roger 28-29, 123
Drueke, Gaber 169
Duncan, Dave 134, 185
Durocher, Leo 24, 77-78, 106
Dwyer, Fran 96, 114, 170
Dwyer, Judy Clarke 96, 114, 170
Dyer, Eddie 82, 85, 87-88

E

Eads Bridge 158, 167
East St. Louis, IL 157
Ebay 186, 191
Ebbets Field 52
Ebbets, Charles 139
Eckert, William D. 117
Edmonds, Jim 25, 158, 162, 174
Eigenbrod, Mike 199
Eighteenth Amendment 63
Eighth St. 167
El Birdos 115, 218
El Hombre 178
Ellis Grove, IL. 190
Encarnacion, Juan 173
ESPN 23, 177, 210
Evans, Sara 176
Eversgerd, Bryan 205
Evert, Jake 192

F

Fairgrounds Racetrack 41
Fall Classic 23, 65, 81, 83, 115, 172, 176, 180, 188, 207
Falstaff Brewery 75, 93
Family Day 164
Fan Appreciation Day 165
Farm System 63-64, 79-80, 82, 86, 91, 178, 203-204

Nineteenth Amendment 56
Nolan, Kelly 192-193
Nolan, Nick 192-193
Noonan, Edward 41
Norris, Stephen A. 165
Northrup, Jim 116
Northwestern League 33
Norworth, Jack 54

O

O'Day, Hank 49
O'Malley, Walter 84
O'Neill, Dan 109
Oakland A's 133, 134, 153, 156, 173, 176-177
Obama, Barack 26, 176, 178, 184
Obama, Michelle 191-192
Office of Defense 81
Ohio 64, 103
Oklahoma 66
Oklahoma City 190
Oliver, Gene 108
Olympics 48
Omaha, Nebraska 105
Opening Day 35, 40-42, 49, 55, 112, 114, 119,
124, 133, 145, 167, 171, 175, 184
Oquendo, Jose 205
Oriole Park 161
Orlando, FL 180, 184
Orta, Jorge 125
Osborn Engineering Company 68
Outrigger Hotel 103
Owens, Brian 192
Ozuna, Marcell 207

P

Pacific Coast League 101
Pagano, Paul 165
Pagnozzi, Tom 150
Paige, Satchel 85
Palm Beach, FL 172
Panama 86
Parcells, Bill 191